Wild Essex

compiled, edited
and designed by

Tony Gunton

Lopinga Books

Published by Lopinga Books
Tye Green House, Wimbish, GB-Essex, CB10 2XE

Jointly with the Essex Wildlife Trust
Fingringhoe Wick Visitor Centre, South Green Road,
Fingringhoe, GB-Essex CO5 7DN

With financial support from BAA (Stansted Airport),
Essex Millennium Festival, Environment Agency and
Essex & Suffolk Water Company

First published 2000

Text & maps © Tony Gunton 2000

Front cover painting © Alan Harris 2000

Photographs © as credited in captions

ISBN 0-9530362-2-7 (softback edition)

ISBN 0-9530362-3-5 (hardback edition)

British Library Cataloguing-in-Publication Data
A catalogue record for this book is available from the British Library

Printed by Healeys Printers Ltd,
Unit 10, The Sterling Complex, Ipswich IP1 5AP

The *Nature of Essex Series* No. 3

Contents

Acknowledgements

Sponsors

The author and publishers are extremely grateful to the four organisations that made donations to support the publication of this book. Their generous support has allowed a very highly illustrated book to be made available at a much more modest price than would otherwise have been the case.

Photographers

All the photographers whose colour photographs are such an important part of this work supported the Essex Wildlife Trust by allowing us to use their work free of charge. Without this generous help the production of this book would have been impossible. We also thank Stuart Luck who flew David Corke on a tour of Essex to take aerial photographs.

Photographers are credited on each photo caption. Some of them earn their living as wildlife photographers. Organisations wishing to contact any of them regarding use of their work in other publications can do so via the Essex Wildlife Trust or Lopinga Books. Andy McGeeney is willing to undertake commissions to take wildlife and environmental photographs.

Other important contributors

Many people have contributed to the making of this book, such as by providing information and by checking the entries for the sites under their care. We would like to thank them all for their generous support and help.

Special thanks are due to Fred Boot, Geoff Gibbs and Chris Gibson for their many helpful comments on the final draft, and David Harris for a final proofreading.

Wildlife conservation charities

The great majority of the sites in this book are owned and managed by wildlife conservation charities. Although these charities encourage visits by non-members they depend on their members to help buy and manage their nature reserves as well as campaigning for wildlife conservation generally.

The Essex Wildlife Trust and London Wildlife Trust are local organisations (although membership is open to anyone, wherever you live). Both are part of the national Wildlife Trusts partnership

The National Trust, Royal Society for the Protection of Birds and the Woodland Trust are each large national organisations which work in Essex and throughout the country.

All these organisations have been very supportive during the preparation of this guide book. If you enjoy visiting the sites in this book, please try to support one or more of the wildlife charities that work for wildlife in the county. See pages 2–3 for sources of membership and other information about these organisations.

Disclaimer

Despite all our best efforts to provide a comprehensive and accurate guide, no doubt errors remain. Information that was correct in September 2000 can also, of course, go out of date. Users of this guide are strongly recommended to make use of the telephone and website contacts, to check the latest situation before setting off on a long journey to visit a site. The author and publishers accept no liability for loss or inconvenience resulting from any errors or omissions in this book.

The maps are designed to give visitors a good indication of what they will find when they visit a site. They must not be taken as a definitive statement of rights of way or of boundaries.

Foreword

From the President of The Wildlife Trusts, Prof. David Bellamy Botanist

Whether you like Canary Wharf or not, the view from the top is breathtaking, east London at your feet and Essex stretching away towards what most people might think is a flat boring horizon of cereal and oil seed rape. Part of the bread and utterly butterly basket of England. Well add this book to your travelling library and prepare to be pleasantly surprised. Then take a trip on one of the wild sides of the metropolis in which I had my roots.

The Essex Wildlife Trust have for over 40 years been working in partnership with all caring people, and that includes many intensive farmers and urban and rural local authorities, to ensure that what is left of the rich wildlife that characterised the area when Julius Caesar sailed up the Thames to found Londinium is in good hands in the future. The real good news is that the partnership is now working hard to put ever more of the landscape back into biodiverse working order

Sit back and get ready to be amazed at the wealth of habitat from the dizzy heights of Canary Wharf to the fabulous holiday coastline which comes complete with wild flowers, creepy crawlies, fish, amphibians, reptiles, birds and mammals which enjoy and are part of the goodlife of the region. A goodlife which thanks to that partnership boasts a patchwork of country parks, greenspace and reserves, no less than 170 sites covering 30,000 acres. There for you to explore, free gratis and, well I can't say for nothing, for with the on-site interpretation and the good services of rangers, wardens, reserve managers and gifted volunteers you will be able to understand the importance of the natural heritage of the two big E's: east London and east Essex. There is one problem growing on the horizon: with all the planting of native trees going on in the area it is getting more difficult to find your way about. Never fear the book is full of detailed maps.

For those of you who are lucky enough to live in the area, boast about it to your friends. Visitors, please send postcards to your friends and let them in on the real wild part of the story of the east-enders.

I must add a public health warning, for once you have seen it for yourselves you will just have to join the Wildlife Trusts partnership.

Thank you for caring.

David Bellamy

Using This Book

What is 'Essex'?

As far as this book is concerned, Essex is the original geographical county of Essex, in other words stretching into Greater London as far as the River Lea in the west, including the London Boroughs of Havering, Barking & Dagenham, Redbridge, Waltham Forest and Newham.

What places are included?

All sites of significant wildlife interest in Essex and that can be accessed without charge are included, although in some cases restrictions are placed on access in the interests of wildlife (such as to limit disturbance at critical times) or in the interests of public safety.

It is the official guide to the nature reserves of the Essex Wildlife Trust, one of the joint publishers, but also includes the nature reserves of other conservation charities, such as the London Wildlife Trust, the RSPB, the Woodland Trust and the National Trust. It also covers those of English Nature's National Nature Reserves that are accessible to the public, plus the country parks, nature reserves and public open spaces managed by local authorities, but excluding those of principally amenity rather than wildlife value.

Some of the smallest or newest sites do not have a full entry, but are listed separately on page 248.

Finding where to go

Sites are arranged in alphabetical order by name in the book, except that some sites that are geographically close have been grouped. Individual sites are indicated on the key map on pages 4–5 by a solid blob, whereas grouped sites are indicated by an open rectangle, beside which the name of the group is shown first with the sites listed beneath in italics. So, for example, to find *Hilly Fields* turn to **Colne Valley** in the book, then look for the Hilly Fields heading under that entry. An index at the end of the book lists all the sites by name, showing also their key features, such as whether they are easy to get to by public transport.

On pages 6–7 you will find a *Quick Guide*, which suggests some of the best places to go at different times of the year.

Keys to the information in the heading for each site and to symbols used on the site maps are on page 8.

Getting there

For each site directions are given for travel by road, while for travel by public transport any convenient stations and/or bus routes are listed. Because timetables and routes change so rapidly, you will need to check details of services. Call the appropriate number below or visit the web sites, some of which provide downloadable route maps and timetables.

Essex Traveline   **0870 608 2 608**
London travel advice
   (not trains)   **020 7222 1234**
National rail
   enquiry service   **08457 48 49 50**
Essex County Council travel information:
   www.essexcc.gov.uk/travel
London Transport
   www.londontransport.co.uk
Railtrack
   www.railtrack.co.uk/travel/index.htm

Information pages

Distributed throughout the book are a number of information pages that explain a little about some of the habitats and management methods (such as coppicing and pollarding) mentioned in the site descriptions. These are listed in the table of contents on page iii and the key terms are included in the index on page 249, so refer to either of these if you come across a term you are not familiar with or want to know more about habitats or background issues.

Species photos

Distributed throughout the book also you will find many photos of particular species of animal or plant. You will find an index to these photos at the back of the book, on page 249.

Visiting safely

Heavy machinery is used to manage many of the sites included in this book, such as to cut the hay in summer, and felling of trees is a necessary part of the management of many woodlands. Please be vigilant, obey warning signs and consider the safety of children and dogs when you visit.

Conservation charities

Telephone numbers of wardens or other contacts for individual sites are given in the entries, where appropriate. If you want to know more about the conservation charities whose nature reserves are included in this book or to ask about membership, please write, telephone, email or access the web sites given below.

Essex Wildlife Trust

Headquarters

Until mid-2001:
Fingringhoe Wick Visitor Centre
South Green Road
Fingringhoe
Essex CO5 7DN
☎ 01206 729678

From mid-2001
Abbotts Hall Farm
Maldon Road
Gt Wigborough
Essex CO5 7RZ
☎ 01206 735456
email admin@essexwt.org.uk
web www.essexwt.org.uk

Visitor Centres

Abberton Reservoir Visitor Centre
☎ 01206 738172

Fingringhoe Wick Visitor Centre
☎ 01206 729678

Hanningfield Visitor Centre
☎ 01268 711001 (from November 2000)

Langdon Visitor Centre
☎ 01268 419095

Thorndon Countryside Centre
☎ 01277 232944

London Wildlife Trust
Harling House
47–51 Great Suffolk Street
London SE1 0BS
☎ 020 7261 0447
email londonwt@cix.compulink.co.uk
web www.wildlifetrust.org.uk/london

The National Trust
36 Queen Anne's Gate
London SW1H 9AS
☎ 020 7222 9251
email enquiries@ntrust.org.uk
web www.nationaltrust.org.uk

East Anglia Office
Blickling
Norwich NR11 6NF
☎ 01263 733471

Royal Society for the Protection of Birds
The Lodge
Sandy
Beds SG19 2DL
☎ 01767 680551
web www.rspb.org.uk

East Anglia Regional Office
☎ 01603 661662

South East England Regional Office
☎ 01273 775333

The Woodland Trust
Autumn Park
Grantham
Lincs NG31 6LL
☎ 01476 581111
Membership freephone **0800 026 9650**
web www.woodland-trust.org.uk

Other organisations

Other key organisations involved with wildlife conservation in Essex, apart from local authorities, are as follows.

English Nature Essex, Herts. & London
Government body responsible for nature conservation in England, including managing National Nature Reserves and overseeing Sites of Special Scientific Interest

Harbour House
Hythe Quay
Colchester
Essex CO2 8JF
☎ 01206 796666

26-27 Ormond House
Boswell Street
London WC1N 3JZ
☎ 020 7831 6922

Enquiry service ☎ 01733 455101
web www.english-nature.org.uk

Forest Enterprise
Responsible for recreation facilities in Forestry Commission woods

Tangham
Rendlesham
Woodbridge
Suffolk IP12 3NF
☎ 01394 450164

Environment Agency
Government body responsible for water quality and pollution prevention; for flood warning and defence; and for recreation and conservation involving water resources

General enquiries ☎ 0845 933 3111

Emergency hotline ☎ 0800 80 70 60
To report all environmental incidents

Floodline ☎ 0845 988 1188
24-hour advice and information on floods

email enquiries@environment-agency.gov.uk
web www.environment-agency.gov.uk

Map of wild places in this book

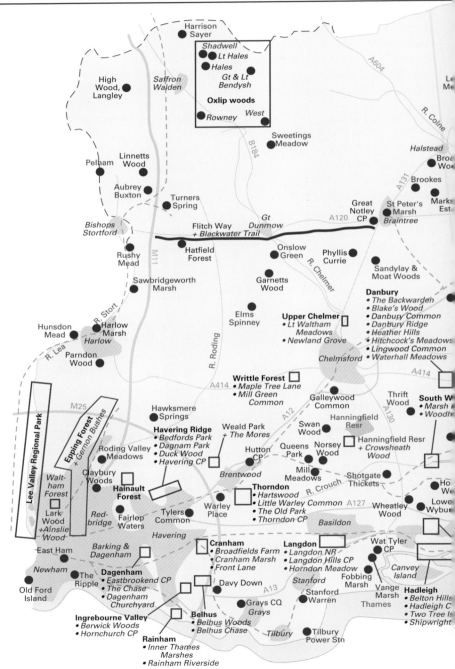

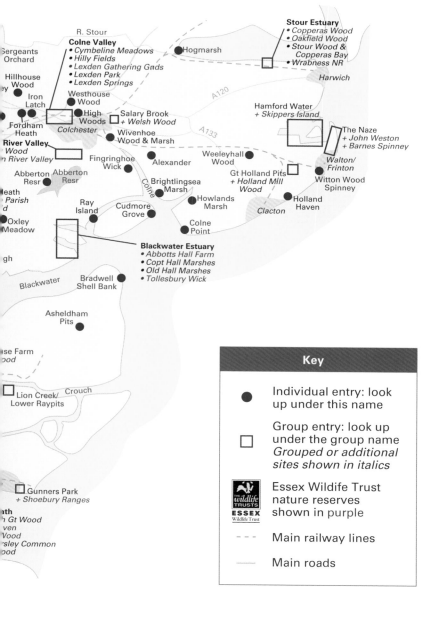

R. Stour

Colne Valley
• *Cymbeline Meadows*
• *Hilly Fields*
• *Lexden Gathering Gnds*
• *Lexden Park*
• *Lexden Springs*

Sergeants
Orchard

Hillhouse
Wood

Iron
Latch

Fordham
Heath

Westhouse
Wood

High
Woods

Salary Brook
+ *Welsh Wood*

Colchester

River Valley
Wood
n River Valley

Wivenhoe
Wood & Marsh

Fingringhoe
Wick

Abberton
Resr

Abberton
Resr

Alexander

Brightlingsea
Marsh

Ray
Island

Cudmore
Grove

Oxley
Meadow

Colne
Point

Howlands
Marsh

Hogmarsh

Stour Estuary
• *Copperas Wood*
• *Oakfield Wood*
• *Stour Wood &*
  Copperas Bay
• *Wrabness NR*

Harwich

Hamford Water
+ *Skippers Island*

The Naze
+ *John Weston*
+ *Barnes Spinney*

Weeleyhall
Wood

Gt Holland Pits
+ *Holland Mill*
Wood

Walton/
Frinton

Witton Wood
Spinney

Holland
Haven

Clacton

Blackwater Estuary
• *Abbotts Hall Farm*
• *Copt Hall Marshes*
• *Old Hall Marshes*
• *Tollesbury Wick*

Blackwater

Bradwell
Shell Bank

Asheldham
Pits

se Farm
ood

Lion Creek/
Lower Raypits

Crouch

Gunners Park
+ *Shoebury Ranges*

ath
Gt Wood
ven
Vood
sley Common
ood

Key	
●	Individual entry: look up under this name
□	Group entry: look up under the group name *Grouped or additional sites shown in italics*
Essex Wildlife Trust	Essex Wildlife Trust nature reserves shown in purple
- - -	Main railway lines
——	Main roads

		South-West
April...	The best show of woodland flowers is in early spring, before the trees put on all their leaves. At this time the woods also fill with birdsong as summer migrants like warblers join the resident birds and sing to attract mates and to mark their territories.	Epping Forest, Thorndon, W● Park, Writtle Forest
May	A different mix of breeding birds is in evidence at more open sites, where birds that nest low down in dense undergrowth, in reed beds or in rough grassland find a suitable niche.	Hainault Forest, Havering Ri● Ingrebourne Valley, Langdo● Lea Valley
June	Many wild flower meadows and grassland sites are at their best in June/July, before they are cut or grazed.	Havering Ridge, Lea Valley, Roding Valley Meadows
July	Heath fritillary butterflies are on the wing mainly from mid-June to mid-July.	
	Saltmarsh is at its most colourful in July, with the sea lavender in flower.	
August	Wetland soils take longer to warm up so the best show usually appears later, in July/August, accompanied by a peak in the numbers of butterflies, dragonflies and other insects.	Cranham Marsh , Lea Valley Stanford Warren
	High summer is the peak time for insects almost everywhere, with butterflies along woodland rides and glow-worms in scrubby sites in the south-east of Essex.	Epping Forest, Grays Chalk Quarry
	Heathlands are at their best in August with the heather in flower and many insects about.	Epping Forest, Galleywood Common
September	Swans and ducks moult ready for migration and for winter.	Lea Valley
	August sees the beginning of the autumn migration, with birds streaming down the coast before crossing to the continent and heading for their wintering grounds further south.	
October	October brings autumn colours in the woods and the main flush of fungi on the woodland floor.	Epping Forest, Hainault Fore● Thorndon
	Brent geese usually arrive in late September to feast on eel-grass before moving on to grazing marsh.	
November	By November large numbers of water birds have settled in for the winter on inland lakes and reservoirs, while wetland birds like bitterns and bearded tits find shelter in large reed beds.	The Chase (Dagenham), Ingrebourne Valley, Lea Val● Stanford Warren
	Many thousands of waterfowl and waders spend the winter on the estuaries and around the coast. Most arrive in September/ October and leave in March/April, with numbers at a peak in January/February.	Rainham

dlife spectacles at different times

South-East	North-West	North-East
es Wood (Danbury), Daws h, Hockley Woods, Norsey d, Swan Wood, Thrift Wood	Broaks Wood, Brookes, Oxlip woods	Chalkney Wood, High Woods CP, Shut Heath Wood, Stour Estuary, Weeleyhall Wood
House Farm, Hanningfield rvoir, South Woodham	Aubrey Buxton, Hatfield Forest	Fingringhoe Wick (nightingales), Great Holland Pits, Marks Hall, The Naze
Meadows, Langdon	Hunsdon Mead, Upper Chelmer	Colne Valley
s Heath, Hockley Woods, t Wood		
Tree Island (Hadleigh)		Blackwater Estuary, Colne Point, Cudmore Grove, Fingringhoe Wick, Ray Island
rhall Meadows (Danbury), Tyler CP	Harlow Marsh, Phyllis Currie, Rushy Mead, Sawbridgeworth Marsh	Alexander, Holland Haven, Roman River Valley
ury, Maldon Wick, Stow es Halt, Hadleigh	Hatfield Forest	Colne Valley, Stour Estuary
ury		Fordham Heath, Tiptree Heath
ingfield Reservoir		Abberton Reservoir
well, Gunners Park		Colne Point, The Naze
ury, Hockley Woods	Brookes, Phyllis Currie	
Tree Island (Hadleigh)		
ingfield Reservoir, Wat CP		Abberton Reservoir, Chigborough Lakes
well, Lion Creek/Lower ts, South Woodham		Blackwater Estuary, Cudmore Grove, Fingringhoe Wick, Holland Haven, Howlands Marsh, Stour Estuary

Main entries in *orange*; sub-entries in *grey*

Blue House Farm

601ac/240ha OS Ex176/La168 GR 856 971 SSSI (part), SPA

THE
wildlife
TRUSTS

ESSEX
Wildlife Trust

Size in acres and hectares

OS Explorer and Landranger map numbers

Grid reference

Designations (see key below)

Organisation chiefly responsible for management

Key to Visiting

How to get there

Public transport

Opening times

Best time to visit

Facilities/notes for disabled visitors

Further information from...
(= leaflet available)

Warnings and guidance for visitors

SSSI — Site of Special Scientific Interest
Area notified by English Nature as important and with statutory protection.

SPA — Special Protection Area
Area protected under the EU Birds and Habitats Directives.

NNR — National Nature Reserve
Nature reserve of national importance, managed by or for English Nature (not always with public access).

LNR — Local Nature Reserve
Nature reserve of local importance, established by a Local Authority (usually with public access).

Key to maps

Vegetation
grass or heath
scrub
woodland
new woodland
marsh or fen
reed bed
saltmarsh
mud
sand or shingle
arable

Water bodies
fresh/ brackish
salt

Site boundary

Facilities
visitor centre 🅥
museum 🅜
bird hide
information board *i*
play area ⊼
picnic area ⊼
pub
drinks
parking 🅿
" informal 🅿
" disabled 🅿&
toilets WC
" inc. disabled

Paths
foot only
in between†
wheelchair
permissive public

Features
sea wall
bank & ditch
slope or cliff
church
golf course
viewpoint
building
built-up area

Entrances
vehicle
other

Roads
surfaced
other/track
bridleway/ horse ride/ multi-use path

† surfaced paths suitable for people with walking difficulties and possibly usable by wheelchairs, e.g. with assistance

ESSEX &
SUFFOLK
WATER

The huge expanse of Essex & Suffolk Water's Abberton Reservoir is one of Europe's most renowned wetland sites. It is of international importance as a safe haven for wild duck, swans and other water birds, whether resident, passing through on migration or over-wintering. The reservoir is situated close to east coast migration routes and, with its surrounding envelope of pasture and tree plantations, is a welcome sight to tired birds.

The sheer numbers of wildfowl in autumn and winter cannot fail to impress. Total numbers of the top seven species – wigeon, teal, mallard, pochard, tufted duck, coot and black-headed gull – can run to many thousands. Added to this there can be hundreds of shoveler, gadwall, goldeneye, pintail and great crested grebe.

In summer there is the unusual sight of 20 or 30 pairs of cormorants nesting in trees, one of the few places in Britain where this occurs. They suddenly began doing this in 1981 and have continued ever since.

Late summer brings the spectacle of large numbers of swans and ducks moulting – replacing their worn-out feathers – on the reservoir. Safety is vital while they do so because they replace all their flight feathers at once, which means that for a while they are unable to fly.

In dry winters water levels fall temporarily to expose large expanses of mud. This attracts large numbers of passage waders such as ruff and spotted redshank to the reservoir from the coast, further confirmation of the great value of the site to birds.

The surrounding farmland, too, is of value to birds. In winter thousands of golden plover may be seen there, along with small numbers of migratory geese and swans.

Finally, for the keen birdwatcher the reservoir boasts an impressive list of rarities visiting briefly in winter or passing through on migration.

Cormorants nesting in trees at Abberton Reservoir
Owen Keen

Wigeon: thousands winter on Abberton Reservoir
Owen Keen

Abberton Reservoir *nature reserve*

9ac/4ha   OS Ex184/La168   GR 963 185

A nature reserve managed by Essex Wildlife Trust is on a well-protected bay of the reservoir. Although only 9 acres, it is surprisingly rich in wildlife. It was created in 1975 with the advice of Sir Peter Scott, when a large pond was excavated close to the reservoir and a wide range of native tree and shrub species of value to wildlife were planted. Many have matured into fine specimen trees. Others have developed into valuable hedges and thickets that attract birds and insects and screen visitors on the nature trail, reducing disturbance to wildlife. A wide range of small birds nest here, particularly warblers, nightingales and finches and, in the tall clumps of gorse, yellowhammers and linnets.

The pockets of grassland provide open, sunlit sites ideal for many insects, including butterflies. In spring and summer you are likely to see small copper and wall brown, and other common species such as common blue, gatekeeper and small skipper.

The largest single feature is the pond. With a central nesting island, it attracts breeding mute swan, canada goose, mallard, moorhen and other waterfowl in spring.

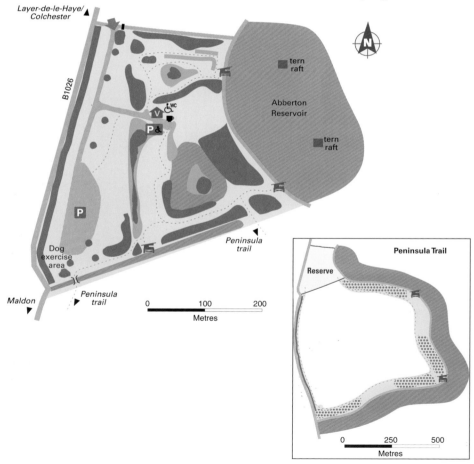

There are three bird hides within the reserve, two of which give views of two floating nesting rafts for common terns. The Trust has built two further bird hides on the peninsula of farmland and grassland adjacent to the reserve, where canada geese and wigeon graze in winter. In spring yellow wagtails, corn buntings and many other small birds nest in the young tree plantations, while in summer many butterflies and dragonflies can be seen among the tall thistles and grasses.

The Visitor Centre, built with the support of Essex & Suffolk Water and Colchester Council, sits right beside the reservoir. It is a birding centre par excellence, winter and summer movements bringing a variety of birds at different times of the year so that interest is always high. If you need binoculars or perhaps a telescope, then the regular Optics Field Days offer a wide range with experts on hand to help you find one that suits. The shop stocks a better range of wildlife books than anywhere else in Essex. Come and have a really good day looking at the wildlife, and get kitted out to improve your knowledge and enjoyment at the same time.

Small skipper: a widespread butterfly of rough grassland, on the wing mainly in July
Tony Gunton

Visiting

Five miles south-west of Colchester on the B1026, a minor road linking Colchester and Maldon, just outside Layer-de-la-Haye. Watch out for brown 'Wildfowl Centre' signs.

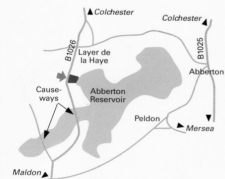

Centre, shop and nature reserve are open 9am-5pm every day except Mondays, Christmas and Boxing Days.

When the Centre is closed, good views can be had from the two causeways which are wide enough for safe parking.

Good all the year round, but especially in winter for wildfowl, May and June for breeding birds, and August for moulting swans and ducks. In dry winters low water levels attract wading birds from the coast.

The Centre is designed for disabled visitors. A boardwalk links the Centre with the large Scott hide. Two bird hides have low-level viewing slots and can be used with assistance by visitors in wheelchairs.

Please note that only guide dogs for the blind are allowed in the Centre and reserve. An enclosed exercise area for dogs is provided in the car park.

The Centre organises a regular programme of events for both adults and children. Call 01206 738172 for details.

Bordering Tenpenny Brook and forming part of a valuable wildlife corridor, this small triangle of freshwater marsh and grassland was left to the Essex Wildlife Trust in 1995 by the late Mrs Daphne Hart (née Alexander). It is a haven for wetland plants and animals with much of it covered in tall marsh grassland plants interspersed with fragments of willow, sallow and blackthorn scrub providing an ideal habitat for warblers and bullfinches. The southern half is often waterlogged and is dominated by sedges and rushes and flowers such as meadowsweet and ragged robin. The drier northern half holds a more varied mix of species on patches of dry ground, including greater birdsfoot trefoil, broad-leaved helleborine, marsh bedstraw, marsh woundwort and marsh speedwell, the only site in the area where this species is known.

Good numbers of moths and butterflies, including speckled wood, orange tip and small copper, can be seen in the summer months along with an abundance of other insects.

During the late annual cut the tiny suspended nests of harvest mice are often found threaded between the stems of taller plants.

Smooth newts are found in the small pond to the east where you may also be fortunate to see a grass snake .

Along the brook there are numerous water vole holes and a quiet approach to the stream can often yield sightings of this timid animal, along with the fleeting glimpse of a kingfisher.

During the winter snipe may be seen on the reserve and the occasional grey wagtail beside the brook, with the bordering alders proving a valuable food supply for flocks of siskins.

Visiting

On the B1027 Clacton-Colchester road at the bottom of Tenpenny Hill, Thorrington, on the Thorrington/Alresford border.

Approx. hourly buses from Colchester stop opposite and at the bottom of Tenpenny Hill.

Access is difficult pending the installation of a footbridge: meantime please call the warden on 01206 251302 for advice.

July for wild flowers.

At times parts of the site can be waterlogged.

Call the warden on 01206 251302 or Essex Wildlife Trust HQ on 01206 735456.

Harvest mouse nest
Sue Ward

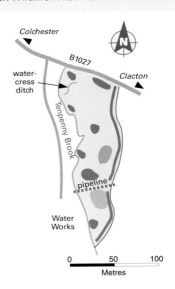

ESSEX
Wildlife Trust

This worked-out gravel pit has a lake occupying about one-third of the site, together with areas of grassland and willow/hawthorn scrub. The lake is bounded on three sides by steep escarpments and sandy beaches and on the other side by a more graduated embankment.

Plant life is varied, including stands of purple loosestrife around the shore and cliffs; St John's wort in the hedgerows; birdsfoot trefoil in the grassland; and sand and corn spurreys on the low-nutrient, open sandy areas. Bird's foot is prolific on the upper heath, which also has many mosses.

Variable numbers of wildfowl, sometimes up to 200, winter on the lake – mainly mallard, tufted duck, pochard and teal, with occasional appearances of shoveler, wigeon, goldeneye, pintail and ruddy duck. Mute swans and great crested grebes breed most years.

Among the butterflies, skippers can be found where the grass is longer, speckled wood in the wooded sections, common blue in the grassy areas and holly blue around the thicker hedges. Other insects include green and Roesel's bush-crickets.

The grassland is mown annually in winter or early spring to a height of about 10 cm: this benefits plants such as bee orchids, which have appeared in large numbers since the practice was adopted. Encroaching scrub is cut back to increase the area of open grassland.

Clearings are made in the willow scrub to promote a more diverse habitat, and short sections of boundary hedge are coppiced annually to ensure continued regeneration.

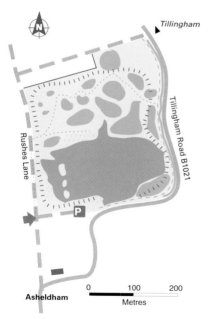

Tillingham

Tillingham Road B1021

Rushes Lane

Asheldham

0   100   200
Metres

Visiting

2 km north of Southminster on the B1021. As you enter Asheldham, the reserve entrance is via a gravel chase (Rushes Lane), which is on the left next to a row of cottages on the corner of a right-hand bend – look for direction sign on fence. The car park is about 150m up on the right.

Accessible at all times.

Southminster station is about 3km distant via Tillingham Road.

From spring through to mid-summer for breeding birds, flowering plants and butterflies.

Call the warden on 01621 779350 or Essex Wildlife Trust HQ on 01206 735456.

Aubrey Buxton

24ac/10ha   OS Ex195/La167   GR 521 264

Originally the pleasure park to Norman House, this reserve is high woodland interspersed with grassland, on a sandy/gravel soil. It has three man-made ponds, probably about 200 years old, and three further ponds dug in the 1950s when it was a wildlife park. It was donated to the Essex Wildlife Trust by Lord and the late Lady Buxton in 1976.

Cowslip, wild strawberry and common spotted orchid grow in the meadows, along with the uncommon lesser lady's mantle and adderstongue fern. Hop sedge, which is very localised in this part of Essex, grows around the ponds.

The many bird species include nuthatch, owls, woodpeckers and a number of summer visitors. There is a rookery.

Twenty-two species of butterfly have been recorded and in good years numbers can be impressive. A nest of wild bees in an old beech tree has been active for some time.

Many mature trees were lost in the storms of 1987 and 1990. This left poplar trees very prone to storm damage and in 1991 many of these were felled. They are gradually being replaced with native trees, and notably a dozen black poplars.

This species formerly played an important part in country life, being planted to give shade to cattle and to provide firewood and charcoal for the home.

The grassland areas are mown annually in the autumn, with small areas mown on rotation during June or July to encourage plant diversity.

Visiting

The reserve is just to the north of Stansted. Turn right (east) off the B1383 (Bishop's Stortford–Stansted–Cambridge) on to Alsa Street. The entrance is 200m up a private road (with white gateposts at its end) on the right.

Accessible at all times.

Spring or summer.

Call the warden on 01799 550378 or Essex Wildlife Trust HQ on 01206 735456.

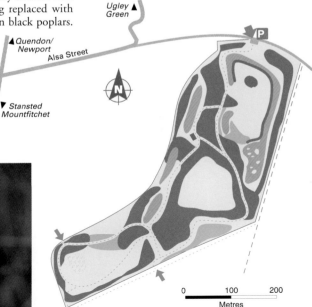

Great spotted woodpecker (male)
Alan Williams

14

Belhus

Belhus, near Aveley in Thurrock, is the site of an historic park landscaped by Capability Brown, now bisected by the M25 motorway. Belhus Woods Country Park occupies the western end, and also has ancient woods and lakes, while part of the eastern section is open access woodland and grassland. Recently the Woodland Trust has acquired additional land to the south of the country park to create a new parkland landscape.

Belhus Woods Country Park

180ac/72ha OS Ex175/La177 GR 565 825 Essex County Council

Belhus Woods was once a deer park, and was landscaped by Capability Brown in the mid-18th Century. It is now a country park managed by Essex County Council's Ranger Service. The main part, to the east of Romford Road, contains ancient woodland, grassland, and three lakes that were created by gravel extraction in the 1980s and added to the country park later. Two of these are used for fishing but the other is reserved for wildlife. There are two further small ancient woodlands on the other side of the road. More land surrounding the park has been added to it recently, some of which is being planted with trees and some kept as hay meadows.

With such a variety of habitats the park is rich in wildlife. Brick Kiln wood with its streams and ponds, dug to extract clay for brickmaking, is alive with insects in summer, as are the meadows nearby. The hazel in Running Water Wood is coppiced to produce timber for thatching and hurdle-making, and the clearings are full of wild flowers, including early purple orchids and ragged robin.

Lake at Belhus Woods Country Park
Tony Gunton

Belhus Chase

134ac/54ha   OS Ex175/La177   GR 567 822

WOODLAND
TRUST

This area of land to the south of Belhus Woods Country Park was acquired by the Woodland Trust in 1998 as part of its 'Woods on your Doorstep' project which is supported by the Millennium Commission and the Sainsbury Family charitable trusts. Part of it has been planted with trees and part has been left as open meadows, to create a parkland atmosphere.

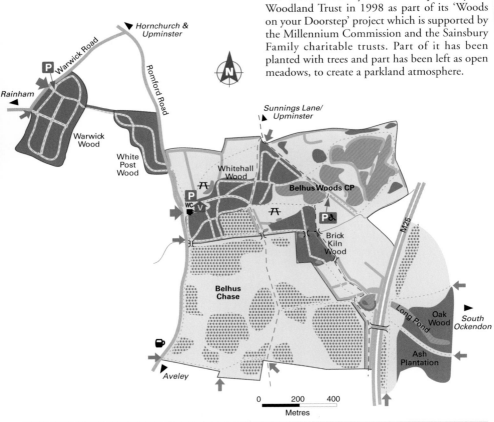

Visiting

The main entrance is on Romford Road about one mile north of Aveley. From Upminster follow Corbets Tey Road (B1421) south, turn right on to Harwood Hall Lane at the Huntsman & Hounds PH, then first left on to Aveley Road which runs straight on into Romford Road.

Buses from Romford to Grays via Upminster station pass the main entrance. Upminster rail and tube station is about 3 miles from the park.

Country park open 8 am until dusk all the year round. Visitor Centre open 10 am–5 pm at weekends and 1 pm–4 pm on Wednesdays from April to October. Belhus Chase and public footpaths accessible at all times.

May–July for birdsong, butterflies and dragonflies. Choose a day with a westerly breeze to carry away the noise from the nearby M25.

Parking area for disabled near the lakes.

Call the Ranger on 01708 865628 for more information or details of activities.

Blackwater Estuary

When the Essex Wildlife Trust acquired Abbotts Hall Farm in early 2000, it added a large piece to a jigsaw of valuable conservation land around the Salcott Channel at the head of the Blackwater Estuary. To the east of Abbotts Hall Farm lie Copt Hall Marshes, owned by the National Trust, and to the south the RSPB's important Old Hall Marshes reserve. Beyond Old Hall Marshes is another Essex Wildlife Trust reserve, Tollesbury Wick Marshes. This makes up almost 3,000 acres of land in total which, along with Abberton Reservoir just a few miles to the north, is of tremendous importance to wildlife, and especially to birds. This area also has several experiments relating to more sustainable flood defence, such as beach recharge and managed retreat (see page 19), and a large part of it belongs to the Blackwater Estuary National Nature Reserve.

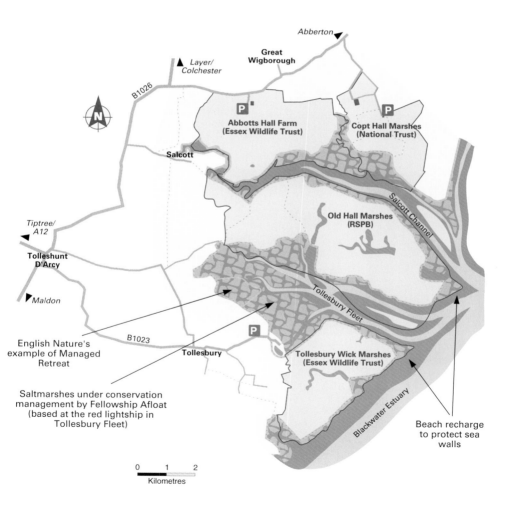

17

Abbotts Hall Farm

700ac/280ha OS Ex184/La168   GR 963 146   SSSI (part), SPA

In early 2000 Essex Wildlife Trust purchased this 700-acre arable farm with a large legacy from the late Miss Joan Elliot and support by WWF-UK, the Environment Agency, English Nature and the Heritage Lottery Fund.

The Trust plans to continue farming about half the area as arable, but features such as hedgerows, field margins, ditches, copses and headlands will be reinstated to show how wildlife can survive alongside arable farming.

Most of the remaining area will be put into 'managed retreat' by controlled breaching of the seawall, creating 300 acres of saltmarsh, saline lagoons and grazing marsh – all nationally threatened habitats. By putting some of these habitats back, the Trust hopes to show how other landowners could do the same and to support wildfowl like brent geese, wigeon, teal and waders like curlew, plovers, godwits and redshank.

The estate dates back to the Domesday Survey of 1085. Abbotts Hall, a grade II listed building, will be converted to form a new headquarters for the Trust and to provide visitor facilities.

Visiting

About 3km south of the causeway across Abberton Reservoir, turn east off the B1026 (Colchester–Maldon) towards Peldon. The entrance to Abbotts Hall Farm is about 1km down on the right.

Not open to the public until mid-2001, when the Joan Elliot Visitor Centre will provide visitor facilities and a start point for a choice of walks. Call Essex Wildlife Trust on 01206 735456 for up-to-date information or check the Trust website at *www.essexwt.org.uk*.

Abbotts Hall Farm as the Essex Wildlife Trust plans it should become

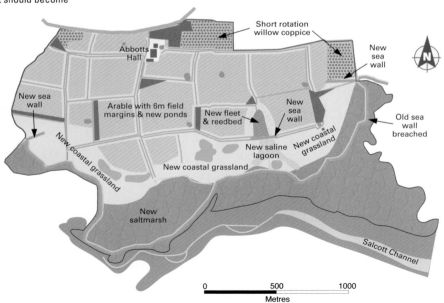

Coastal Squeeze and Managed Retreat

The sea level is rising all around the Essex coast partly because south-east England is sinking slightly and also because of the expansion of the seas caused by global warming. Saltmarsh plants cannot survive being regularly submerged in salt water, so as the sea level rises these plants die and the saltmarshes begin to disintegrate or rot. If there was no sea wall on our Essex coastline, then over a period of years the saltmarshes would migrate back to slightly higher land. But ever since the 13th Century we have built sea walls to protect low-lying land against flooding and to capture new land for agriculture. As a result the saltmarshes have nowhere to migrate to and instead they are squeezed against the sea wall. This is known as *coastal squeeze*. Some of our Essex estuaries have now lost over 60% of their saltmarshes due to rising sea levels and coastal squeeze.

The rise in sea levels also puts up the cost of maintaining the sea defences, to such an extent that the Environment Agency has adopted a policy known as *managed retreat*. Managed retreat means abandoning some sections of sea wall and retreating to a more defensible position further inland, and they are now considering

Eroding saltmarsh on the Blackwater
Pat Allen

Now

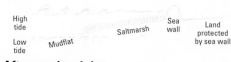

After sea level rise

which of the 460 km of sea walls in Essex should be abandoned in this way and which should continue to be maintained.

This is why the Environment Agency, WWF-UK, English Nature and Essex Wildlife Trust have agreed to work together at Abbotts Hall Farm. Together they are looking for a more sustainable way of managing a 3km section of coastline. They will remove the restriction of the sea wall so that saltmarshes can once more develop on higher land behind the current line of sea defence. This will result in massive wildlife gain because saltmarshes will be created on arable land and it will result in reduced costs because there will be no sea wall to maintain.

Copt Hall Marshes

400ac/160ha OS Ex184/La168   *GR 981 146*   *SSSI (part), SPA*

T his working farm to the north of the Salcott Channel is owned by the National Trust. The Trust encourages its tenants to farm in a wildlife-friendly way, with conservation headlands and well-managed hedgerows.

Wildfowl such as brent geese over-winter on the grazing marsh and waders frequent the saltmarsh beyond the seawall. 'Red hills' on the grazing marsh, produced by the fires used to heat the salt pans, are evidence of salt extraction in the past.

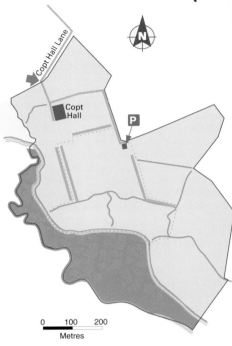

Visiting

Lies south of the minor road that joins the B1026 to the B1025 south of Abberton reservoir via Peldon. Turn off on to Copt Hall Lane and follow signs to the car park at Lower Barn.

Occasional bus services from Colchester to Mersea Island pass the end of Copt Hall Lane.

Accessible at all times.

Winter for wildlfowl.

A waymarked circular route runs across the grazing marsh and along the sea wall. To reduce disturbance, visitors are asked to use a shorter route in winter.

Brent geese on one of the fleets
at Old Hall Marshes
Pat Allen

Old Hall Marshes

1148ac/459ha   OS Ex184/La168   GR 959 124   NNR, SSI, SPA

Old Hall Marshes is a peninsula of grazing marsh at the head of the Blackwater Estuary, protected by 10km of sea wall. Within the walls are large areas of ancient 'unimproved' grassland, reedbeds and open water and it has just about all the designations you can think of, including SSSI, NNR and SPA. It was bought by the RSPB in 1984 and is run as a working farm as well as a nature reserve. Grazing by cattle and sheep is managed to produce swards of different lengths to suit different bird species, and the water regime is managed to try to keep levels consistent summer and winter.

As a result the reserve attracts wildfowl and waders to breed and overwinter in internationally and nationally important numbers. Numbers of wintering brent geese, for example, average more than 4,500 and, of the 60 species of bird that breed there, numbers of garganey, shoveler, pochard, avocet and bearded tit are of national importance.

The reserve also supports scarce plant and insect species and has thriving populations of brown hare and water vole, both of which are in decline nationally.

Visiting

Access by car is restricted to holders of permits only, obtainable by writing to the warden, 1 Old Hall Lane, Tolleshunt D'Arcy, Maldon, Essex CM9 8TP, but there is a public footpath running right round the reserve on the seawall and this can most easily be reached from Tollesbury. From Tollesbury the full circuit is over 10 miles, but a shortcut can be taken across the centre.

Bus services run to Tollesbury from Maldon, Colchester and Witham.

Accessible at all times via the public footpaths.

Winter for overwintering brent geese and other waterfowl on the fleets and on the estuary; spring and summer for breeding birds.

The sea wall path can be very muddy in winter.

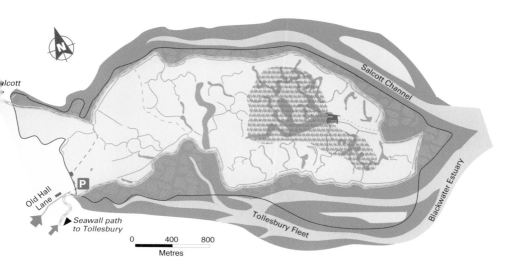

21

Tollesbury Wick

599ac/240ha OS Ex176/La168   **GR 970 104**   **SSSI, SPA**

This is a rare example of an Essex freshwater grazing marsh, worked for decades by traditional methods sympathetic to wildlife and now owned by Essex Wildlife Trust. Wildlife is abundant in the 600 acres of rough pasture, borrowdykes, sea walls, wet flushes, pools and saltmarsh.

Large areas of rough pasture suit small mammals such as field vole and pygmy shrew. In winter, they in turn attract hunting hen harriers and short-eared owls.

Dry grassland on the slopes of the sea walls supports a wide variety of insects, including butterflies, bush crickets and grasshoppers. In spring spiny restharrow, grass vetchling, slender

Visiting

🚗 Follow the B1023 to Tollesbury via Tiptree, leaving the A12 at Kelvedon, then follow Woodrolfe Road towards the marina and car park at Woodrolfe Green.

🚌 Bus services run to Tollesbury from Maldon, Colchester and Witham.

🕐 Accessible at all times along the footpath on top of the seawall. A permissive footpath across the grazing marsh is under construction (see map).

📅 May for birdsong; July for saltmarsh colours and for insects; winter for wildfowl and waders.

⚠ Sheep ticks can be a problem in April–June: keep out of the long grass or wear light-coloured (so the ticks can easily be seen) long trousers for protection.

🚻ℹ from Essex Wildlife Trust visitor centres. For more information, call the warden on 01621 868628.

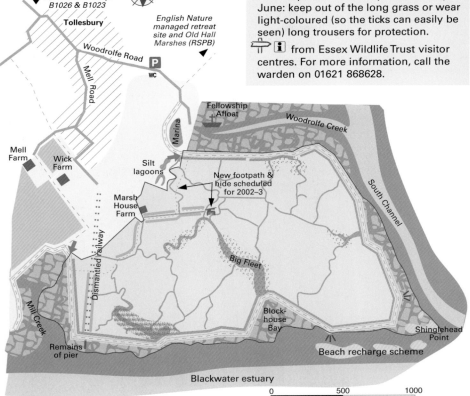

hare's-ear and many other wild flowers can be found in ungrazed areas.

Borrowdykes trace the inland edge of the sinuous seawall for its entire length. Common reed, sea clubrush and fennel pondweed are typical plants of these brackish areas where reed warbler and reed bunting nest in spring, and heron and little grebe search for food. Wet flushes, dykes and small pools in the pasture support aquatic plants such as water crowfoot, and breeding populations of dragonflies and other aquatic species.

Golden plover, lapwing, brent geese and wigeon feed or roost on the winter-wet grassland.

On the other side of the seawall, and within the reserve boundary, creeks, salt marsh and exposed mud support typical communities of coastal mud-dwelling invertebrates, coastal birds and salt marsh flora. Scattered shingle spits have yellow-horned poppy, and also a small breeding colony of little terns.

The main pillars of management are water level control and getting the right level of grazing to create suitable conditions for birds and other wildlife.

Dredgings being used to recharge
the beach at Tollesbury Wick
Geoff Gibbs ▼

Dark-bellied form of brent goose
▼ *Gerald Downey*

Brent geese feeding at Tollesbury Wick, with the lightship 'Fellowship Afloat' in the background
Jonathan Smith ▼

Blue House Farm

601ac/240ha   OS Ex175-6/La168   GR 856 971   SSSI (part), SPA

Blue House Farm was bought by the Essex Wildlife Trust in 1998 with support from the Heritage Lottery Fund and many other donors. It is a working farm, mainly coastal grazing marsh with an area in arable production. Most of the farm was originally saltmarsh until sea walls were constructed to capture land from the sea. It was then used as grazing pasture, this practice continuing today. Some of the higher, drier fields are used for crops and about 90 acres are in cereal production.

The farm is a Site of Special Scientific Interest (SSSI) as part of the River Crouch Marshes, notified for its wetland bird species and rare water beetles. It is within the Essex Coast Environmentally Sensitive Area (ESA) which encourages land owners to retain and recreate coastal pastures and to increase areas of conservation wetlands.

The flat fields between the farmhouse and the sea wall are used in winter as a feeding ground by brent geese. Often more than 2,000 geese are seen, together with large numbers of wigeon grazing on the short turf.

Throughout the year hares are abundant and are most easily seen on these fields where cover is scarce. Skylarks also thrive, and are often heard singing high overhead in spring and summer.

The fleets provide deep water which is important for diving birds including tufted duck and little grebe. Our smallest duck, the teal, and our largest, the shelduck, are both commonly seen. At high tide sea birds move on to the fleets from the mudflats beyond the sea wall.

The creeks and ditches within the traditional grazing marsh are important habitats for rare water beetles and other water insects like the

Visiting

🚗 Take the B1012 east from South Woodham Ferrers and after about 3 miles turn right to North Fambridge. Access is via a track on the left off Fambridge Road 200m south of Fambridge station.

🚌 An hourly train service runs to Fambridge via Wickford.

🕐 Accessible at all times via public footpath along the seawall. The permissive footpath giving access to bird hides overlooking the fleets is open from April 1st to October 31st.

📅 Between mid-October and March for brent geese and wintering wildfowl. From April to June for breeding birds and for hares.

📋 Please take care to close gates behind you as this is a working farm as well as a nature reserve.

ℹ️ from Essex Wildlife Trust visitor centres. For more information call the warden on 01621 740687.

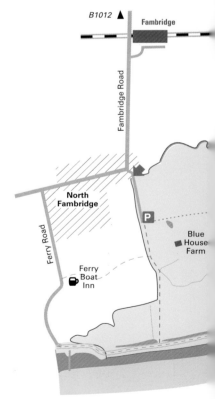

hairy dragonfly and scarce emerald damselfly. Those with thick vegetation support water voles and may, in time, again give shelter to otters, known to have lived here at least until 1963.

The marshy fields attract wading birds such as redshank, curlew and snipe which feed on creatures within the boggy ground. The saltmarsh and intertidal mud beyond the seawall provide abundant food for wading birds like these and for oystercatchers and black-tailed godwit.

Like most coastal grazing marsh the land was extensively drained for agriculture. The Trust is putting in sluices to raise and control water levels, vital for the wildlife. The level of grazing is also critical, so the Trust is working towards a balance between good livestock farming and good conservation.

Hairy dragonfly
Dr Chris Gibson/English Nature

Bridgemarsh Island

River Crouch

0   250   500
Metres

25

The fleet at Blue House Farm
Nick Robson

On your way to Blue House Farm, why not drop in at ...

Hall Wood

8ac/3ha   OS Ex175/6/La168 GR 854 987

ESSEX
Wildlife Trust

This wood, managed by Essex Wildlife Trust, mainly comprises oak with some ash and elm (now mostly dead), and with field maple and spindle on its edge.

It contains one of the largest rookeries in Essex and usually several grey heron's nests – the main heronry is in the adjoining wood. Woodland birds are well represented and all three species of woodpecker are seen.

Spring brings a fine display of bluebells, and it is unusual to see colonies of foxgloves and, particularly, stinking iris this far east in Essex.

Visiting

🚗 On the left (south) of the Burnham-Wickford road 300m west of its junction with the Maldon-North Fambridge road.

🚌 An hourly train service runs to Fambridge station (about 1km away) via Wickford.

🕐 Accessible at all times

📅 Spring for bluebells and other early flowers

📋 Rooks and herons are easily disturbed when nesting: please do not linger near them or their nests.

☎ Call the warden on 01621 741351 or Essex Wildlife Trust HQ on 01206 735456.

Shell and shingle

Silt and sand are carried into estuaries both by the river and by the sea. Fine silt is deposited in sheltered waters to form mudflats that are covered and uncovered by each succeeding tide, but towards the sea conditions are more turbulent, so only the coarser material can settle. As a result shell or shingle spits develop at the estuary mouth. These spits have only a tiny area compared with the mudflats, but they are of major importance for nesting seabirds like little terns and ringed plovers, which need an undisturbed beach on which to lay their eggs.

▲ Yellow horned-poppy: grows only on shingle and shell banks
Jonathan Smith

◄

Little terns breed on shingle spits where thay are highly vulnerable to predation and disturbance
Alan Williams

Ringed plovers nest on sand or shingle all round the Essex coast
Owen Keen
▼

Often the spits remain sterile because they are constantly shifted by the tides, but sometimes they do become stable enough to support vegetation, like those within the Essex Wildlife Trust reserves at Colne Point and Bradwell. Then unusual plants like yellow horned-poppy and sea campion manage to colonise, with sea beet and sea rocket down nearer the tideline.

Bradwell Cockle Spit

200ac/80ha   OS Ex176/La168   GR 035 081   SSSI

This nature reserve on the Dengie peninsula consists of some 30 acres of shell bank, together with extensive saltmarsh. The shell bank is continuous between Tip Head and Gunner's Creek, but further south consists of a series of small cockle spits, many of which are separated by deep creeks and gullies. The adjoining saltings in some places are several hundred yards wide.

The reserve is run jointly by Essex Wildlife Trust and the Essex Birdwatching Society. The latter also operates Bradwell Bird Observatory, situated in the grounds of Linnett's Cottage on the edge of the reserve.

Little terns, ringed plovers and oystercatchers breed on the shell banks, and the saltings support a wide variety of species including redshank, yellow wagtail, meadow pipit, reed bunting and linnet. In autumn and winter large flocks of up to 20,000 waders roost on the reserve at high tide. Snow bunting are regular winter visitors; shore lark and lapland bunting visit occasionally.

A wide range of raptors frequent the area, among them hen harrier, merlin, peregrine and short-eared owl in winter, and marsh harrier, sparrowhawk and hobby at other seasons.

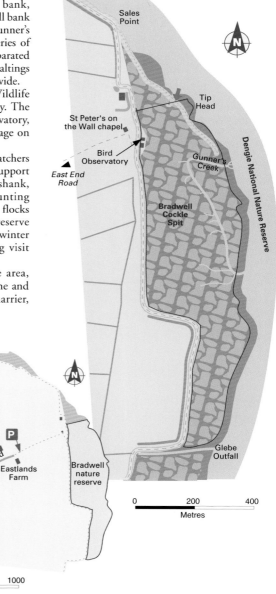

Visiting

Head for Bradwell-on-Sea (a mile inland!) via Latchingdon or Southminster, following the B1010/B1018 from Chelmsford or Maldon. Turn right in Bradwell by the church and follow East End Road to its end and park at Eastlands Farm. The reserve is entered via the Saxon chapel of St Peter's on the Wall – a distance of about 800m from there. To reach the reserve, walk northwards along the seawall to Sales Point, then southwards along the public beach to Tip Head Creek. This can be crossed quite easily at low tide and gives access to the first few hundred yards of the reserve, as far south as Gunners' Creek. *This creek is wide, with deep mud in parts, and no attempt should be made to cross it!*

Accessible at all times. If you are interested in seeing waders, time your visit to coincide with high tide. At Bradwell this is just before Southend and about 90 minutes before London Bridge (the nearest places usually included in newspaper tide tables).

Access for the disabled can be arranged through the warden: call 01277 354034 or Essex Wildlife Trust HQ on 01206 735456.

In order to protect breeding shore-birds, between April and August inclusive please keep to the sea wall overlooking the reserve, or where no wall exists to the edge of the saltings.

The more stable parts of the shell banks support a rich flora that includes yellow horned-poppy, slender birdsfoot trefoil, grass-leaved orache, sea rocket, marram grass and occasional clumps of the locally rare sea kale. A wide range of specialised species can be found on the saltmarsh.

The mud and sandflats to the east of the reserve, extending some 3km from the shore, are part of the Dengie National Nature Reserve. These are internationally important for overwintering waders, and notably for grey plover, knot and bar-tailed godwit. Sales Point is a good spot from which to watch waders feeding, ideally when the tide is rising to cover the mudflats. As well as the waders just mentioned, you may see dunlin, redshank, oystercatcher and curlew.

As you continue along the seawall you may also find turnstone, sanderling and ringed plover. Flocks of brent geese could be on the fields, mud or the sea. The small thicket between the Bird Observatory and Sales Point is used as a refuge by many migrating birds

The barges sunk just offshore are there to protect the saltmarsh and seawall from erosion.

Grey Plover
Alan Williams

Yellow wagtail
Alan Williams

29

Brightlingsea Marsh

75ac/30ha   OS Ex184/La168   GR 076 164   NNR

ENGLISH NATURE

This area of grazing marsh right next to Brightlingsea is part of the Colne Estuary NNR. Redshank and shoveler breed there in summer, while in winter it is used by brent geese and other wildfowl. It has a huge density of ant hills, and these in turn attract green woodpeckers, for which ants are a favourite food. Its flowering plants include spiny rest-harrow and, on the ant hills, lady's bedstraw.

It is grazed by cattle or sheep in the traditional way. High water levels are maintained using overspill water from a gravel works nearby, to create good conditions for wading birds. The adjacent grazing marsh, outside the NNR, is managed in a similar way.

Visiting

In Brightlingsea, follow the Promenade towards Westmarsh Point, parking near the Martello Tower.

Regular buses to Brightlingsea from Colchester and Clacton, or rail to Great Bentley and bus from there.

Good views at any time from the sea wall path. Access to the site requires a permit from English Nature's Colchester office: call 01206 796666.

May to July for breeding birds; winter for wildfowl.

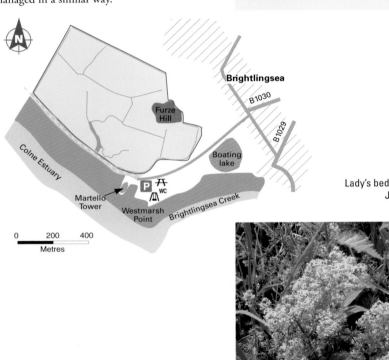

Lady's bedstraw, flowering June–September
Tony Gunton

30

Broaks Wood

155ac/62ha   OS Ex195/La167   GR 784 317

Forestry Commission

This woodland, much of it ancient in origin, is managed for the Forestry Commission by Forest Enterprise. It is a working woodland with an average of 500 tonnes of timber harvested annually, but conservation is given a high priority. Where introduced timber trees are harvested, for example, the original native broadleaved trees and woodland plants are replanted or allowed to regenerate naturally. The traditional method of coppicing is used also, on species such as sweet chestnut, hazel and ash.

As a result the wood is rich in wildlife, including familar plants such as bluebells and primroses, and also some rarities. For example, it has a scattering of wild service trees and, in the stream valley to the east, opposite-leaved golden saxifrage. It is also a good place to see bats, feeding in the glades and along the rides at dusk.

Visiting

The main entrance is on Hedingham Road (A1017 Braintree–Hedingham) two miles east of Halstead.

A bus service from Braintree to Castle Hedingham runs along Hedingham Road.

Accessible at all times.

Spring for woodland flowers and birdsong; summer for butterflies and other insects in glades and rides.

A 3km waymarked nature trail (red posts) takes in the most interesting sights and should take an hour or so. **i** from Forest Enterprise (01394 450164).

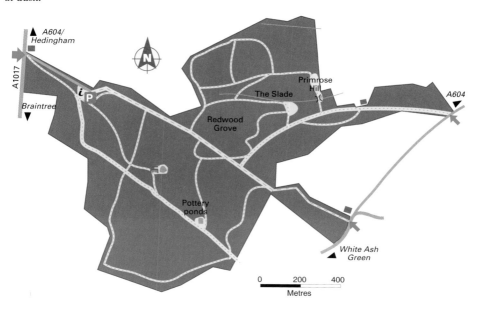

Brookes Reserve

59ac/24ha   OS Ex195/La168   GR 813 266   SSSI (part)

THE WILDLIFE TRUSTS

ESSEX
Wildlife Trust

This nature reserve, owned by the Coda Wildlife Trust and managed by Essex Wildlife Trust, comprises over 40 acres of ancient woodland and some 18 acres of arable fields, part of which has been planted up with native trees. The woods are known locally as Brooks's Woods, and the reserve is named after Thomas Brookes, the 18th-century owner.

Most of the wood is ash and hazel coppice. Areas of small-leaved lime and hornbeam add variety, and there are also more than 20 wild service trees. A network of historic green lanes, one a bridleway, crosses the woods. Thirteen ponds and the wet surface are evidence of the chalky boulder clay soil.

Bramble, pendulous sedge and dog's mercury dominate the ground flora, with primrose over large areas. Some notable species are greater butterfly orchid, twayblade, herb paris, sweet woodruff, wood small reed, hard shield fern, narrow buckler fern and at least six different varieties of sedge.

Nuthatch, treecreeper and lesser spotted woodpecker nest on the reserve along with many summer migrant songbirds. Brown hares and large herds of fallow deer are often seen.

The wood is coppiced on rotation to produce charcoal and firewood.

Visiting

Between Stisted and Greenstead Green north-east of Braintree: from Greenstead Green the reserve is 2km down on the right and from Stisted 3km down on the left just past Tumbler's Green.

Saturday only bus service Halstead to Braintree.

Accessible at all times. Car park may be locked at night to discourage misuse.

For songbirds, a sunny morning in April/May; a warm summer afternoon for butterflies; early October for autumn colours.

Please do not let children play near ponds as they could be dangerous. Please keep to the paths and keep dogs on a lead. Waterproof footwear essential in wet weather.

For more information call the warden on 01787 472012 or Essex Wildlife Trust HQ on 01206 735456.

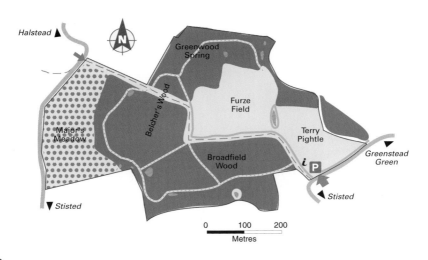

Alexandra's pond, the best and largest of 13 in Brookes Reserve
David Self

Nuthatch: nests in open woodland and parkland
David Harrison

Primrose, flowering mainly in early spring but occasionally in autumn or winter
Tony Gunton

Burnham Country Park

40ac/16ha   OS Ex176/La168   GR 942 961

**Maldon
Council**

Maldon Council has recently landscaped and planted up this country park next to the Crouch Estuary at Burnham. It is largely open countryside with a few small copses and a small wetland area with open water, marsh and reedbed.

Skylarks nest in the rough grassland and the wild flowers, shrubs and young trees attract seed-eating birds such as linnets and goldfinches. Gulls and other birds visit from the estuary. In summer insect life is good with many butterflies over the grassland and dragonflies and damselflies over the wetland.

Visiting

🚗 Entering Burnham-on-Crouch on the B1021, turn right just past the station into Foundry Lane or (for disabled parking) about 200m further on into Millfields.

🚌 Burnham station (from Liverpool Street via Romford and Wickford) is about 15 minutes walk via Foundry Lane.

🕐 Accessible at all times.

📅 Summer for birds and insects.

♿ Easy access trail runs north-south.

☎ Call Maldon Council's parks team on 01621 875823.

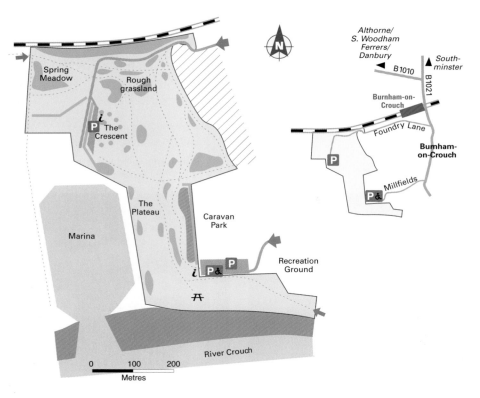

34

Chalkney Wood

200ac/80ha   OS Ex195/La168   GR 872 273   SSSI   Essex County Council

Forestry Commission

Chalkney Wood has both great historical and great wildlife interest. It was owned from the Norman conquest until 1570 by the De Veres, Earls of Oxford. They used it to breed and rear wild boar, which were extinct in the wild at the time. There are none there now, of course, but there is still evidence of its history in features such as ancient woodbanks and the narrow tracks winding through the wood, which probably follow the same routes as in the Middle Ages.

The south-western part of the wood is owned by Essex County Council and managed as a public space. The remainder, running down to the River Colne, is owned by the Forestry Commission who have planted up much of it with conifers. As these conifers are harvested the original native trees are being allowed to grow through and take their place.

Chalkney Wood is unusual in its great variety and in that it contains the greatest concentration of small-leaved lime trees in the county. Small-leaved lime used to be widespread across lowland

Visiting

Main entrance about a mile down a minor road leaving the A1124 (Colchester–Halstead) between Earls Colne and White Colne, heading south. It can also be entered from the north via a footpath running south from the A1124 at White Colne to Chalkney Mill.

Several bus services between Colchester and Halstead run along the A1124.

Accessible at all times.

Late March through to May for spring flowers and birdsong.

Coppiced
small-leaved
lime
Pat Allen

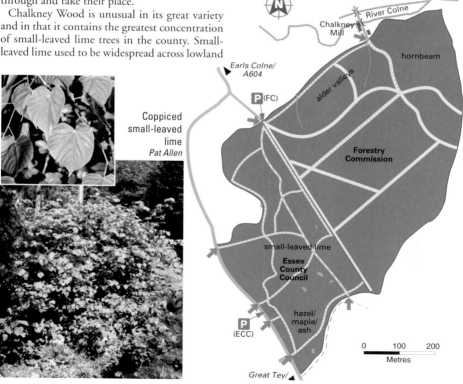

35

England but is now restricted to just a few woods. It has little timber value and was rarely planted, so it survives almost solely in woods that have not been reshaped by man for many centuries. Small-leaved lime is the dominant species in much of the Essex County Council section of the wood, which is on a boulder clay soil. This gives way to London Clay as the land falls towards the River Colne in the north, and as it falls so the natural vegetation contains more and more hornbeam.

The southern corner contains a mix of ash, hazel, holly, field maple and wild cherry, with wild currant growing beneath them. This is probably because of a patch of particularly chalky soil. Along the north-western edge are a number of alder valleys fed by springs. Here and there are patches of aspen, a wild service tree or two, oak, sweet chestnut and elm, invading from the edges. There are ponds, pits and depressions all over the place.

As a result of its long history of coppicing the wood has great natural richness. Bluebells, anemones and primroses cover the woodland floor in different parts of the wood, especially in the areas that have been coppiced recently.

Wild cherry
Gordon Reid

Chigborough Lakes
▼ *Phil Luke*

Chigborough Lakes

46ac/18ha   OS Ex183/La168   GR 877 086

This Essex Wildlife Trust reserve consists of worked-out flooded gravel pits to the north of the Blackwater Estuary. It has a variety of habitats including willow carr, open water, small ponds and marshy areas, rough grassland, and willow and hawthorn scrub. It lies on a relatively thin layer of non-glacial terrace sands and gravels deposited on London clay, and hence the lakes are shallow and likely to dry out in summer.

Extraction has left some low-nutrient areas with an interesting flora, including common spotted orchid, bee orchid and southern marsh orchid, heath speedwell, blue fleabane and wild strawberry. More than 200 species of plant have been recorded, among them round-leaved wintergreen, golden dock, lesser reedmace and wild service tree. There are 11 types of willow, notably almond willow, purple willow and naturalised cricket-bat willow.

Over 120 species of bird have been recorded, and more than 40 of these have bred at some time, including great crested and little grebes, kingfisher and water rail. Ruddy duck can be numerous when the water level is high. Conversely greenshank and other waders increase when the shallow-water margins are wider. Sedge and reed warblers can be seen or heard in spring and summer, together with whitethroat, reed bunting and willow warbler.

Grass snakes have been seen in large numbers, and common lizards appreciate the rough grassland areas.

There is a variety of insects including good numbers of common blue, small copper and ringlet butterflies and many dragonflies.

Visiting

About a mile up the B1026 from Heybridge towards Tolleshunt d'Arcy, turn north into Chigborough road. Continue past the fishery entrance and Chigborough Farm buildings, until you see the entrance gate to Chigborough Quarry. The reserve entrance is about 50m beyond this, on the left.

Buses from Colchester to Maldon Leisure Centre run along the B1026.

Accessible at all times.

April–July for birds, flowers and butterflies; October–February for wintering wildfowl.

During working hours, please take care not to obstruct the view or access of lorries using the gravel pit entrance.

from Essex Wildlife Trust visitor centres. For more information call the warden on 01621 853969 or Essex Wildlife Trust HQ on 01206 735456.

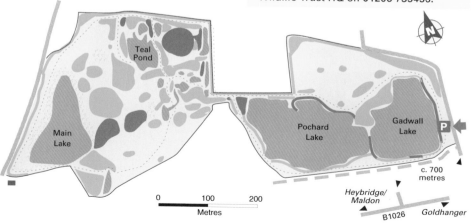

Claybury Woods

42ac/17ha   OS Ex174/La177   GR 435 911

London
Wildlife Trust

This ancient woodland in the grounds of Claybury Hospital, now part of the 420-acre Claybury Estate, is managed by London Wildlife Trust. It was originally part of the Royal Forest of Hainault and contains old hornbeam coppice and ancient oaks. It is carpeted with bluebells, wood anemones and ramsons (wild garlic) in spring, and also has unusual plants such as wild service tree, southern woodrush and broad-leaved helleborines.

Visiting

In the grounds of Claybury Hospital, east of Woodford Bridge. Footpath and cycle route access is possible across the south of the site from Riding Lane and Tomswood Road.

Hainault tube station (Central line) about 1 mile.

For events and workdays only at present. Telephone 020 7261 0447 for more details and up-to-date information.

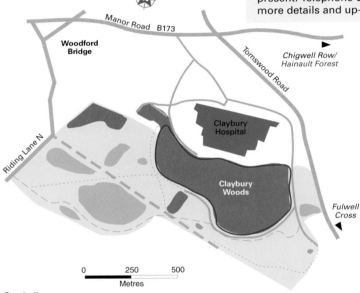

0   250   500
Metres

Sea holly
Owen Keen

Golden samphire
Dr Chris Gibson/English Nature

This large and important Essex Wildlife Trust reserve at the mouth of the Colne Estuary and at the south-western end of the Tendring peninsula consists of a shingle ridge enclosing a considerable area of saltmarsh, through which Ray Creek flows. The shingle and sand is nearly all that remains of a much larger area between Walton-on-the-Naze and St Osyth that existed at the end of the 19th century but has now mostly been developed by the seaside holiday industry.

For anyone wishing to explore the movement of shingle and the development of shingle structures, Colne Point is of great interest. It is the best developed spit on the Essex coast and includes various stages of stabilisation.

The reserve is rich in plants and animals, including many species that are rare nationally or locally. The saltmarsh is a typical example of the habitat in Essex and holds good populations of golden samphire and small cord-grass (both nationally scarce) as well as sea wormwood, sea lavender and thrift, amongst others. The shingle and sand ridge has many attractive plants which are now highly localised. Sea holly, sea bindweed, sea spurge, yellow horned-poppy and sea kale are all well established. Nationally scarce species include sea heath, dune fescue, curved hard-grass, sea barley and rock sea-lavender. The stands of shrubby seablite are some of the best on the east coast.

The exposed mudflats, shell banks and shingle

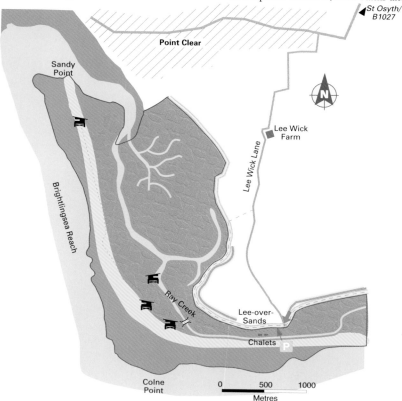

39

pools total some 250 acres and hold a large range of marine invertebrates and algae. These inter-tidal areas provide a feeding ground for large numbers of waders that arrive in autumn and winter. Colne Point is on a major migration route for finches, chats, pipits, skylarks and hirundines and in autumn movements are diurnal with birds constantly streaming through the reserve when the weather conditions are right. Birds of prey are also frequently seen, particularly at passage times. The saltmarsh is used as a winter feeding ground by brent geese and various ducks, with grebes and divers offshore. In summer there is a small nesting colony of little terns, on the shingle with oystercatchers and ringed plovers. Other breeding birds include redshank, skylark, reed bunting and linnet.

The reserve is important as well for its invertebrate populations, with particularly good numbers of spiders, beetles and moths recorded. A variety of solitary bees and wasps find the sandy substrate ideal for nesting. Many of these invertebrates are rare, nationally or locally, and a number of Red Data Book species (the rarest of the rare) are present.

Colne Point from the air
David Corke

Visiting

Access via the road running to Lee Wick Farm from St Osyth. A car parking space is provided just inside the reserve on the seaward side of the sea wall, but is liable to flood at very high tides. Please use the car park and do not drive along the track past the chalets which the Trust does not own. Please drive slowly and leave all gates as you find them.

Bus from Colchester to St Osyth village, then another bus to Lee Wick Lane. From here it is a two-mile walk to the reserve.

Except for Essex Wildlife Trust members access is by day permit only, available from Trust HQ (01206 735456).

Migration periods for birds; summer for saltmarsh plants and insects.

During the breeding season (March to September) visitors are asked to walk below the last high tide mark as eggs and chicks are extremely difficult to see and are easily trampled.

At high tides various parts of the reserve can be flooded for some time, including around the car park and either end of the footbridge (the only access to the main part of the reserve), so consult a tide table before you visit. It is advisable to wear wellingtons or waterproof boots as it may be muddy, or even necessary to wade, at any time of the year.

Colne Valley

As it approaches Colchester from the west the River Colne meanders across a broad flood plain, forming a green space that runs almost to the centre of the town. At its heart is Cymbeline Meadows, former farmland that Colchester Council is managing much like the ancient flood meadows that used to occupy this land. Close by are three other open spaces the Council manages for wildlife – Hilly Fields, Lexden Springs and Lexden Park – and an Essex Wildlife Trust nature reserve, Lexden Gathering Grounds.

Lexden Gathering Grounds

22ac/9ha   OS Ex184/La168   GR 966 253

This was formerly a 'gathering ground' for water from constantly flowing springs and used as a water source from the turn of the century until the mid-1970s. It is owned by Anglian Water, who operate the covered reservoir and treatment works nearby, and managed by Essex Wildlife Trust.

In the 1960s parts of the site were planted with scots pine and with beech and oak. Between the woodlands lies a valley with semi-natural woodland of birch and ash on the steep slopes and a partially wooded marsh at the bottom, with a meadow beyond it.

The valley has bluebell and climbing corydalis, an uncommon plant typical of old woodland on sandy soils. The marsh has moschatel and old hazel and alder coppice. The meadow grassland is acidic with sheep's sorrel dominant over large areas.

Great and lesser spotted woodpeckers, sparrowhawk and smaller woodland birds are present. Fox and badger forage on the site. In the meadow in summer you will see the commoner brown butterflies and small copper, whose caterpillars feed on sheep's sorrel.

The plantation is being thinned to improve the mix of trees and the ground flora. Rides have been widened and are kept open to help butterflies and other invertebrates. Water levels have been raised in the marsh and a pond has been dug, fed by the original springs. Shading is kept down by clearing surrounding trees and scrub. The meadows are grazed.

Visiting

The reserve is in Lexden west of Colchester. The entrance is on Cooks Lane off Cymbeline Way (A133), about 50m from its junction with the A12 at Lexden Road.

Bus services run along Lexden Road to the south.

Accessible at all times..

Call the warden on 01206 861990 or Essex Wildlife Trust HQ on 01206 735456.

Lexden Springs

11ac/4.5ha   OS Ex184/La168   GR 973 253   LNR

Colchester Council

This ancient meadowland with a freshwater spring, just north of Lexden, is owned and managed by Colchester Council. Grassland like this is now very scarce and is generally rich in wild flowers. Here you will find a large colony of devilsbit scabious and also harebell and pignut.

Visiting

Via Spring Lane, a turning off Lexden Road (A1124), Colchester.

Bus services run along Lexden Road.

Accessible at all times.

Phone 01206 853588.

41

Lexden Park

18.5ac/7ha   OS Ex184/La168   GR 973 250   LNR

Lexden Park has some old parkland and mature woodland adjoining a wildflower meadow and an ornamental lake. It was declared a Local Nature Reserve in 1991 and is being managed for wildlife by Colchester Council.

The mature oaks in the south-eastern corner, probably 400 years old, are a particular feature and from near here there are also views of Lexden Dyke, an earthwork dating from the 1st century AD.

Visiting

🚗 On Church Lane, Lexden.

🚌 Regular bus services run along Lexden Road to the north.

🕐 Open from 8am to dusk daily.

♿ Facilities for people with limited mobility including level access and a modified picnic area.

🚏 ℹ Call 01206 853588 for information or help.

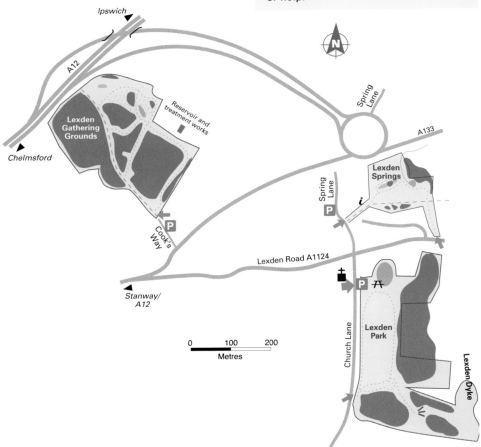

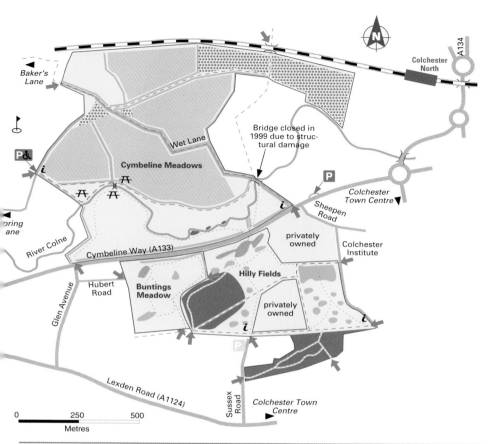

Hilly Fields

40ac/16ha   OS Ex184/La168   GR 884 253

Colchester
Council

This public open space, owned by Colchester Council, shares the ridge on which the town of Colchester developed, overlooking the flood plain of the River Colne. It is part of the Sheepen site that was an industrial and commercial area of Colchester in Iron Age and Roman times: most of it is a Scheduled Ancient Monument.

Since farming stopped about 40 years ago it has developed a mosaic of varied habitats. Much of it is grassland partially invaded by scrub and woodland, but the eastern section towards the town has very sandy soils and patches of heathland have developed, with broom and gorse patches.

At the foot of the slope against Cymbeline Way is a marsh fed by springs. Ponds that had silted up over the years have now been restored.

Buntings Meadow to the west has a butterfly trail. Noctule and pipistrelle bats feed over the ponds: visit late on a warm evening to see them.

Visiting

Accessed via Sussex Road, that runs north off Lexden Road (A1124).

Frequent bus services from Colchester Town Centre to Lexden and Stanway run along Lexden Road.

Accessible at all times.

Most paths are unsuitable for wheelchairs because of the steep terrain.

Call 01206 853588 for information or help.

43

Cymbeline Meadows

159ac/63.5ha OS Ex184/La168   GR 980 260

This area bordering the River Colne has been farmed for hundreds of years and is now owned by Colchester Council. Most of it is being farmed by the Council's tenant farmer in a wildlife-friendly way, with limited use of pesticides and features such as 'conservation headlands' – strips along the edge of arable fields sown with non-invasive wild flowers that serve as reservoirs of beneficial insects.

In the north-east corner south of the railway a new wood of over 12,500 trees has been planted, known as Charter Wood. Smaller woods and copses have been planted elsewhere, including beside the Colne.

The river and its bankside meadows form a wildlife corridor running through urban Colchester and they are home to kingfishers and water voles. The river is important as a flood channel and the meadows used to flood regularly in winter, encouraging a rich flora, but in these times of reduced rainfall this has been sporadic.

Visiting

Can be reached via a public footpath from Cymbeline Way (A133) or via public footpaths leading in from the north and west.

Within easy walking distance of Colchester North station.

Accessible at all times.

A parking area for disabled visitors can be reached via Baker's Lane (Spring Lane exit from the Lexden roundabout) and a surfaced pathway leads down to the river from there.

A farm trail has been laid out starting from Baker's Lane. **i** available from the Council or phone 01206 853588.

Devlisbit scabious, flowering in late summer
Tony Gunton

Grey heron: a familliar sight along rivers like the Colne, waiting for fish to come within reach of its dagger-like bill
David Harrison

Colne Valley Railway

5.24ac/2ha   OS Ex195/La168   GR 868 292

This length of former railway embankment north of Earls Colne was last used in the late 1960s in the age of steam when it carried the main line from Colchester to Cambridge. It is now an Essex Wildlife Trust nature reserve and is largely wooded apart from the central path.

From the embankment there are fine views over the attractive undulating countryside that surrounds it. It has woodland flowers such as yellow archangel, ramsons (wild garlic) and dog's mercury, and is used by many of our commoner birds.

Apart from keeping open the central path, the Trust is managing the woodland to maintain a variety of vegetation from mature trees through dense scrub to open glades.

Visiting

800m from Earls Colne village. The entrance is on the left 100m up the Colne Engaine road from its junction with the A604 Colchester–Cambridge road, about five miles from Halstead.

Accessible at all times.

A clear day in spring or summer.

Call the warden on 01787 224696 or Essex Wildlife Trust HQ on 01206 735456.

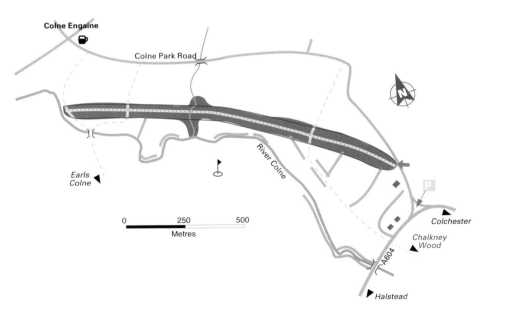

Cranham

There are three very different sites in the Green Belt near Cranham. Cranham Marsh is an Essex Wildlife Trust nature reserve with ancient woodland and marshland, contrasting with Broadfields Farm, the headquarters of the Thames Chase Community Forest team, which has new woodland and grassland on former arable land. The third site, on Front Lane, is a Woodland Trust site of pastureland with mature hedgerows.

Cranham Marsh

32ac/13ha   OS Ex175/La177   GR 567 856

ESSEX
Wildlife Trust

Cranham Marsh is all that remains of a marshland habitat that once covered many square miles of southern Essex, but which has now mostly been converted to arable farming. It contains a variety of habitats including marsh, sedge fen (one of the best surviving in Essex) and damp woodland.

The largest of the reserve's three small ancient woods, Spring Wood, consists mainly of hazel and alder coppice, together with some very large oak and ash trees and a few wild cherry standards. Dogwood, guelder rose, spindle and midland hawthorn are also found here, indicating that it is very old woodland. (Bonus Wood is apart from the main reserve and there is no public access.)

The grassland across the south of the reserve is bisected by old reed-filled drainage ditches leading into the main stream, which runs through the reserve roughly from east to west.

It contains a large concentration of betony and, in the wetter patches, southern marsh orchids, marsh marigold and ragged robin. The grassland also supports three large patches of the rare yellow loosestrife. Fine-leaved water dropwort and golden dock grow along the stream and in the ponds.

The reserve attracts marshland birds such as sedge and reed warblers, alongside woodpeckers (all three species) and treecreeper in the woods. Kestrels and sparrowhawks breed in the reserve regularly, and sometimes hobbies and nightingales.

Grass snakes are often seen in the grassland and there is abundant insect life. Twenty-three butterfly species have been recorded, including small copper, wall brown and speckled wood.

Because of changes in land use around the marsh it is not as wet as it used to be. To make the most of the available water, dams have

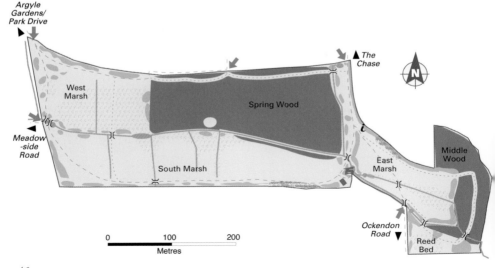

been built along the main stream. The meadows are cut annually for hay, and the sedge beds and rough grassland less frequently, to create a mosaic of varying habitats. A coppice cycle has been resumed in parts of the woods.

Visiting

Access via Argyle Gardens or The Chase, both of which run south off St. Mary's Lane (B187), with footpaths leading on to the reserve.

Yellow loosestrife: flowers in July/August
Tony Gunton

Upminster station (District Line tube and Fenchurch St) is about 15 minutes walk away. Buses from Romford via the station run along St. Mary's Lane.

Accessible at all times.

April and May for early flowers and birdsong; July and August for later flowers and insects.

Please keep to the marked paths. Please keep your dog under strict control and out of the long grass, where birds may be breeding.

from Essex Wildlife Trust visitor centres and at the interpretation board in the reserve. For more information call the warden on 01708 220897 or Essex Wildlife Trust HQ on 01206 735456.

Betony growing at Cranham Marsh: flowers June–August
Tony Gunton

47

Front Lane, Cranham

12ac/5ha   OS Ex175/La177   GR 573 886

WOODLAND
TRUST

These horse pastures that have begun to scrub over, with luxuriant hedgerows and a few patches of damp ground, were acquired by the Woodland Trust as part of its Woods on Your Doorstep millennium project.

Some trees have been planted to screen the A127 to the north and horse grazing will continue to keep the flower-rich grassland open. A good selection of birds nest in the hedgerows and scrub.

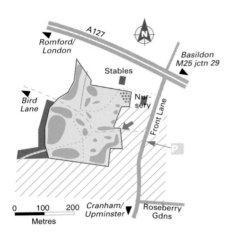

Visiting

Reached via a footpath running east from Front Lane, Cranham. Front Lane can be entered from the A127 westbound about 1km beyond M25 junction 29 or from the B187 (St Mary's Lane) about 2km east of Upminster centre.

Bus from Romford via Upminster station stop on Front Lane a short way from the entrance footpath.

Accessible at all times.

Broadfields Farm
Pat O'Brien

48

Broadfields Farm
140ac/56ha   OS Ex175/La177   GR 583 862

This former arable farm is now the headquarters of the project team for Thames Chase, the Community Forest. New woodlands have been planted over part of the site, and its broad rides and occasional glades have been sown with a grass and wildflower mix.

Just south of the farm buildings is a new orchard of traditional Essex varieties, and this and a few open areas are intended to be grazed. There are two ponds alongside the stream that runs down through the centre of the meadows and into the golf course under construction to the north, one with a hide and one a pond-dipping platform. A visitor centre is planned for the future.

Such a large site should develop a great deal of wildlife interest as it matures. Already skylarks nest in the open grassland, and birds such as green woodpecker, yellowhammer, willow warbler and whitethroat exploit the young woodland. Adders, grass snakes, great crested newts and smooth newts have been seen.

Visiting

The main entrance is off Pike Lane, a narrow lane running south from St Mary's Lane (B187) about a mile east of Upminster centre.

Half-hourly buses from Romford to Grays via Upminster Station run along St Mary's Lane. Get off at Thatched House PH. Upminster station is about 20 minutes' walk.

Accessible at all times. Forest Centre open weekdays 9 am–5 pm – at other times park in laybys in Pike Lane.

Green woodpecker
Alan Williams

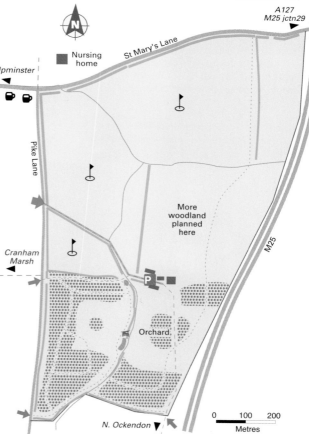

49

Thames Chase, the Community Forest

The Forestry and Countryside Commissions launched the Community Forests initiative in 1989. An area of Essex was chosen for one of the first of the new Community Forests, extending from Dagenham in the west through Havering and out into London's Green Belt between Brentwood and Thurrock, and known as Thames Chase. Wildlife conservation forms an important part of the aims for Thames Chase, alongside forestry, sport and recreation, landscape and others.

In some respects the community forests resurrect the concept of the mediæval forest, since they are not intended to be continuous woodland but a patchwork of woodland, farmland and public open spaces. In other respects they are very much of our time because they will not be imposed by government decree, as the Royal Forests were. Instead grants and other incentives are being used to encourage farmers and other landowners to consider the business opportunities available in forestry and in the leisure activities that will take place in the Community Forest. There is also strong emphasis on the rehabilitation of damaged land, the area having more than its fair share of former gravel pits and waste tips.

The Thames Chase project team operates in partnership with the five local authorities whose territory falls within the community forest area: Brentwood, Barking & Dagenham, Havering and Thurrock Councils, and Essex County Council. Between them, the local authorities own over a quarter of the land, Essex County Council being the largest single landowner in Thames Chase.

Five established wildlife sites lie within the Thames Chase area, namely Belhus Woods, Thorndon and Hornchurch country parks, all of which have new sites developing nearby, and Cranham Marsh and The Chase nature reserves. The Chase is now cheek-by-jowl with the new Eastbrookend country park in Dagenham. New sites are also being developed at Broadfields Farm near Cranham, the headquarters of the Thames Chase project team, at Davy Down in Thurrock and at Kennington Park near Belhus Woods.

For more information about Thames Chase, call the project team on 01708 641880.

Demonstration woodland at Broadfields Farm, designed to promote small-scale local forestry projects
Pat O'Brien

Cudmore Grove country park takes its name from a small grove of elms growing on the cliff top. This was the only woodland on the island, but the original elms have died and even some of the replacement oaks have been lost as the sea has eroded the cliff. With its flower-rich grassland and its views across the Colne estuary towards Brightlingsea and Colne Point, it is always worth a visit, but it and the Colne Estuary National Nature Reserve (NNR) alongside are really exceptional for birdlife in winter. It became a country park in 1975 and is managed by Essex County Council's Ranger Service.

The damp pastures at the northern end are managed for brent geese, and also attract golden plover and snipe in winter. If you take the seawall path beyond them you are likely to see birds all around you – waders feeding on the mudflats, songbirds finding cover in the saltmarsh, and sea ducks like goldeneye and red-breasted merganser on the estuary.

Visiting

Bear left to East Mersea after crossing The Strood on to Mersea Island (B1025 from Colchester). The country park is beyond East Mersea village, off Bromans Lane.

Regular bus service from Colchester to West Mersea passes within 2 miles of Cudmore Grove – get off at Blue Row. Some services run to East Mersea.

Country park open from 8 am until dusk, all the year round.

January/February for waders and wildfowl; autumn and spring migration times for unusual birds; July for salt-marsh colours. Plan your visit for round about high tide, when the birds will be closest (tide tables available from local shops).

The Strood is sometimes covered by spring tides.

Information room open daily. Ranger telephone: 01206 383868.

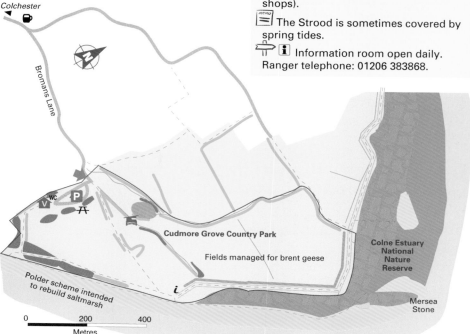

Colchester

Bromans Lane

WC V P

Cudmore Grove Country Park

Fields managed for brent geese

Polder scheme intended to rebuild saltmarsh

Colne Estuary National Nature Reserve

Mersea Stone

0   200   400
Metres

51

Dagenham Corridor

The Dagenham Corridor is a swathe of green land running through London from the Ford factory on the Thames north to rural Essex. Migrating birds use this corridor in spring and autumn to cross London, many stopping off at the lakes of The Chase nature reserve and Eastbrookend country park for rest and refuelling.

The Chase

120ac/48ha OS Ex175/La177   GR 515 860

London
Wildlife Trust

The Chase is an area of almost 120 acres lying between Dagenham and Hornchurch that has been shaped by gravel extraction. When extraction finished in the late 1960s some of the pits escaped infilling and formed a valuable wetland habitat of ponds, lakes and marshes. The area was turned over to horse pasture and this kept the grassland open until it became a nature reserve in the mid-1980s. Most of it is owned by Barking and Dagenham Council and the remainder by Havering, and it is managed by the London Wildlife Trust – the largest reserve under the Trust's care.

The Chase is of interest principally for its birds, with around 170 species recorded. These include teal and shoveler in winter, woodpeckers and kingfisher all year, and unusual migrants such as the long-eared owl.

For those not especially interested in birds, it is a haven of quiet within easy reach of much of urban East London.

Visiting

🚗 Access from Dagenham Road which runs south from Rush Green Road (A124 Upminster–Hornchurch–Dagenham). Turn off left just before the Farmhouse Tavern.

🚌 District line to Dagenham Heathway and then bus to Rush Green, getting off after the Farm House Tavern PH; or 15-minute walk from Dagenham East station via the footpath alongside the perimeter fence around the chemical works.

🕐 Accessible at all times.

📅 May for breeding birds on the lakes, with gorse and hawthorn in flower; September to March for birds on passage and wintering in the reserve.

📝 To avoid disturbing the birds, please do not go inside the fence around The Slack and keep dogs under strict control.

ℹ️ For details of events and workdays please call 020 8593 8096.

Dagenham Village Churchyard

2ac/.8ha   OS Ex175/La177   GR 500 844

London
Wildlife Trust

This tranquil refuge in a busy residential area of East London is managed for people and wildlife by London Wildlife Trust. Kestrels sometimes nest in the mature trees and small birds in the church tower.

Visiting

🚗 Reached via Church Lane off Ballards Road (B178), Dagenham.

🚌 Dagenham East station is a few minutes' walk. Buses run along Church Lane.

📅 Accessible at all times.

Eastbrookend Country Park

190ac/76.1ha OS Ex175/La177   GR 510 860

Barking & Dagenham Council

Eastbrookend is a new country park created by Barking and Dagenham Council on land between Dagenham and Hornchurch damaged by gravel extraction.

Fels Field to the north of Dagenham Road has large grassland areas used by skylarks and meadow pipits.

Eastbrook Grove to the south houses the visitor centre, built with the support of the Lottery Fund and designed to showcase environmental features such as low energy use. It has several large water bodies and the eastern section, adjoining The Chase nature reserve, has a heath-like character.

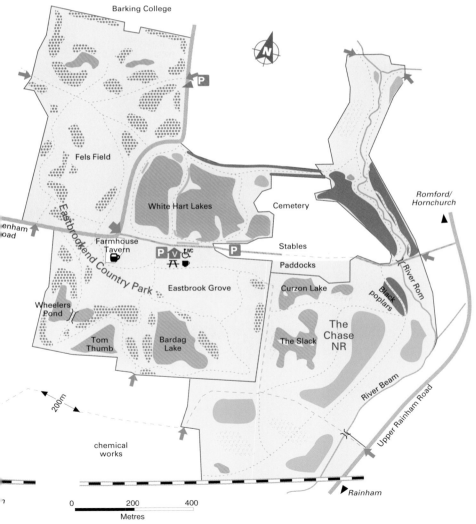

53

Danbury

Danbury is fortunate in still being surrounded by several fine areas of common and heath. Like most such areas they have been heavily invaded by trees and scrub in recent decades, since grazing and the other uses of common land declined, but the conservation organisations that manage them now – the National Trust and the Essex Wildlife Trust – have been working hard to rehabilitate them. In the areas that they have tackled heathland plants have started to recolonise, and it takes only a small effort of the imagination to visualise what they must have looked like in their prime.

But Danbury has a great deal to offer over and above heathland. It also has some fine areas of ancient woodland, with valley bogs and luxuriant stream valleys, and some of the best wild flower meadows in Essex. Danbury, in short, is a wildlife experience not to be missed.

Blake's Wood
104ac/42ha OS Ex183/La167   GR 775 064   SSSI

ESSEX
Wildlife Trust

Blake's Wood is owned by the National Trust and managed by the Essex Wildlife Trust. It is famous for its spring flowers, when sheets of wood anemones give way to spectacular displays of bluebells, while in summer its more open areas are dense with foxgloves. It has a range of other flowering plants, including yellow archangel, early purple orchid, twayblade, moschatel and wood spurge, and several unusual species of rush and fern. In autumn the wood is rich in fungi.

Most of the wood is ancient with well defined banks and ditches. Much of it consists of hornbeam and sweet chestnut coppice, with oak, ash and birch standards.

Breeding birds include warblers, nightingale, all three species of woodpecker and treecreeper. Butterflies include purple hairstreak.

One of the main management tasks is to re-establish a traditional coppicing regime. The great storm of October 1987 felled an estimated 4,000 trees and forestalled a plan to reintroduce coppicing on a major scale. It took four years to clear the fallen trees, with some areas deliberately left untouched and one area of about two acres planted with seedling trees taken from elsewhere in the wood. Although at first seen as a calamity, in the event the storm has resulted in an increased variety of habitats.

Visiting

To the north of Riffham's Chase, Little Baddow. Approach either via junction with The Ridge, one mile north of Eve's Corner on the A414 at Danbury, or via Riffham's Lane, turning off the A414 further west.

The most frequent bus services are from Chelmsford to Maldon and Chelmsford to S. Woodham Ferrers. Get off at Riffham's Lane.

Accessible at all times.

April to June for wild flowers and songbirds; October for fungi.

Call the warden on 01245 352174 or Essex Wildlife Trust HQ on 01206 735456.

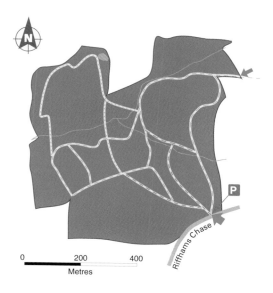

Danbury Common

218ac/87ha   OS Ex183/La167   GR 781 041   SSSI

anbury Common is owned by the National Trust. It is an excellent illustration of the way commons were formed, criss-crossed by roads, tracks and paths, with long straggling boundaries funnelling out along the roads, and with houses in enclaves.

The southern part still remains typical of a traditional open common, but the northern part has seen natural progression to woodland.

Grazing by stock kept the commons open from Saxon times until the early 1900s but today, as it is difficult to protect animals on common land, the best that can be done is to simulate grazing by mowing at different heights and times throughout the year and removing the clippings.

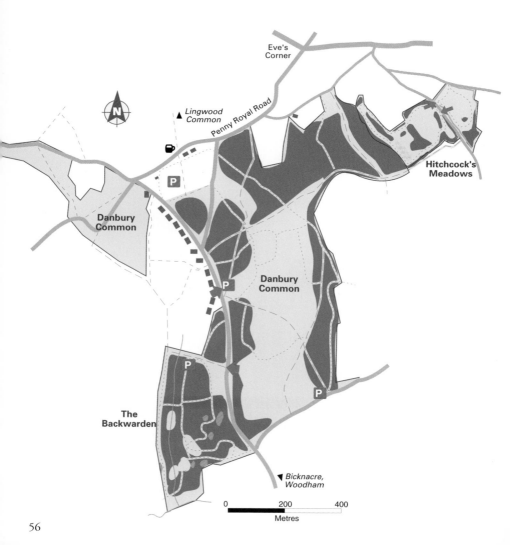

Backwarden

30ac/12ha   OS Ex183/La167   GR 781 041   SSSI

ESSEX
Wildlife Trust

The south-western part of Danbury Common is known as The Backwarden and is leased to the Essex Wildlife Trust by the National Trust. It has a great variety of habitats for its size. There are a number of pools and bogs, some of which have formed in old marl or gravel workings; relic heathy tracts with an increasing growth of heather; a small marsh; both old and secondary woodland, and notably some aspen groves; and blackthorn thickets.

Visiting

🚗 The common is on both sides of the road running south from Danbury to Bicknacre.

🚌 Chelmsford–Maldon bus to Eve's Corner, and take the road signposted Danbury Common and Bicknacre. Chelmsford–South Woodham Ferrers bus passes the common.

🕐 Accessible at all times.

📅 May for birdsong; July–September for heathland plants; October for fungi and leaf colours.

🚸 ℹ️ Waymarked nature trails have been set up both round the main part of the common and round The Backwarden. *Backwarden*: for more information call the warden on 01245 352174 or Essex Wildlife Trust HQ on 01206 735456.

It has a wide variety of flowers, including heathland species such as tormentil and heath milkwort and wetland species like marsh willowherb, fine-leaved water-dropwort, pennywort and common and lesser skullcap. It also boasts no fewer than 18 species of sedge and many fungi and mosses, including seven of the nine Essex species of sphagnum moss.

The reserve is outstanding for its reptiles, with adders, grass snakes, slow worms and lizards much in evidence. Dormouse, yellow-necked mouse and water shrew are present and nesting birds include nightingale, blackcap and the three woodpecker species.

It is rich in insects, including the green hairstreak butterfly. Because of the many alder buckthorn trees, which are the foodplant of its caterpillars, many brimstone butterflies appear in spring.

Dormouse: still doing well at Danbury
Dr Chris Gibson/English Nature

Tormentil
Owen Keen

Hitchcock's Meadows

15ac/6ha   OS Ex183/La167   GR 788 049   SSSI

On hilly land adjoining the eastern and south-eastern boundaries of Danbury Common, about half the area of this reserve is flower-rich ancient unimproved pasture and the remainder is secondary woodland, scrubland and marsh. In 1998 the Trust acquired the Dell and Dell Meadow on the other side of Gay Bowers Lane as an extension to the reserve.

The main meadow, Toot Hill, a former lookout area from which the North Downs can be seen, contains green-winged orchid, common and heath dog violets, eyebright, common milkwort and autumn lady's tresses, among many other grassland plants. Ketley's Mead consists of relic grassland and scrub. Here you will find hoary cinquefoil, wood sage (food plant of the speckled yellow moth) and sweetbriar.

The marsh is dominated by the bright emerald green of giant horsetail, with a patch of devil's-bit scabious.

The small laneside meadow, Broken Back, has several uncommon clovers, pignut and knapweed and is excellent for butterflies.

The luxuriant hedgerows and thickets harbour a good number of bird species and the reserve is rich in insect life, including glow-worms.

Visiting

From Eve's Corner, Danbury, head east down the main road (A414), then turn right and continue 200m down Gay Bowers Lane. Enter by the small gate carrying the Trust notice board and turn right over the stile.

Accessible at all times.

Late April–September for wild flowers (plus butterflies July–August and glow-worms in July).

Leave the path if you wish, but please take care where you walk during the flowering season.

Call the warden on 01245 323906 or Essex Wildlife Trust HQ on 01206 735456.

Hitchcock's Meadows in bloom
Geoff Pyman

Danbury Country Park
41ac/16ha   OS Ex183/La167   GR 771 048

Essex County Council

What is now Danbury Country Park was once a deer park belonging to the estate of Danbury Manor, dating back to the Norman conquest of 1066. It was re-landscaped in Elizabethan times, and some massive oaks in the park today are believed to date from then, along with exotics such as cedar of Lebanon and redwood. Essex County Council Rangers manage it now.

The eastern part of the park is dense woodland, extending also along the southern boundary. This is dominated by hornbeam and oak, including the massive ancient trees mentioned above. There are three ornamental lakes, used for angling and north of them, next to Danbury Palace, is an ornmental garden. A wildflower meadow to the west is full of St John's wort, field scabious and wild carrot.

The very old trees in the park and associated dead wood form a valuable habitat for invertebrates such as beetles, including a number of rarities. One rarity here of particular note is a tiny pseudo-scorpion called *Allochemus widerii*. Big old trees are also valuable to bats as roosting sites and a trip to the lakes on a warm summer evening should be rewarded by seeing some feeding over the water. The mix of woodland, open grassland and ornamental garden attracts a good selection of birds.

Visiting

🚗 Entrances on Woodhill road (the Sandon Road) west of Danbury Common.

🕐 Accessible at all times via public foot-path. Car parks open 8am to dusk.

📅 Spring and summer for birds; warm summer evenings for bats.

♿ Easy and moderate trails, toilets and picnic benches designed for wheelchair users. Battery operated buggies phone first (01245 222350) to ensure gates are opened.

📋 Guided walks available on request. School groups welcome by arrange-ment. Call the Rangers on 01245 222350.

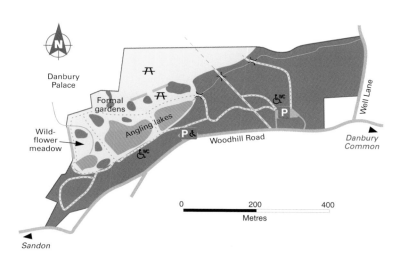

59

Danbury Ridge Complex

250ac/100ha OS Ex183/La167   GR 775 064   SSSI (part)

The Essex Wildlife Trust manages a block of nearly 250 acres of nature reserves on Danbury Ridge, a mosaic of woodland, common and heathland, streams, bogs and farmland.

Woodham Walter Common, a gravel-covered plateau sloping down to stream valleys on both north and south sides, forms the eastern section. It is principally secondary woodland, with a few open areas that are being kept open to encourage low-growing plants, and especially ling heather. It is noted for its sessile oak trees, with many rowan and a scattering of wild service and alder buckthorn.

The northern valley bog has been reinstated, and contains sphagnum moss, as well as marsh fern and other uncommon ferns, smooth sedge, and common and lesser skullcap growing side by side.

Birch Wood at its north-east corner consists mainly of hornbeam coppice. In spring there is a superb display of flowers, including wood anemones, wood spurge, wood sorrel and climbing corydalis. The wood also contains a strong colony of the localised golden-scaled fern.

Pheasanthouse Wood to the west is mixed woodland with three raised bogs. The largest of these has been restored and has dense hummocks of sphagnum moss and large numbers of the rare lesser skullcap, and smooth and star sedges. The other main feature is lily-of-the-valley, covering several acres.

Pheasanthouse Farm beyond is also owned by the Trust and is farmed by a tenant. It consists entirely of grassland, currently grazed by sheep and other livestock, including rare breeds.

Little Baddow Heath forms most of the southern section, descending steeply from north and south to a superb stream valley containing primrose, fen bedstraw, ragged robin and several species of fern, and alive with insects in summer. North of the stream was once grass heathland that has developed into secondary woodland over the past 20–30 years. A section has been restored and here can be found many wild flowers, including unusual plants such as heath milkwort and goldenrod.

Poors Piece sits in the angle to the west of Little

Baddow Heath. It contains many oak pollards, suggesting that it was once used as wood pasture. In its southern corner is a marsh full of wetland plants, and notably hemp agrimony, hop sedge and lady fern.

The southernmost tip is Scrubs Wood, consisting mainly of hornbeam and chestnut coppice with oak standards, plus some wild service trees. It is fairly flat except for the gently sloping bank on its southern boundary which has a fine display of wood anemones. Other flowering plants include tormentil, creeping cinquefoil and broad-leaved helleborine.

Spring Wood, added most recently, is nine acres of secondary woodland towards the south-west corner.

Dormice, once common but now much reduced in numbers, are found in many parts of the reserve. The birdlife includes nuthatch, hawfinch, all three species of woodpecker, migrant warblers and, intermittently, nightingale. There are good numbers of butterflies including brimstone, ringlet and small copper.

Lily of the valley is a special feature of Danbury Ridge, and other unusual wild flowers here include yellow archangel, greater butterfly orchid and wood sanicle.

Lily of the valley
EWT library

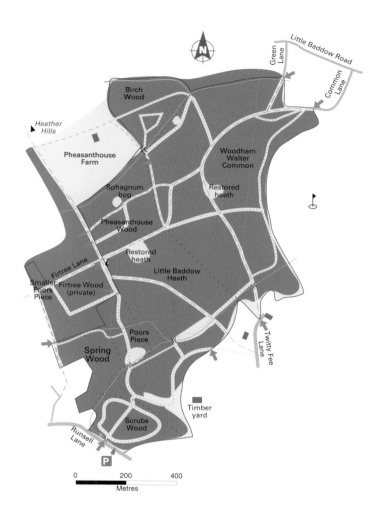

Visiting

Foot access from the west via Fir Tree Lane, a turning off The Ridge; from the east via Common Lane, Woodham Walter; and from the south via Twitty Fee Lane or Runsell Lane, a turning to the right 600m along Little Baddow Road from Eve's Corner. Roadside parking on Runsell Lane.

Regular bus services Chelmsford–Maldon and Chelmsford–S. Woodham Ferrers. Get off at Eve's Corner.

Accessible at all times.

May for breeding birds and wild flowers; June for ferns and bog plants and for butterflies; autumn for fungi.

Pheasanthouse Farm is a working farm and access is only permitted via the public footpath that crosses it. Please keep dogs on a lead.

ℹ from Essex Wildlife Trust visitor centres. For more information call the wardens on 01245 222808 or 01245 222328, or Essex Wildlife Trust HQ on 01206 735456.

Heather Hills

16ac/6ha   OS Ex183/La167   GR 780 077

ESSEX
Wildlife Trust

This reserve, recently licensed to Essex Wildlife Trust by Little Baddow Council, is divided in two by a very steep stream valley, on either side of which are slopes once covered in heather but which is now restricted to the summit and edges. As well as many native trees and shrubs, including a row of elms, it has stands of mature beech, Scots pine and European larch.

Flowers include moschatel, climbing corydalis and heath bedstraw. Several species of fern grow along the stream together with a variety of wetland plants.

Priority is being given to restoring heather to the slopes, with limited clearance of overgrown areas including parts of the stream valley.

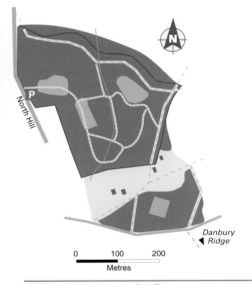

Danbury ◀ Ridge

0   100   200
Metres

Visiting

🚗 On the east side of North Hill, Little Baddow. The main entrance is off North Hill, using a trackway known as York Street. Parking at St Andrews Parish Room on North Hill.

🚌 Regular bus services Chelmsford–Maldon or Chelmsford–S. Woodham Ferrers, getting off at Eve's Corner, or bus to Little Baddow.

🕐 Accessible at all times

📅 Spring for early flowers; August for heather.

⚠ Take great care when descending the steep scarp to the valley floor.

☎ Call the warden on 01245 264238 or Essex Wildlife Trust HQ on 01206 735456.

Lingwood Common

100ac/40ha   OS Ex183/La167   GR 780 858   SSSI

Lingwood Common is another former heath that has 'tumbled down' to woodland. Like Danbury Common it is under the care of the National Trust, and the Trust has opened up several clearings along the bridleway that runs from one end to the other, and some of the heathland plants have returned. The woodland is mainly oak with birches to the west, and aspen and willow down the stream valleys.

Just stroll round it, or use it as a link between Danbury Common to the south and Blake's Wood and the Danbury Ridge reserves further north.

Visiting

🚗 From Eve's Corner walk west along Main Road (A414) for a couple of hundred yards, and turn down a steep footpath on the right just before the road turns sharp left. The footpath leads through farmland and woodland on to the common.

🚌 Buses to Eve's Corner.

🕐 Accessible at all times.

📅 High summer

Waterhall Meadows

5.7ac/2ha   OS Ex183/La167   GR 759 072

These ancient unimproved flood meadows on the west bank of Sandon Brook, with a small spinney and an area of blackthorn thickets, are managed by Essex Wildlife Trust. Formerly flooded regularly, they rarely flood today.

Cowslip and meadow saxifrage flower in the meadows in spring, lady's bedstraw is conspicuous in mid-summer, and devil's-bit scabious and pepper saxifrage appear later. At the far corner of the meadow is a small pond in which grow amphibious bistort, great water dock and fine-leaved water dropwort. Goldilocks buttercup flowers nearby in spring and a little further on hemp agrimony and spindle grow together by the brookside.

Among the 84 bird species recorded are eight species of warbler, at least six of which nest regularly. The kingfisher is a regular visitor and has bred in the reserve.

The reserve is rich in insect life. Its dragonflies and damselflies are particularly notable: 17 species have been recorded including the localised white-legged damselfly, present in large numbers.

Visiting

The reserve is in Little Baddow. Turn off the A414 into Hammonds Road at the roundabout signposted Boreham, and after 1 mile turn right into Hurrells Lane. Entrance is by a stile on the right before a ford through Sandon Brook. There is limited parking by the entrance and across the ford on the left.

Accessible at all times

Spring and summer for flowers, and summer for dragonflies, most likely to be found along the edge of the brook.

For more information call Essex Wildlife Trust on 01206 735456.

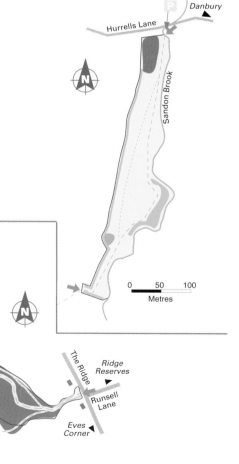

Davy Down

30ac/12ha   OS Ex175/La177   GR 588 803

Thurrock Council

This former farmland in the Mar Dyke valley has been planted and landscaped by Thurrock Council and Essex & Suffolk Water, supported by local volunteers and Thames Chase, the Community Forest team. It also includes a pumping station containing huge diesel pumps, now disused, and is overlooked by an impressive railway viaduct dating from 1892.

It has meadows running along the Mar Dyke, maturing woodland, ponds and a small wetland, and is a particularly good place to see water voles, both in the ponds and along the Mar Dyke.

Visiting

On the B186 (Pilgrims Lane) between South Ockendon and Chafford Hundred. Leave the A13(T) or the M25 at their junction and head east on the A1306 towards Chafford Hundred/Grays, turning right where it crosses the B186. The entry is on the left about 200m up.

Several bus services between Romford and Grays run along Pilgrims Lane.

Accessible at all times.

Surfaced paths run all round the site.

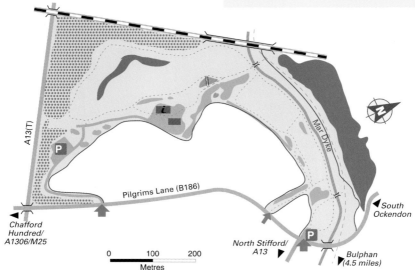

Daws Hall

20ac/8ha   OS Ex196/La155   GR 887 366

ESSEX
Wildlife Trust

Daws Hall is an educational nature reserve on an attractive stretch of the River Stour where it forms the Essex/Suffolk boundary. It has a well equipped field centre staffed by full-time teachers supported by the Essex Education Authority and is owned by the Daws Hall Trust.

It consists of a mixture of habitats developed on land that was farmed until the mid-1960s. The land slopes gently to the north and east down into the river flood plain. The lower lying areas are planted with cricket-bat willow and include a stretch of Losh House Brook where the attractive bankside vegetation includes common valerian. The Stour itself has true bulrush, lesser reedmace and arrowhead.

A narrow strip of unimproved meadow contains yellow rattle, now rare in north-east Essex. The central area of the reserve is now managed as a wild flower meadow, cut for compost and grazed by sheep in winter.

A steep tree-clad bank provides superb views both of the reserve and into Suffolk. Another hide overlooks the flood plain to the north, where grey heron, kingfisher, and winter flocks of golden plover, lapwing and snipe can be seen. A third hide gives good views of a shallow scrape, constructed in 1985 and visited by wildfowl and waders. Nesting birds include reed warblers, which are common along the river, with garden warbler common within the wooded areas. In autumn/winter large flocks of redwings and fieldfares can be seen. The reserve attracts a wide range of insects, including red-eyed damselfly and white-legged damselfly.

Beside the river is a small area developed as a clone bank for the native black poplar, our rarest timber tree. Here cuttings from mature trees throughout Essex and Suffolk are growing to provide material for replacement and additional planting.

Visiting

Take the minor road between Bures and Sudbury on the Essex side of the River Stour. From Bures, the entrance is 500m on the right-hand side beyond Lamarsh church.

Bures BR station is 2.5 miles from the reserve, but there is no bus service that passes the entrance.

Access only on annual open days and, for Essex Wildlife Trust members only, by prior arrangement with the warden – please call 01787 269213 giving date and time of visit. Teachers interested in visiting should ring the Field Centre on 01787 269766.

Something to offer throughout the year. Spring is the time for nesting birds. The meadowland is at its best in early summer and the brookside vegetation in late summer. Autumn and winter are good for migrant birds.

The Field Centre has toilets for disabled visitors. The tree hide has a lift for wheelchair access, by prior arrangement only.

Great care should be taken when walking beside the river and on to Pitmire Island. A small patch of giant hogweed is growing on the island. Impressive in flower, it can cause a painful irritation to the skin after contact. Warning signs are present.

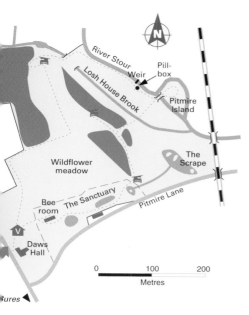

Black poplar
Dr Chris Gibson/English Nature

Daws Heath

The ancient woodlands in and around Daws Heath have much in common. They are all 'working woods', coppiced for centuries to supply wood for a range of purposes, and they all occupy land that was unattractive for agriculture – gravelly slopes or plateaux of infertile soil, running down into damp stream valleys. Yet they are also very different from one another, showing what effect man's treatment of a wood can have on its character and its wildlife, even many decades after. Nearby is Thundersley Common, a fragment of old common land with some of its original heathland vegetation still intact.

Thundersley Common

35ac/14ha   OS Ex175/La178   GR 798 896   SSSI

Castle Point Council

Thundersley Common packs great variety and interest into a relatively small area. Like most commons it was used by local people to graze their animals, collect firewood and so on. When these practices stopped it was invaded by trees and scrub, but most of this was cleared in 1972 and some of the original heathland plants reappeared. Now it is owned and managed as a public open space by Castle Point Council.

The northern slope has many heathland plants in the uncut islands of heather and gorse in the grassland, including milkwort, cross-leaved heath and common cow-wheat.

The woodland in the central section is dominated by oak, hornbeam and hawthorn, but there is also alder buckthorn, food plant of the brimstone butterfly, and, on the western boundary, a pollarded wild service tree.

The southern plateau has some marshy pools with lesser spearwort and on the drier ground you will find tormentil and a small patch of heather.

Visiting

On Kingsley Lane, the first turning on the right off Rayleigh Road (A129) just south of the Rayleigh Weir roundabout on the A127 Southend Arterial Road.

Regular bus service serving Rayleigh station and Southend bus station via the A13; get off at Sainsbury's.

Accessible at all times.

June–August for flowers and insects.

Hadleigh Great Wood

92ac/37ha   OS Ex175/La178   GR 820 875   SSSI, LNR

Southend Council

Hadleigh Great Wood is the main survivor of a group of ancient woods forming a large stretch of woodland in the southern part of Rayleigh Hills, like Hockley Woods to the north. Several of the other woods have been destroyed for housing, and the remnants of others lie in Belfairs Park to the east. Along with Dodds Grove at its north-west corner it is managed as public space by Southend Council, forming Belfairs Nature Reserve.

Apart from a hiccup in the 1930s, the wood has a history of many centuries of uninterrupted coppicing. As a result a wide range of flowers and shrubs grow amongst the trees, including sheets of wood anemones, and it attracts a very wide range of birds and butterflies.

West Wood, Daws Heath

79.4ac/32ha   OS Ex175/La178   GR 805 880

Castle Point Council

West Wood has been managed as coppice woodland for at least two hundred years, except that a large area of the northern part was clear felled in the 1930s, removing the standards as well as the coppice. Like Hadleigh Great Wood it is owned by the Church Commissioners. It is managed as a public open space by Castle Point Council.

Pound Wood

55ac/22ha   OS Ex175/La178   GR 816 888

ESSEX
Wildlife Trust

Pound Wood was acquired by the Essex Wildlife Trust in 1993 following a public appeal. Its complex geology gives it a great variation in woodland types. Sweet chestnut and birch occur on the plateaux and ridges, hornbeam and holly on the slopes, and hornbeam, ash, willow, aspen and hazel in the three stream valleys. The wild service tree is notably abundant in some areas. The oaks are mostly sessile, with pedunculate in the valleys. The south-west section is very old secondary woodland, almost indistinguishable from the ancient woodland. The wood suffered in the 1987 storm, and most of the fallen or leaning trees are where the wind left them.

There are fine early mediæval woodbanks, several ponds and many dells. Bramble, bracken and bluebell dominate the woodland floor, with common cow-wheat, yellow archangel, angelica, wood spurge and figwort where light can penetrate this once neglected wood.

Before it was bought by the Trust, Pound Wood was owned by the Church Commissioners, who had taken over its management from the Dean and Chapter of Westminster Abbey in 1875, who had probably acquired it in the 13th century. The name Pound Wood first appears in the mid-18th century.

Coppicing has been neglected in recent decades and the overgrown trees have made it very dark and bare. Helped by many volunteers, the Trust is now restoring it.

Little Haven

92ac/37ha   OS Ex175/La178   GR 811 889

ESSEX
Wildlife Trust

This reserve was formerly part of Lower Wyburns Farm and is leased from the Little Haven Children's Hospice by the Essex Wildlife Trust. It became a nature reserve in 1996 with the building of the hospice. It comprises 15 meadows, a network of fine old hedgerows and two woods.

Starvelarks Wood is mainly sweet chestnut and is probably a 19th-century plantation that has been under coppice management.

Wyburns Wood contains a complex range of tree and plant species, indicating its ancient origins. It is very damp in places and here it supports a rare type of woodland known as plateau alder wood, which has a ground flora of male fern and pendulous sedge.

Coppicing has been reinstated in Starvelarks Wood. The meadows are cut for hay and some hedgerows are coppiced or laid.

Visiting

Turn south off the A127 at Rayleigh Weir on to Rayleigh Road (A129) and turn left on to Daws Heath Road at the Woodmans PH mini-roundabout. Or join the A129 from the A13, and turn right on to Daws Heath Road. Park on local streets with consideration for residents.

Bus services run along Rayleigh Road. For Pound Wood and Little Haven, half-hourly daytime service exc. Sundays from Rayleigh, Leigh, Chalkwell and Westcliff stations, and Southend bus station; get off at Rivers Corner for Pound Wood or Ann's Mini-market for Little Haven. Evenings and Sundays use the service serving Rayleigh station and

Southend bus station via the A13 and get off at Woodman's Arms.

Accessible at all times.

April to June for spring flowers and woodland birdsong

Wheelchair access gate to Little Haven opposite Ann's Mini-Market

To minimise disturbance to wildlife, please keep to the designated paths and keep your dog under control.

from dispensers in the reserves or from EWT visitor centres. Call the Little Haven warden on 01702 716678 or the Pound Wood warden on 01268 773375.

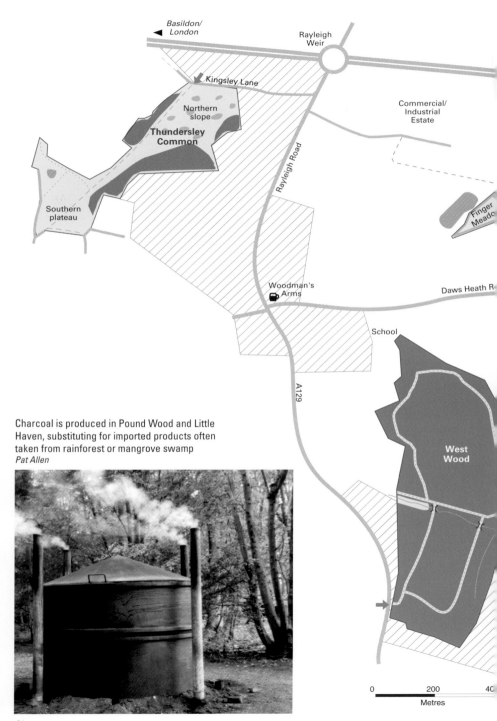

Basildon/
London ◄

Rayleigh
Weir

Kingsley Lane

Northern
slope

**Thundersley
Common**

Commercial/
Industrial
Estate

Rayleigh Road

Finger
Meado

Southern
plateau

Woodman's
Arms

Daws Heath R

School

A129

West
Wood

Charcoal is produced in Pound Wood and Little
Haven, substituting for imported products often
taken from rainforest or mangrove swamp
Pat Allen

0   200   40

Metres

Lower Wyburns
(see p.171)

Wood ants are widespread
in all these woods
Pat Allen

A127

Little
Haven
NR

Wyburns
Wood

Starvelarks
Wood

Tile
Wood
East

Southend

Ann's

Rivers
Corner

Pound
Wood

Daws Heath

Bramble Road

Poors Lane North

Dodds Grove

Belfairs Park

Poors Lane

Prittle Brook

Hadleigh
Great Wood

Hadleigh

East Ham

20ac/8ha   OS Ex162/La177   GR 429 824

The church of St Mary Magdalene in East Ham has the largest churchyard in London and this has been turned into a nature reserve, managed by Newham Council. It has grassland, hedges, scrub, mature and young trees, a small raised pond and, of course, gravestones, a distinct microhabitat supporting mosses and lichens. Here you will find a good selection of insects, reptiles such as slow worms, grass snakes and common lizards, and sometimes migrant birds like blackcap and whitethroat stop off to nest.

Visiting

Entrance on Norman Road, just north of the A13 near Beckton Alps.

District line to East Ham; DLR to Beckton; several bus services.

Open Tuesday to Friday 10am–5pm (summer), 10am–4pm (winter); Sundays 2pm–5pm (summer), 1pm–4pm (winter).

Wheelchair trail; member of sympathetic hearing scheme; tapping board for white stick users; guide dogs for the blind welcome (no other dogs permitted).

Visitor Centre telephone 020 8470 4525.

East Ham (and tube)

High Street South (A117)

P &

London

Dagenham/Southend

Newham Way (A13)

Slow worm, a legless lizard
David Corke

Grass snake, recognisable by its yellow/orange collar
David Corke

Elms Spinney
1.7ac/1ha   OS Ex183/La167   GR 615 140

ESSEX
Wildlife Trust

This small Essex Wildlife Trust reserve on a bend of the brook-sized River Can is a wildlife oasis on boulder clay surrounded by arable fields. Once a wet, undrainable field corner, it has been used as a farm dump and a willow plantation and today consists of an area of rough grassland surrounded on three sides by thorn scrub.

140 plant species have been recorded including a strong stand of the rare (despite its name!) common meadow-rue, as well as lady's smock and ragged robin. In spring, open areas are covered with the flowers of ground ivy and lesser celandine. Primrose and sweet violet can be found at the north end of the path.

Butterflies include ringlet and speckled wood. The occasional pair of stock doves breed in nest boxes. Summer migrants include blackcap and whitethroat. The diminutive harvest house is notable among the mammals.

Visiting

Off the road between the villages of Good and High Easter. The nearest main road is the A1060. There is a Trust sign on an ash tree near the meadow entrance. Park on the roadside verge, but please do not block the gate entrance. Access is along top of meadow and then field edge alongside river, entering over a small planked bridge.

Accessible at all times.

Spring and early summer

Access may be difficult in summer, walking along the edge of farm crops.

Call the warden on 01245 281314 or Essex Wildlife Trust HQ on 01206 735456.

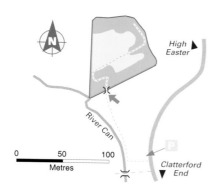

High Easter

River Can

0   50   100
Metres

Clatterford End

Harvest mouse
David Corke

71

Curlew: a common passage migrant and winter visitor with several thousand present from August through to March
Alan Williams
▶

Redshank: widely distributed around the coast all year, with large numbers wintering and some nesting, mainly on grazing marsh and saltmarsh
David Harrison
◀

Dunlin, a small, busy wader: thousands pass through on migration and stay over winter
Alan Williams
▶

Avocet: a success story in Essex, with a steady growth in numbers breeding since 1975, and over 500 wintering, most on Hamford Water
David Harrison
◀

Shelduck, our largest duck: breeds all around the coast and on large inland water bodies such as reservoirs
Alan Williams
▶

Teal, our smallest duck (male on right): large numbers pass through on migration and over-winter, with just a few pairs breeding
Owen Keen
◀

Epping Forest

Epping Forest covers more than 6,000 acres of land, the main part running in a crescent about 12 miles long from Wanstead in the south to Epping in the north. Although some of the original wildlife diversity of the Forest has been lost, it is still a wonderful place with much to see and enjoy. The many ancient pollard trees are its most striking feature, and especially the great beeches on the higher ground in the central parts.

CORPORATION
OF LONDON

Epping Forest is set on a ridge of high land between the river valleys of the Lea and Roding, with its highest point a mile or so south of Epping. The ridge consists of patches of gravel laid down by the Thames aeons ago on top of beds of sandy clay, and it has a network of springs and water courses.

Probably declared a Forest by Henry I, it was originally part of Waltham Forest, a much larger area, although the wooded area has probably never been much larger than it is now. As Forest Law – the regulations that protected the deer for hunting – declined so parts of it were enclosed and by 1850 no more than 2,000 acres remained unaffected by enclosure.

In 1851 most of the neighbouring Hainault Forest was grubbed out and turned into farmland. This caused a public scandal and many people determined that Epping Forest should not suffer a similar fate. In 1871 a number of local commoners, including the Corporation of the City of London, took action against the lord of the neighbouring manors to prevent them from enclosing and building on the Forest.

The lawsuit succeeded and led directly to the Epping Forest Act of 1878 which established general public access and appointed the Corporation of London as 'Conservators of the Forest'. The campaign to save the forest can now be seen as the birth of the modern conservation movement.

The Act placed emphasis on maintaining the 'natural aspect' of Forest – in other words it was not to be turned into a public park. In the earlier years of the Corporation's stewardship we did not know as much about the management of ancient woodlands as we do now, and unfortunately this was interpreted as meaning 'leave it to nature'. Without continued cutting of pollard and coppice trees the canopy closed and the woodland floor lost most of its wild flowers and became dark and bare. Primroses, wood anemones and bluebells used to be widespread but are now few and far between.

About one-sixth of the original Forest consisted of open areas. As grazing declined, so most of these were invaded by birch and thorn scrub and today heathland plants like heather are very scarce as well.

Attempts have been under way for some time to reverse the damage and are beginning to show real success, but the road back is slow and difficult after so many years of neglect. Very old pollards, for example, can easily die when repollarded, and birch is very difficult to eradicate from former heathland once established.

For all that, Epping Forest remains an unmissable experience. Here we cover the best sections of the Forest, starting with the Green Lanes and the Lower Forest to the north and working southwards down to Leyton Flats and Wanstead Park in the heart of east London.

With the overview maps that follow are some brief notes on other parts of the Forest and its buffer lands that are also worth a visit.

Overview maps

Buffer Lands

One of the aims of the Corporation of London is to protect the 'natural aspect' and the integrity of Epping Forest by acquiring neighbouring land. These 'buffer lands', shown shaded yellow on the maps, consist of a mixture of farmland and woodland. The farmland is used to grow crops or raise livestock and the woodland to produce timber, but in such a way as to benefit wildlife and enhance the local landscape. Public access to some of the buffer lands is possible via public and other footpaths – the main access paths are shown on the maps.

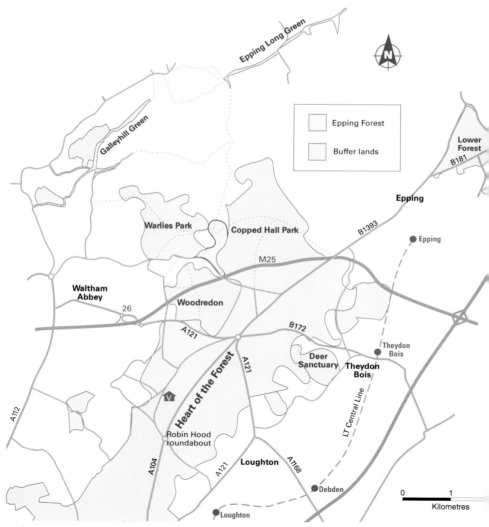

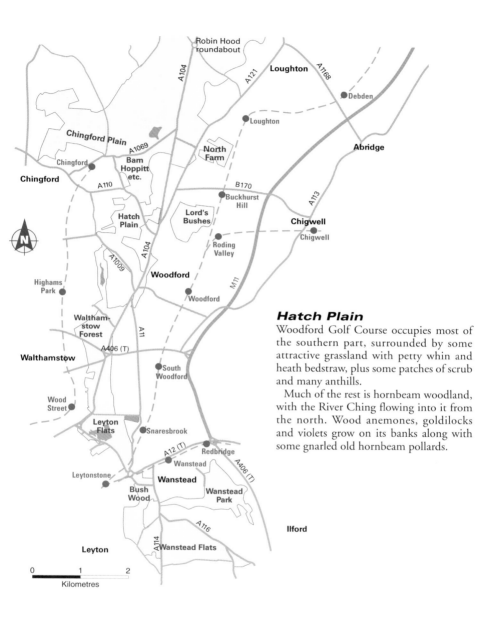

Hatch Plain

Woodford Golf Course occupies most of the southern part, surrounded by some attractive grassland with petty whin and heath bedstraw, plus some patches of scrub and many anthills.

Much of the rest is hornbeam woodland, with the River Ching flowing into it from the north. Wood anemones, goldilocks and violets grow on its banks along with some gnarled old hornbeam pollards.

Bush Wood

Bush Wood used to be part of Wanstead Park. It is a mature woodland with some grassy glades and some massive trees, including some very large sweet chestnut trees. Its birdlife is good, including great spotted woodpeckers and long-tailed tits.

Wanstead Flats

Wanstead Flats consists of over 400 acres of grassland with some patches of trees. Much of it is maintained as playing fields and the rest is grazed by cattle. It has three water bodies all of which are short of water but which are to be restored. It is an important London site for skylarks.

Wood-pasture

Wood-pasture is the term used to describe woodland in which commoners have kept grazing or browsing animals. With such animals in the wood the trees have to be managed in a particular way, because if the animals are allowed in amongst coppiced trees they eat the young shoots and kill the trees.

One method used to prevent this from happening was to cut the trees at head height or above, where the animals cannot reach, rather than at ground level. This practice, known as pollarding, has a similar effect to coppicing in that it produces a regrowth of straight branches and prolongs the life of the tree. Pollarding results in trees with a distinctive shape, consisting of a massive trunk with all the main branches radiating from a swollen crown about an axe length above head height, which anyone who has visited Epping, Hainault or Hatfield Forests will recognise.

Animals grazing beneath the pollards prevent other trees or shrubs from growing, creating a landscape of pollard trees scattered across open grassland. This landscape, known as wood-pasture or tree-pasture, still exists in Hatfield Forest and is being restored in both Epping and Hainault Forests, where most of the pollards have become overgrown so that few plants can grow on the woodland floor.

Recently pollarded tree
Jeremy Dagley

Overgrown beech pollards in Epping Forest
David Corke

Green Lanes
88ac/35ha   *OS Ex174/La167*   *GR 440 060/396030*

These Green Lanes are now completely separated from the rest of the Forest, running in an arc starting near Fishers Green in the Lea Valley and finishing north of Epping. They consist of pleasant green lanes interspersed with grassy areas, small woods and occasional ponds. Surrounded as they are by intensive farmland their wildlife value is high. Yellowhammers and linnets, for example, are still seen along them regularly in summer but have almost disappeared elsewhere.

Linnet (male)
Alan Williams

Visiting

Park at Fishers Green (see Lea Valley p.158) and walk from there.

Harlow–Waltham Abbey bus to Eagle Lodge or Holyfield. Harlow–Epping bus to Epping Green.

Accessible at all times.

Lower Forest

478ac/191ha   OS Ex174/La167   GR 475 035   SSSI

The Lower Forest north of Epping is predominantly wood-pasture of oak and hornbeam, much of it dense with holly and scrub. Two broad Green Lanes, bordered by a number of re-pollarded hornbeams, divide it into four. One of these – Stump Road, once the main road from London to Cambridge – runs alongside Cripsey Brook which has many flowers on its margins, including primroses, dogs mercury, sanicle and angelica. It runs into Wintry Wood Common which is also flower-rich.

Epping Plain at its south-west corner was once open grassland that has been heavily invaded by oak. It has several large ponds with unusual aquatic plants like water violet and a wide range of dragonflies.

Visiting

Between High Rd (B1393) and Epping Road (B181) north-east of Epping. There is a parking area on The Woodyard south of the B181.

Buses between Epping and Harlow run along the B1393.

Accessible at all times.

Spring and summer for woodland flowers and insects.

Gernon Bushes

79ac/32ha   OS Ex174/La167   GR 478 030   SSSI

ESSEX
Wildlife Trust

This is the last remnant of the old Coopersale Common that once linked Epping Lower Forest (now cut off by the disused Central Line tube) along the hill ridge to Ongar Park, managed as a nature reserve by Essex Wildlife Trust. It has many ancient hornbeam pollards plus some more recent woodland and a network of ponds originally dug for gravel extraction, and descends steeply from the plateau of the ridge across pebbly clay drift and claygate beds to London Clay lower down.

In the north of the reserve the gravel workings

Pollarding at Gernon Bushes
Janet Spencer

Visiting

Turn off the B181 towards Coopersale village and turn left on to Garnon Mead 200 yards after passing under the railway bridge.

A bus service runs to Coopersale from Harlow via Epping.

Accessible at all times

Spring for songbirds; summer for marsh and bog plants.

Call the warden on 01245 281314 or Essex Wildlife Trust HQ on 01206 735456.

have developed into sphagnum bogs. In the south two springs rise on the edge of the plateau and their streams descend steep-sided valleys through a series of bogs with extensive patches of the rare marsh fern. Other notable plants include lady fern, bogbean (in one of its very few Essex sites), marsh valerian, marsh marigold and ragged robin.

It has a good variety of resident and summer migrant birds. Hawfinch and sparrowhawk are among the many species that have been recorded.

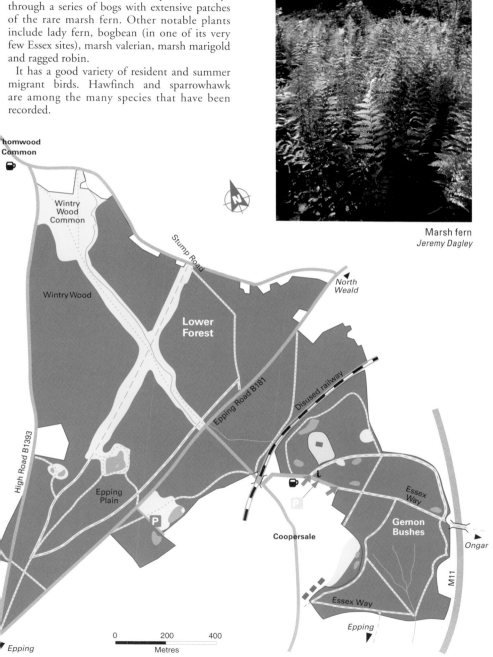

Marsh fern
Jeremy Dagley

Heart of the Forest

6250ac/2500ha   OS Ex174/La177   GR 412 981   SSSI

The heart of Epping Forest, with its massive ancient trees, lies to the west of the Epping Forest Conservation Centre at High Beach. To see many of the best of the Forest's habitats, follow Three Forests Way – signposted Loughton – from the High Beach car park and turn left at Debden Slade on to Green Ride. Follow Green Ride all the way to Long Running, then return via St Thomas' Quarters and Verderer's Ride.

Loughton Camp

Loughton Camp is a circular earth bank believed to date from the late Iron Age. It is set in a woodland of tall beech pollards, with occasional clumps of heather. Below it is Debden Slade, a grassy glade beside a stream where oaks and hornbeams have been repollarded. Many streams run through this area, some with boggy flushes full of ferns, sedges and wetland flowers.

Honey Lane Quarters

Honey Lane Quarters slopes down steeply to the west with good views over the Lea Valley. It is wood-pasture, with beech at the top and hornbeam lower down. A broad ride leads down to the grassy plain and stream at its foot.

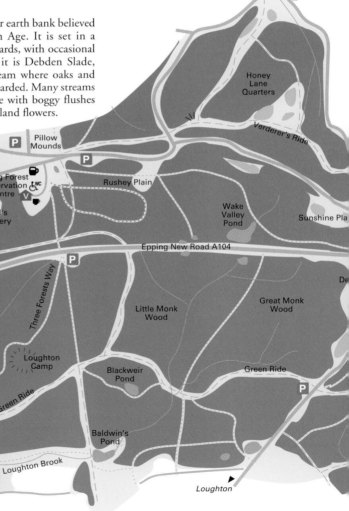

80

Wake Valley

The Wake Valley is a mosaic of beechwood and heathland with a number of ponds. These have good dragonfly populations, and especially Wake Valley Pond, in which the downy emerald breeds. The marsh to the the north has a good range of wetland plants including ragged robin, lesser spearwort, marsh violet and marsh fern.

St Thomas' Quarters

This is mostly beech wood-pasture, with some very large beech pollards. It has a number of streams with boggy flushes and two fine valley bogs east of Lodge Road. Visitor pressure is relatively low so it serves as a refuge for fallow deer.

Furze Ground & Copley Plain

These are restored heathland, surrounded by ancient pollards and some 'coppards', that is trees that have first been coppiced then the multiple stems have been pollarded.

Visiting

🚗 Leave the M25 at junction 26 and head east along the A121 towards Loughton. This brings you to the Wake Arms roundabout where the A121 meets Epping New Road and the road to Theydon Bois (B172). The Wake Road turns off the A121 on the right just before the roundabout and leads to the Conservation Centre.

🚌 Chingford station (BR Liverpool St) is a short walk from Queen Elizabeth's Hunting Lodge. The central parts of the Forest are a longer walk from Loughton or Theydon Bois stations on the Central Line, and bus services run from Debden station on the same line.

🕐 Forest accessible at all times.

📅 Worth a visit at any time of year.

☎ Call Forest Information Centre on 020 8508 0028. (The Conservation Centre is run by the Field Studies Council for school visits: phone 020 8508 7714.)

Long Running

Long Running has probably the best areas of restored heathland in the Forest. One section is being grazed by cattle and others have been cleared of invading birch and the original vegetation of cross-leaved heath and ling has reappeared. In the open areas there is a good chance of seeing tree pipits, a once-common bird that has become very scarce in Essex in the last 20 years, and they also support many reptiles.

Gt & Lt Monk Woods

Here you will find many very old beech and oak pollards, a good number of which have died, creating small clearings in which dense stands of young trees spring up. A number of streams cut deeply into the gravelly slopes.

Loughton Brook

Loughton Brook meanders in a deep valley cut through beech and hornbeam wood-pasture, bordered by ferns, sedges, flag iris and heather. Kingfishers and grey wagtails nest along its banks. It leaves the Forest at Staples Pond which has marsh marigolds and a good range of dragonflies.

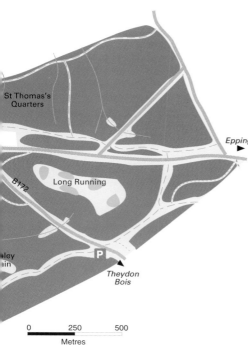

St Thomas's Quarters

B172

Long Running

Epping

...ley ...in

P

Theydon Bois

0   250   500
Metres

Longhorn cattle grazing Long Running (the birch
trees serve as songposts for tree pipits)
Jeremy Dagley

Deershelter Plain
Jeremy Dagley

Massive oak pollards in Barn Hoppit
Jeremy Dagley

Heather and pollards on Warren Hill
Jeremy Dagley

Around Chingford

1000ac/2500ha   OS Ex174/La177   GR 397 948   SSSI

It is estimated that about one-sixth of Epping Forest was originally open country, and kept so by grazing by deer and cattle. As grazing declined, so scrub and then trees have moved in and taken over most of this area. There is still attractive, rolling open country in the south of the main part of the forest, though, near Chingford.

This area is particularly good for birds, because of the variety of habitats, ranging from mature woodland via scrub to open grassland, much of it damp. Try a tour from Queen Elizabeth's Hunting Lodge via Connaught Water, Fairmead Bottom and Almshouse Plain to Yardley Hill (from where there are good views west across the Lea Valley), returning via Chingford Plain.

Yardley Hill

Once open farmland, Yardley Hill is now virtually covered with oak and thorn scrub. It has patches of chalky soil where plants such as clematis and sweet violet grow. From the top there are good views across the Lea Valley reservoirs into north London.

At its foot is Yate's Meadow, which is full of wild flowers in summer and where skylarks and meadow pipits breed.

Visiting

Queen Elizabeth's Hunting Lodge is on the A1069 next to the Royal Forest Hotel. Leave the M25 at junction 26 and head east along the A121. At the Wake Arms roundabout head south down the A104 then turn right on to the A1069.

Chingford station (Liverpool St line) is a short walk from Queen Elizabeth's Hunting Lodge.

Accessible at all times.

May to early June for breeding birds. Come in the very early morning and avoid sunny weekends if you want to miss the crowds.

Many paths are very boggy in winter, and some all year round.

Chingford Plain

Chingford Plain was under arable cultivation until 1878. Part of it forms Chingford golf course and some of it has returned to scrubland which attracts many birds. In early winter large numbers of fieldfares and redwings, visiting from Scandinavia, often gather on the golf course.

Epping Forest from the west, looking across the William Girling reservoir
David Corke

The Plains

Almshouse Plain, Whitehouse Plain and Fairmead Bottom are interconnected areas of grassland, some of it damp. They are dotted with large patches of scrub and crossed by flower-lined ditches and are good territory for insects and small mammals. There is a scattering of ponds, the best of which is Fairmead Pond, where grass snakes are common.

Connaught Water

Connaught Water is a large shallow lake with wooded islands, made in 1880. The grass around it is cropped short by canada geese, and mallard and moorhen breed on its wooded islands. In the winter the Forest's considerable population of mandarin ducks roost there.

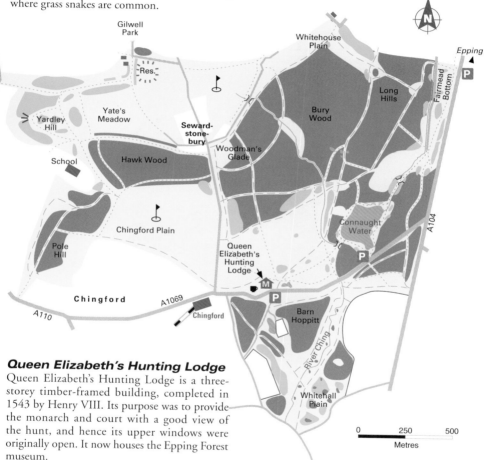

Queen Elizabeth's Hunting Lodge

Queen Elizabeth's Hunting Lodge is a three-storey timber-framed building, completed in 1543 by Henry VIII. Its purpose was to provide the monarch and court with a good view of the hunt, and hence its upper windows were originally open. It now houses the Epping Forest museum.

Barn Hoppitt & Whitehall Plain

Barn Hoppitt and Whitehall Plain were part of the Forest's 'plains': open areas used for grazing cattle. Barn Hoppitt is the best example of oak wood-pasture in the Forest, with well-spaced ancient oak pollards over sparse grassland with many anthills and a mosaic of scrub patches.

The River Ching meanders through from north to south and its corridor supports unusual shrubs like spindle, buckthorn and purple osier.

Once open grassland, Whitehall Plain has been invaded by thorn scrub which has driven out most of its flowering plants, but these are starting to return now that it is being cut for hay.

Lord's Bushes & Knighton Wood
133ac/53ha   OS Ex174/La177   GR 413 935   SSSI (part)

Lord's Bushes is oak and hornbeam wood-pasture on a light soil, with many beech trees as well, some of the largest of which are well past their best. Wide pathways cross the wood, fringed by gorse, sheep's sorrel and fine grasses.

Knighton Wood to the west was owned and landscaped by E. N. Buxton, once a Verderer, and returned to the Forest after his death in 1930. It has a mixture of trees – predominantly oak, hornbeam and beech with a scattering of exotics like red oaks and copper beech – and an attractive lake with islands.

Visiting

North of Woodford, east of A121 High Road Woodford Green

Buckhurst Hill or Roding Valley tube stations are a few minutes' walk.

Accessible at all times.

An easy access path runs in a loop alongside the lake in Knightons Wood.

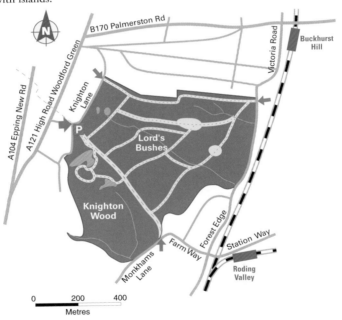

Highams Park
88ac/35ha   OS Ex174/La177   GR 393 922

Higham's Park is pollard woodland of oak and hornbeam that was landscaped by Humphrey Repton in the 1790s. The River Ching flows into it from the north to feed one of the largest lakes in the Forest, which supports many species of dragonfly. It has carpets of bluebells in spring, along with red campion, wood anemone and periwinkle.

The woodland to the south has some large oaks, hornbeam coppice and some planted conifers. The small ponds in the open grassland in the south-east corner are rich in wildlife, including great crested newts.

86

Walthamstow Forest

128ac/51ha   OS Ex174/La177   GR 391 910   SSSI (part)

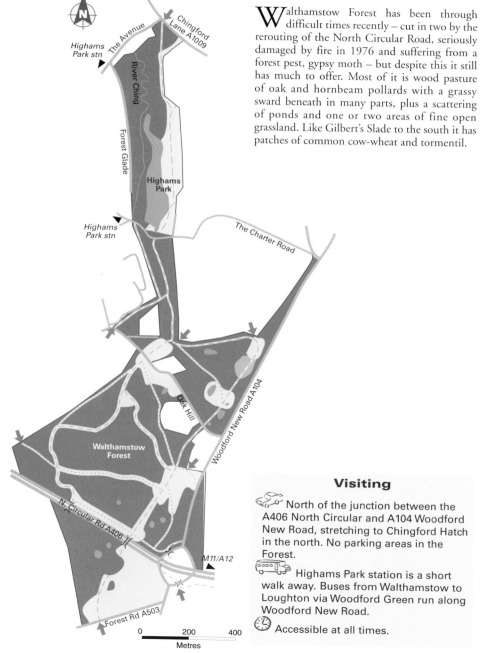

Walthamstow Forest has been through difficult times recently – cut in two by the rerouting of the North Circular Road, seriously damaged by fire in 1976 and suffering from a forest pest, gypsy moth – but despite this it still has much to offer. Most of it is wood pasture of oak and hornbeam pollards with a grassy sward beneath in many parts, plus a scattering of ponds and one or two areas of fine open grassland. Like Gilbert's Slade to the south it has patches of common cow-wheat and tormentil.

Visiting

North of the junction between the A406 North Circular and A104 Woodford New Road, stretching to Chingford Hatch in the north. No parking areas in the Forest.

Highams Park station is a short walk away. Buses from Walthamstow to Loughton via Woodford Green run along Woodford New Road.

Accessible at all times.

87

A bout one-quarter of Britain used to be some form of wetland. Some of the greatest English wetlands are in East Anglia, which has the Fens, extending inland for many miles all around The Wash, and the Norfolk Broads. Much of South Essex also was fen and marsh, but now only tiny fragments remain.

If they are not polluted, wetlands teem with life. Their natural vegetation is luxuriant; their natural structure a complexity of pools, reedbeds, grassland, thickets and damp woods. Much of our natural vegetation is adapted to varying degrees and seasons of waterlogging and many animals either live in water or, like wildfowl, move between wetlands seasonally. Since unpolluted wetland is now so scarce, it follows that many wetland plants and animals have either disappeared or are in decline.

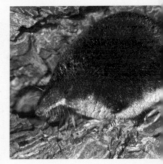

Water shrew: rarely seen but may be more common than we think
David Corke

Otters went extinct in Essex in the 1970s, but have recently begun recolonising rivers in the north of the county at surprising speed, so the omens look good.
Alan Williams

◄

Water voles, once common, have declined massively. They are suffering from loss of bankside vegetation that gives them cover and fluctating water levels that expose their nest tunnels to attack from enemies like weasels and rats. They are also vulnerable to american mink that are spreading into Essex from the north-west, apparently inexorably, although recent evidence suggests that competition from otters may hold them back.
Ken King

F ens (where water is at surface level most or all of the year) and marshes are rich in insect life, because insect larvae benefit from damp soil. This in turn provides plenty of food for birds, who also benefit from the tall and dense vegetation of aquatic plants such as reed and willowherb, which provide good cover and prevent disturbance by people.

The electric blue of a kingfisher ▲ along a river is a good sign that it is healthy, because it means that fish are present and the water is clear enough to catch them.
Gerald Downey

Reed warblers, tiny but noisy birds that are a favourite host for cuckoos' eggs, breed in many Essex wetlands.
David Harrison
▶

Another bird heavily dependent on reeds is the bearded tit, also known as the reedling. They can be seen in winter at Ingrebourne Marshes and Stanford Warren and on the fleet next to Wat Tyler Country Park.
Gerald Downey

Gilbert's Slade & Rising Sun Wood

128ac/51ha   OS Ex174/La177   GR 394 898   SSSI

Gilbert's Slade, to the east of Woodford New Road, is open woodland with many fine old gnarled oak and hornbeam pollards and an open glade at its centre. It has many patches of common cow-wheat and tormentil, with heather here and there.

Rising Sun Wood across the road also has many old pollards, principally hornbeam, and because it was grazed until very recently it still has the feel of old wood-pasture. It too has an open glade, Canada Plain, surrounding Bulrush Pond.

Leyton Flats

188ac/75ha   OS Ex174/La177   GR 395 885   SSSI

Most of Leyton Flats is acid grassland, until recently (when BSE put an end to it) kept open by grazing by commoners' cattle. It has large patches of gorse and broom, which are well used by birds for nesting, and is also the London stronghold for creeping willow. The northern section has mature oak woodland and an interesting marshy area of shallow pools and willow scrub. It has two large ponds: Hollow Pond, used for boating, and Eagle Pond. Eagle Pond, one of the oldest in the Forest, is quite deep in places and has a large concentration of mute swans.

Horseriders in Epping Forest
David Corke

90

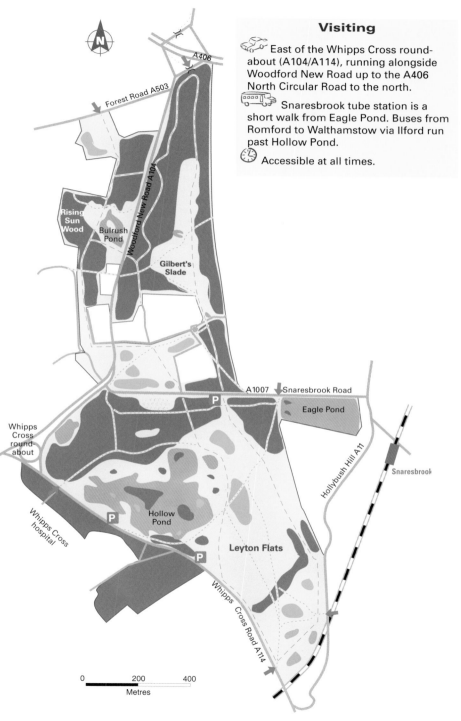

Visiting

East of the Whipps Cross round-about (A104/A114), running alongside Woodford New Road up to the A406 North Circular Road to the north.

Snaresbrook tube station is a short walk from Eagle Pond. Buses from Romford to Walthamstow via Ilford run past Hollow Pond.

Accessible at all times.

A406

Forest Road A503

Woodford New Road A104

Rising Sun Wood

Bulrush Pond

Gilbert's Slade

A1007 Snaresbrook Road

Eagle Pond

Whipps Cross round-about

Hollybush Hill A11

Snaresbrook

Whipps Cross hospital

Hollow Pond

P

Leyton Flats

Whipps Cross Road A114

0   200   400
Metres

Wanstead Park
140ac/56ha OS Ex174/La177   GR 415 875

Once the renowned 18th-century gardens of Wanstead House, Wanstead Park is managed now by the Corporation of London as part of Epping Forest. It has several large lakes, with secluded inlets, islands and marshy areas. These are surrounded by a mixture of mature woodland, parkland and open acid grassland where harebells grow. The River Roding runs along its eastern boundary.

This combination makes for rich wildlife, despite the constant visitor pressure. Birdlife is particularly good, with kingfishers seen regularly throughout the year, wildfowl visiting the lakes in winter and hobbies in summer, and both water birds and migrant warblers nesting in summer.

Visiting

South of the A12 (Eastern Avenue)/M11 interchange. Can be reached from Wanstead Park Road to the east via an overbridge, from Woodlands Avenue/Northumberland Avenue to the south and from Warren Road to the north-west. No parking on the site.

Central line tube to Wanstead. Several bus services run to this station also.

Accessible in daylight hours only.

Autumn/winter for visiting wildfowl; April/May for woodland flowers and bird-song.

A good network of surfaced paths.

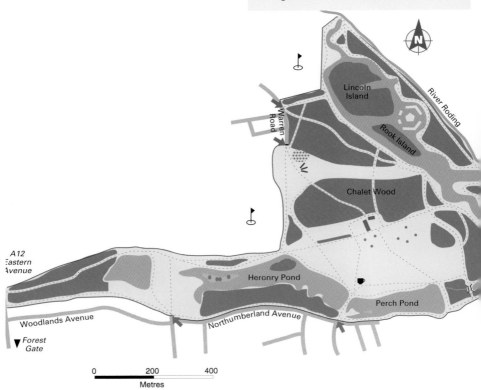

92

Creeping willow on Wanstead Flats
Jeremy Dagley

Downy emerald dragonfly: breeds
in the Wake Valley pond
Andy McGeeney

Wanstead
Park Road

Ilford

Fairlop Waters
100ac/40ha OS Ex174/La177   GR 460 905

Redbridge Council

Fairlop Waters is on the site of the former Spitfire base, RAF Fairlop. It has a large lake, used for sailing, a smaller one, used for angling, and a golf club. It also has a new country park, landscaped and planted up by Redbridge Council. It is an important refuge for some of our declining birds, including sand martins, skylarks, corn buntings and linnets, and also has adders and brown hares.

Its future is in doubt because in 1999 a planning application was filed for a major leisure development. This has been turned down by Redbridge Council but may go to appeal. Check before you visit!

Visiting

Off Forest Road, which runs from the Fulwell Cross roundabout in Barkingside south of Hainault to join the A1112.

Fairlop tube station is a short walk up Forest Road from the main entrance.

Accessible at all times.

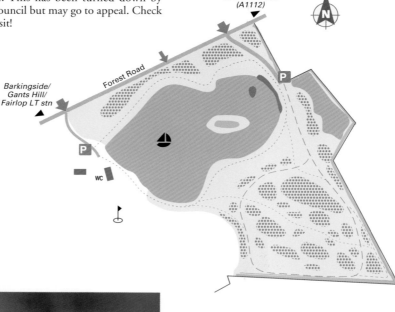

Skylark
Alan Williams

0   200   400
Metres

94

Fingringhoe Wick is the Essex Wildlife Trust's flagship reserve on the west shore of the Colne Estuary, created out of disused gravel workings. From the dust and turmoil of 40 years of gravel extraction the Trust inherited a barren moonscape. But bare gravel, clay, mud and sediments are inviting seedbeds for wild plants, and today the disturbed, undulating terrain is largely buried in woodland, thickets and dense scrub. The reserve has an immense range of habitats, including patches of grassland, gorse heathland, reedbeds and – a vital wildlife feature – ponds and a large lake. There is a mixed plantation of trees, including conifers. The river frontage provides additional habitats such as saltmarsh, foreshore and inter-tidal mudflats.

Strategically placed on sloping ground overlooking the wild expanses of the Colne Estuary, The Wick offers one of the finest saltmarsh panoramas in eastern England.

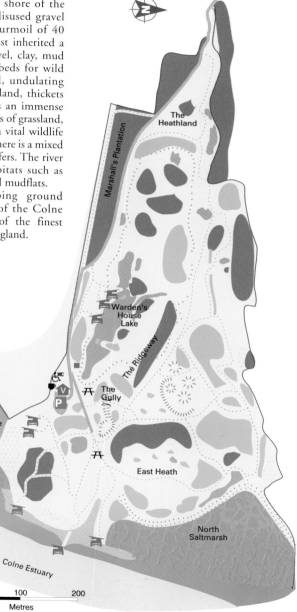

95

Over 200 species of birds have been recorded, of which 50 species nest each year. Come in spring to hear the massed nightingale chorus and for other breeding migrants. Watch the ponds for the darting blue flash of a kingfisher. Kestrels nest, as well as tawny owls, little grebes and sparrowhawks. Between June and September, migrant waders find the Scrape attractive. The estuary, quiet for much of the year, comes into its own in winter. Thousands of wintering waders and wildfowl rely on the expanses of mud and saltmarsh for food or for roosting. This includes up to 700 avocets, viewable from the shore hides. Sea duck can be seen in mid-river.

You will see many rabbits and grey squirrels, and maybe a fox. There are regular sightings of brown hare, stoat and weasel. And watch out for common seals in the estuary.

At least 350 species of flowering plants have been recorded. Common spotted orchids and bee orchids are present. The shaded, humid conditions in the thickets suit ferns, mosses and lichens. Visit in spring for tiny unobtrusive clovers, medicks and trefoils. Summer is best for colourful species, especially sea lavender on the saltmarsh, and masses of dog roses.

The Wick teems with insect life. The dragonflies and damselflies are renowned: thirteen species breed on the reserve. Many common butterflies flourish, together with the more localised green hairstreak. The sandy, eroding cliff faces are attractive to many bees, ants and wasps.

Strangely, frogs are almost unknown at The Wick, although there is a tiny breeding population of toads. Common lizards, slow worms, and smooth newts are abundant. Great crested newts, adders and grass snakes are reported regularly.

On a site like this an annual programme of management is essential to let in sunlight and to create areas of new young growth. Scrub must be controlled and ponds must be maintained.

Occasionally large-scale projects become necessary. For example, the Trust has re-profiled the lake shore to benefit wildfowl and has created a sand martin cliff and a scrape (a shallow lake) for wading birds.

Winter wet pond at Fingringhoe Wick
Laurie Forsyth
▶

East Heath at Fingringhoe Wick
Laurie Forsyth
▼

Visiting

Three miles south-east of Colchester, signposted from there with brown Nature Reserve signs. Take the B1025 from Colchester towards Mersea for three miles. After crossing the Roman River turn first left and follow the signs to the reserve. The lanes between Fingringhoe village and the reserve are narrow – please drive with caution. A 10 mph limit is in force on the reserve itself.

The Visitor Centre is open daily except Mondays from 9 am – 5 pm and the reserve from 9 am to 5 pm (winter) or 7 pm (summer), excluding Christmas Day and Boxing Day. All visitors to the nature reserve are required to enter the Fingringhoe Centre first, to obtain a day permit. The Trust invites donations from non-members of £1 or more for adults and 50p for children.

Worth visiting at any time of the year, but the highlights for many are the nightingale chorus in May and the flocks of brent geese in winter.

A short nature trail (leaflet available) is suitable for people in wheelchairs. Two bird hides that overlook the lake have concrete access paths and low-level viewing slots. A wheelchair is available in the centre on request.

For details of a regular programme of events for adults and children or for any other information, call 01206 729678. Waymarked nature trails start from the centre (i available).

Group visits of parties of more than ten people are welcome, but please advise in advance by calling 01206 729678.

Dogs are allowed within the nature reserve only on a lead. Please use the signposted dog route. They are not permitted elsewhere, nor in Centre or hides.

Flitch Way

40ac/16ha   OS Ex195/La167   GR 519 212–760 227

Essex County Council

The Flitch Way follows the route of the old railway line all the way from Bishop's Stortford to Braintree – a distance of 15 miles. This makes it by far the longest country park in Essex! The railway was built in the 19th century and dismantled in 1969. Since then nature has taken over, with more than a little help from Essex County Council's Ranger Service.

Sections of the line run on embankments with fine views over the surrounding countryside. In the west, for example, it runs across the northern edge of Hatfield Forest.

Other parts run in secluded cuttings, the longest of which is near Dunmow. Here conditions are very wet, and plants like water mint growing alongside the path scent the air.

Many animals make use of this man-made green corridor. Muntjac and fallow deer use it to get about between woods and copses nearby. Foxes use the old drainage pipes as earths.

The south-facing banks form a sun trap and are ideal for slow worms, grass snakes and lizards, which can often be seen basking in the open. They also attract many butterflies.

Visiting

Can be entered from a number of points along its length – see map.

Trains run to Braintree from Witham and to Bishop's Stortford from London. Regular bus services run between Bishop's Stortford and Braintree.

Accessible at all times.

May–July for wild flowers, birds and butterflies.

Call the Rangers on 01376 340262.

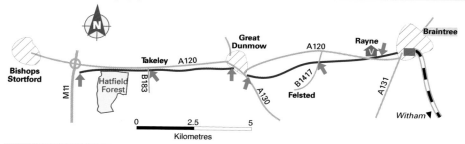

0   2.5   5
Kilometres

Blackwater Trail

20ac/8ha   OS Ex183/La168   GR 848 081–825 151

Essex County Council

The Blackwater Trail follows the disused Maldon–Witham railway line. It is still under development by Essex County Council and the route is not yet continuous, but sections starting from north of Maldon and from east of Witham were available as this book went to press. For the latest information call the Rangers on 01376 340262.

Visiting

Access at the Maldon end from the B1018 just north of its junction with the A414, and at the Witham end from the B1318 south-west of its junction with the A12. No formal parking yet available.

Buses from Maldon to Hatfield Peverel and Chelmsford pass the Maldon access and Chelmsford–Colchester buses pass the Witham access.

Accessible at all times.

Fobbing Marsh

187ac/75ha   OS Ex175/La177   GR 732 846   SSSI (part)

ESSEX
Wildlife Trust

This is one of the few remaining Thameside grazing marshes, set on the north-west edge of Fobbing Creek, part of which was dammed in the aftermath of the 1953 floods. As well as the grazing meadows it has areas of rough grassland (the largest of which is the bed of the dammed creek), saltings, sea walls and an adjoining small reedbed. It is managed by Essex Wildlife Trust.

Its flowering plants are typical of Thameside marshes, including hairy buttercup, knotted hedge parsley, slender hare's-ear and sea barley, together with the normal range of saltmarsh plants and, in early summer, large colourful patches of vetches and tares. It also supports corn chervil and the nationally rare least lettuce.

In summer there are many dragonflies and damselflies along the borrow dykes. The scarce emerald damselfly is a local speciality and is also rare nationally, as are some of the other invertebrates found in the dykes. The rank grass along the sea walls is a haven for grasshoppers and bush-crickets.

Corn bunting and yellow wagtail breed regularly, and the marsh is used by wintering raptors, wildfowl and waders. Visiting passage migrants include wheatear and whinchat.

The fields are cut for hay and then grazed, continuing the traditional method of managing Essex marshland.

Visiting

🚗 Down Marsh Lane, 800m north of Fobbing Church and about a mile from the A13. Park in Fobbing High Road near the top of Marsh Lane (GR 716 845). Please leave the entrance to Marsh Lane clear as it is used by wide farm machinery. Walk down Marsh Lane and at the bottom take the left-hand fork and follow the track until you see the reserve noticeboard – this is almost a mile from the High Road.

🚌 A bus service from Basildon and Stanford-le-Hope stops at Marsh Lane.

🕐 Accessible at all times

📅 December and January to see raptors and waders; March, April and September for birds on passage; summer for insects and wild flowers.

🚫 Please do not walk along the top of the sea walls as this disturbs and frightens away the wildlife.

☎ Call the warden on 01268 554424 or Essex Wildlife Trust HQ on 01206 735456.

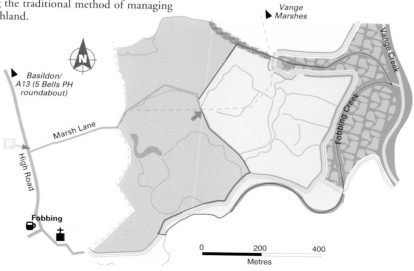

Fordham Heath

36ac/14ha   *OS Ex184/La168*   *GR 944 263*

Eight Ash Green Council

This is a surviving remnant of ancient wet heathland, granted to Eight Ash Green Parish Council by Act of Parliament in 1965. It is managed by the parish council with assistance from the River Colne Countryside Project.

Until the 1940s the heath was dominated by heather and gorse and was grazed by commoners' cattle, but when grazing ceased it was invaded by trees such as oak, birch, blackthorn and aspen which dominate its wooded areas today. But large open areas still remain and are being cut regularly to encourage the regrowth of the original heathland species.

Over 150 different species of wildflower have been recorded in the mosaic of rough grassland, scrub and woodland, including sneezewort, a plant typical of damp rough grassland that is now very scarce.

The woodland in the northern section is being coppiced on a cycle of 12–15 years. This keeps the trees healthy and encourages a diversity of wildlife. Birds that breed here include whitethroat and nightingale.

Visiting

Turn north off the A1124 Colchester–Halstead road in Eight Ash Green, about 800m north of its junction with the A12. The heath is about 400m on.

Buses from Colchester to Fordham and Wakes Colne run past the heath.

Accessible at all times.

Paths may be wet and muddy at any time of the year.

Sneezewort
Owen Keen

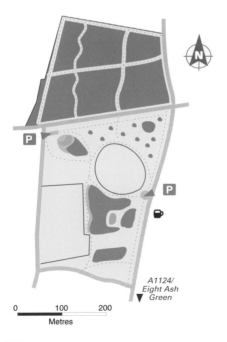

A1124/
Eight Ash
▼ Green

0   100   200
Metres

Galleywood Common

Chelmsford Council

60ac/24ha   OS Ex183/La167   GR 704 025   LNR

This fine piece of common land a mile or so south of Chelmsford is a typical common in its irregular shape, including several enclaves containing buildings, and in the many pits and depressions caused, no doubt, by commoners digging out gravel in the past. It packs a great variety of habitats into a relatively small space.

These include mature and more recent woodland with ponds, a bog and some marshy areas, lowland heath, bracken-covered areas and open grassland.

It is managed by Chelmsford Council.

Visiting

Leave the A12 at its junction with the B1007 and turn north towards Galleywood and Chelmsford.

Buses from Chelmsford to Basildon, Billericay and Wickford run down the B1007 past the common.

Accessible at all times.

Galleywood/ Chelmsford

B1007

Lowland heath on Galleywood Common
Tony Gunton

Brentwood/ London

Colchester

A12

Stock

0   200   400
Metres

Garnetts Wood

60ac/24ha   **OS Ex183/La167**   **GR 635 185**   **SSSI**

Essex County Council

This ancient coppice woodland is owned and managed by Essex County Council. It is not as rich as Chalkney Wood nor as well restored, but coppicing has been resumed and it is an attractive woodland with considerable variety. There are several damp areas full of sedges and a scattering of ponds and streams.

Visiting

On High Easter Road, a minor road running between Barnston and High Easter. Barnston is a village lying on the A130 (Gt Dunmow–Colchester) a mile or two south-east of Great Dunmow.

The nearest bus service (Bishop's Stortford–Chelmsford) runs through Barnston nearly 2 miles distant.

Accessible at all times.

April–May for early flowers and songbirds.

Paths can be very wet in winter and spring – waterproof footwear essential.

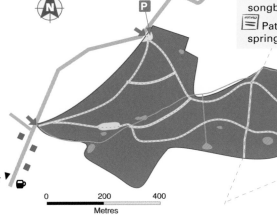

A130/Barnston

High Easter

| 0 | 200 | 400 |

Metres

Pyramidal orchid
Alan Sadgrove

Graylings mating
Alan Sadgrove

102

Grays Chalk Quarry

40ac/16ha   OS Ex162/La177   GR 611 787   SSSI

ESSEX Wildlife Trust

Grays Chalk Quarry is managed as a nature reserve by Essex Wildlife Trust. Now long disused, it is heavily wooded with an imposing chalk cliff at the northern end. Above the cliff is a narrow strip of chalk grassland. A sizeable shallow pool on the quarry floor contains marestail.

The reserve is extremely important because of its wealth of chalk-loving plants. Kidney vetch, chicory, greater knapweed and sainfoin, among many others, create a riot of colour along the access path. The quarry boasts a number of orchid species, several of them rare, including man orchid, pyramidal orchid and bee orchid. It also contains a number of other localised Essex plants such as round-leaved wintergreen, deadly nightshade, yellow-wort, common milkwort and autumn gentian.

It is rich in insect life, having a number of species associated with chalk downland including the chalk carpet and burnet companion moths and some noteworthy micromoths. It also has green hairstreak and marbled white butterflies, while graylings occur in the north-west corner, which is not so heavily wooded. Birds, mammals and reptiles are also well represented.

Trust volunteers maintain the paths and keep larger areas open by clearing scrub and cutting the grass. All plant debris is removed to ensure that the chalk does not become enriched with humus – this would encourage invasion by coarser plants.

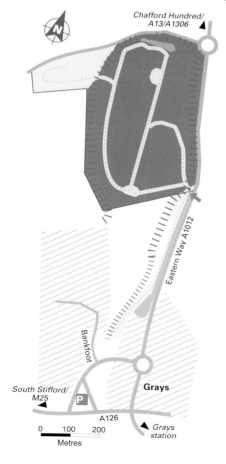

Visiting

Parking is available in the public car park on London Road near Grays town centre and the rail station. Cross the road to the entrance to the new housing estate and you will find the access path a short distance in on the right.

Grays bus and rail stations are within easy walking distance.

For reasons of safety, special permits are required to enter the reserve, obtainable from Trust HQ (01206 735456). These include full details of access.

June to August for orchids and other rare plants.

Arrangements can be made via the warden (01375 408879) for disabled visitors, but note that all paths are difficult to negotiate.

Children must be supervised properly, especially near the cliff faces and flights of steps.

Call the warden on 01375 408879 or Essex Wildlife Trust HQ on 01206 735456.

103

Great Holland Pits
40ac/16ha   OS Ex184/La169   GR 204 190

ESSEX
Wildlife Trust

Except that it does not border an estuary, this Essex Wildlife Trust reserve is in many respects a smaller version of Fingringhoe Wick. Gravel was worked here until about 1964 but the scars have virtually disappeared beneath vigorous growth. Habitats include heathy grassland, pasture, a remnant of old woodland, large and small pools, and wet depressions. From the high ground there are attractive views of Holland Brook meandering through water meadows.

It has a wide variety of flowering plants, including localised Essex species such as moschatel, yellow archangel, small-flowered buttercup, mousetail, carline thistle, several small clovers, true bulrush, and soft shield and hart's-tongue ferns.

There is a good variety of birdlife, with the nightingale among the summer visitors, and several aquatic species including kingfisher, coot and little grebe. Woodcock frequently use the reserve in winter.

As you would expect in such a varied site, there are many butterflies, moths and other invertebrates.

Visiting

🚗 The reserve entrance is 800m west of the Lion's Den pub at Great Holland, north of the Little Clacton Road.

🚌 Buses stop at the Lion's Den on the route from Clacton to Walton.

🕐 Accessible at all times.

📅 Spring and summer for flowers, birds and insects.

☎ Call the warden on 01255 436494 or Essex Wildlife Trust HQ on 01206 735456.

Holland Mill Wood
10ac/4ha   OS Ex184/La169   GR 202 195

WOODLAND
TRUST

Holland Mill Wood, a new wood of about 10 acres planted by the Woodland Trust, can be reached via Great Holland Pits.

Great Notley Country Park

100ac/40ha   OS Ex195/La167   GR 733 210

This new country park is being developed by Braintree Council. It has two lakes, several new copses planted on top of earth mounds and some open grassland. Already skylarks and reed buntings have colonised the site, and its wildlife value can only grow as it does.

A Discovery Centre embodying sustainable principles such as solar heating has been built in the north-east of the park and will provide interpretation and other facilities for visitors. Call Braintree Council on 01376 552525 for the latest information.

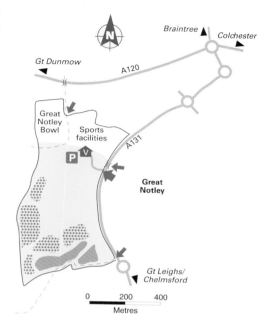

Visiting

On the A131 a short way south of its junction with the A120, 2 miles south-west of Braintree.

Nearest rail station is Braintree. Buses run via the station to Great Notley, from where it is a 15-minute walk.

Accessible at all times.

Little grebe, also known as dabchick (in summer plumage)
Alan Williams

Reed bunting (male)
Alan Williams

105

Gunners Park

50ac/20ha   OS Ex176/La168   GR 933 849   LNR (part)

This former MoD land in Shoeburyness is now a public open space managed by Southend Council. It is all that remains of a large area of common and rough grazing stretching from Southend to Shoebury, consisting of a barrier beach and spit backed in some places by marshland. It used to be part of the MoD rifle ranges and therefore is untouched by agriculture.

It is mainly grassland, divided by ditches and dykes lined with reed and with patches of dense scrub and clumps of trees. This combination makes for good bird and insect life in summer. Goldfinches, linnets and whitethroats nest in the scrub, and kestrels and barn owls hunt over the grassland. It is also a good place to see unusual passage migrants in autumn and spring.

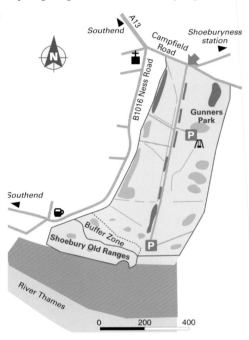

Visiting

Entrance in Campfield Road, Shoeburyness, just beyond the end of the A13.

10 minutes' walk from Shoeburyness station. Buses run from Southend centre.

Accessible at all times.

May to August for birdsong and insects; autumn for passage migrant birds.

Shoebury Old Ranges

22ac/9ha   OS Ex176/La168   GR 931 841   SSSI

This is an old common area that has never been ploughed, together with a buffer zone. It is leased from the MoD by Southend Council and managed by Essex Wildlife Trust.

It contains coastal features such as shell banks and sand dunes with wetter slacks between. The vegetation is mainly short species-rich turf, closely grazed by rabbits and with lichens predominating in small areas.

The area was saved as a nature reserve because of its botanical richness. It contains local and regional rarities such as meadow saxifrage, yellow horned-poppy, suffocated clover, fenugreek, dune fescue and bulbous meadow-grass.

It is also one of the richest areas for invertebrates in Essex, holding species once much more widespread in this south-eastern corner of the county.

Visiting

The vegetation in this reserve is very sensitive and easily damaged, so access is only by prior arrangement with the warden (call 01702 295259), but you can see into the reserve from the buffer zone in Gunners Park or over the old sea wall from the B1016 opposite the Shore House PH.

106

Less common butterflies

Ringlet: a butterfly of woodland glades and rides
Ken Wooldridge

Small copper: a butterfly of rough open places, where its foodplant, sorrel, grows
EWT library

Purple hairstreak: colonies live in oak trees and may be seen flying above the treetops
Iris Newbery

Green hairstreak: found on heath and downland with scattered patches of scrub
Alan Sadgrove

Speckled wood, a butterfly of dimly lit woodland and shady hedgerows
Phil Luke

White-letter hairstreak: breeds on elm trees and spends most of its life in the treetops
Ken Wooldridge

Hadleigh

Alongside the Thames between South Benfleet and Leigh lies Hadleigh Castle Country Park and, to its south-east, Two Tree Island. The country park, with its rough grassland, scrub and grazing marsh, attracts a variety of wildlife, while the eastern part of the island adjoins the saltmarsh and mudflats of Leigh National Nature Reserve, which is an important feeding ground for brent geese.

Hadleigh Castle Country Park

300ac/120ha OS Ex175/La178   *GR 799 870*   *SSSI (part), SPA*   Essex County Council

The main part of Hadleigh Castle country park is hillside running down, steeply in places, to grazing marsh, seawall and a narrow strip of saltmarsh alongside Benfleet Creek. It is managed by Essex County Council's Ranger Service.

From the open areas on the hillside there are views of industrial Canvey on the other side of Benfleet Creek, but these are quickly forgotten as you explore the mosaic of grassland, scrub and light woodland on the hillside. The hay meadows and rides are full of flowering plants such as restharrow, trefoils and self-heal. On a sunny summer's day many butterflies such as comma, speckled wood and white-letter hairstreak feed along the rides, and adders slither out to sun themselves.

At the foot of the hill you emerge into a pastoral landscape where cattle graze the marshland behind the seawall. In summer pipits and skylarks nest in the grazing marsh and it is alive with insects, including the scarce emerald damselfly, once thought to be extinct in Essex, and the shrill carder bee, a rare species selected for priority national conservation action.

Little grebes and reed warblers breed among the dykes and ponds. Unusual migrant birds are often seen here, and merlins come to hunt in winter.

Shrill carder bee, a very scarce bumblebee still present at Hadleigh Castle Country Park
Ted Benton

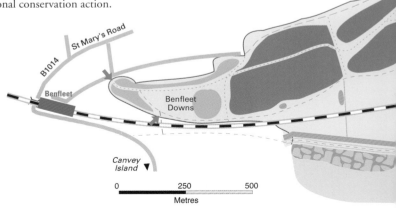

Rest-harrow, a plant of dry grassland such as Benfleet Downs
Owen Keen

Visiting

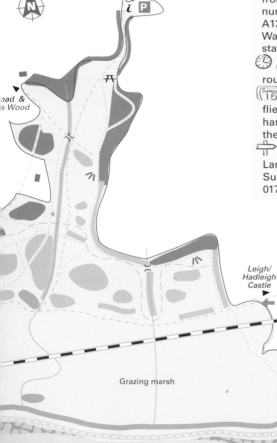

The main entrance is via Chapel Lane, which leaves the A13 opposite the Waggon and Horses PH in Hadleigh. It can also be reached from the footpath running along the seawall between Benfleet and Leigh

Benfleet station (Fenchurch St–Southend line) is a few minutes' walk from the western arm of the park. A number of bus services run along the A13 through Hadleigh (get off at the Waggon and Horses) and to Benfleet station.

Open from 8 am until dusk all year round.

Midsummer for wild flowers, butterflies and other insects; winter (for the hardy) for birds, ideally at high tide when they are closest.

Information room at the Chapel Lane car park, open 10am–5pm on Sundays from April to October. Call 01702 551072 for more information.

Map labels:

Hadleigh/ A13
Chapel Lane
Benfleet Road
N
...ad & ...s Wood
Leigh/ Hadleigh Castle
Leigh/ Two-Tree Island
Grazing marsh
...nfleet Creek

Two Tree Island from the south-west, with in front the saltmarsh
and on the extreme right the eelgrass beds of Leigh NNR.
David Corke

*During your visit to Hadleigh Castle
CP why not pop over to …*

Shipwrights Wood

30ac/12ha   OS Ex175/La178   GR 795 871

**Castle
Point
Council**

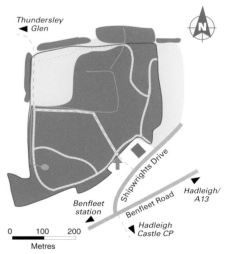

Thundersley
◀ Glen

Shipwrights Drive

Benfleet Road

Benfleet
station

Hadleigh/
A13

Hadleigh
Castle CP

0   100   200
Metres

What is now called Shipwrights Wood in fact comprises two pieces of ancient woodland, now owned and managed by Castle Point Council. The original Shipwrights Wood forms roughly the southern half and the eastern section to the north is part of Jervis Wood, with more recent woodland and a flower-rich meadow making up the remainder. It has many ridges, slopes and hollows and some marshy areas, and this makes for very varied vegetation and wildlife.

Visiting

🚗 Access from Shipwrights Drive off Benfleet Road (B1014) or by following the footpath north-west from Hadleigh Castle country park.

🚌 Regular (except Sundays) buses along Benfleet Road. Get off at Shipwrights Drive.

🕐 Accessible at all times.

Two Tree Island

634ac/254ha   OS Ex175/La178   GR 824 852   SSSI (part), NNR, SPA

Essex County Council

Two Tree Island typifies the history of many Essex coastal sites. It was captured from the sea in the 18th century when a sea wall was built around saltmarsh, and was used for rough grazing until 1910 when a sewage farm was built on its eastern tip. In 1936 Southend Council acquired the whole island and used it as a rubbish tip until the 1970s.

The western part belongs to Hadleigh Castle Country Park. At its tip is a lagoon with a bird hide, from which you can see birds such as redshank and heron feeding.

The eastern part, with the adjoining saltmarsh (170 acres) and a large area of inter-tidal mudflats (464 acres) belonging to Leigh NNR, is a nature reserve managed by Essex Wildlife Trust.

The island consists mainly of grassland and scrub, with the former rubbish tip supporting a number of interesting alien plants and 'escapes'. A wide variety of birds is seen, and particularly migrants. Kestrels hover over the grassland and short-eared owls visit during the winter, hunting for field voles. Insects of note include the marbled white butterfly, Roesel's bush-cricket, the house cricket and the lesser marsh grasshopper.

Visiting

The island is south of Leigh. Turn off the A13 down towards Leigh station, then cross the bridge over the railway and follow the road past the golf range and over the bridge on to the island.

20 minutes walk from Leigh station (Fenchurch St–Southend), which is also served by a number of buses.

Accessible at all times.

Migration periods and winter for birds – the brent geese are normally present from late September to mid-November; July for saltmarsh colours and butterflies.

To avoid disturbing the birds, please keep strictly to the marked footpaths in the nature reserve.

Call the warden on 01702 557208 or Essex Wildlife Trust HQ on 01206 735456.

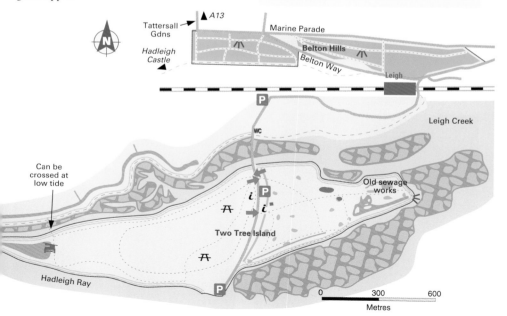

The saltmarsh along the southern shore of the island is one of the best surviving in the Thames Estuary. Among many typical saltmarsh plants it has golden samphire, sea wormwood, sea aster, common and lax-flowered sea lavenders and sea purslane.

The mudflats support dense beds of eel grass and provide a valuable feeding ground for wildfowl and waders, including the dark-bellied brent goose. The concentration of thousands of these birds arriving on their autumn migration is of international importance, representing up to 5% of the world population of this species. Waders such as curlew, dunlin, redshank, grey plover and knot occur in significant numbers outside the breeding season.

Belton Hills

50ac/20ha   *OS Ex175/La178*   *GR 825 860*   *LNR*

Southend Council

Essex County Council

This steep hillside overlooking the Thames estuary at Leigh-on-Sea has covered over with scrub and is now a Local Nature Reserve managed by Southend Council.

In summer birds sing from almost every thicket – migrants like whitethroats and blackcaps and residents like yellowhammers and linnets. Paths have been cut through the scrub and these are lined with wild flowers and frequented by butterflies, including the marbled white – one of the few places in Essex where it can still be seen.

Some characteristic coastal plants that are rare in Essex grow here, including deptford pink (flowering June–August) and bithynian vetch (flowering May–June),

Visiting

South of Marine Parade, Leigh-on-Sea. Turn off the A13 on to Tattershall Gardens or Thames Drive, which lead down to Marine Parade.

Leigh station is ten minutes' walk via Belton Way.

Accessible at all times.

May/June for birdsong; summer for butterflies (mid-June to mid-July for the marbled white).

Call the ranger on 01702 551072.

Deptford pink
Dr Chris Gibson/English Nature

Marbled white butterfly
Alan Sadgrove

Hainault Forest

What remains of Hainault Forest lies on the north-eastern boundary of Greater London on a miniature version of the ridge that forms Epping Forest – a cap of gravelly and sandy soils over London clay. Part is managed by Redbridge Council as a country park and the northern section comprising the ancient pollard woodland is managed by the Woodland Trust.

Hainault Forest

319ac/128ha OS Ex175/La177   *GR 473 924*   *SSSI*

WOODLAND TRUST

Most of Hainault Forest was destroyed for housing and farming after it was 'disaf-forested' in 1851. What remained, which runs across to the north of the present Hainault Forest Country Park, was managed as wood pasture until about 1900. Local commoners had lopping rights to the hornbeam and used to cut above head height to protect the new growth from cattle and other animals browsing on the forest floor. The limbs were cut before they grew above 10cm – the maximum size useable for charcoal burning and firewood in London. This means a cutting cycle of between 18 and 25 years. Pollarding stopped in the early part of this century as the markets for charcoal and firewood declined.

Now the woodland is being managed by the Woodland Trust, with the help of Forest Enterprise, who plan to reinstate a pollard cycle.

In time pollards form massive trees with a swollen head from which extend huge gnarled limbs. The ancient woodland to the east is dominated by hornbeam pollards and oak standards, with holly, bracken and bramble growing beneath them.

Much of the woodland floor is bare because of the dense shade cast by the overgrown pollards, but it has many damp areas and ditches that are greener and more varied, often lined with pendulous sedge. If you look around you will find unusual plants like wood speedwell, hartstongue fern, marsh pennywort and butcher's broom.

In some of the open areas you can see old hornbeams that have been repollarded. This was started experimentally in 1989 but had to be suspended because too many trees died. Pollarding normally rejuvenates trees but after a long gap it is very risky. and better results may be obtained by starting afresh by pollarding

young trees. There are also large areas where trees are being allowed to regenerate naturally and are forming dense thickets.

In the western part the woodland is very different. It has regenerated on sections that were cleared and is dominated by oak and birch with some aspen, poplar and ash.

Ancient hornbeam pollards
Tony Gunton

113

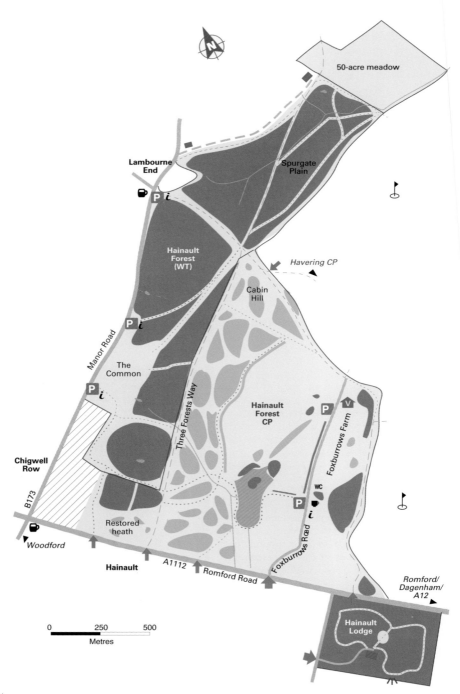

50-acre meadow

Lambourne
End

Spurgate
Plain

Hainault
Forest
(WT)

Havering CP

Cabin
Hill

Manor Road

The
Common

Three Forests Way

Hainault
Forest
CP

Foxburrows Farm

V

WC

Chigwell
Row

B173

Woodford

Restored
heath

Hainault

A1112 Romford Road

Foxburrows Road

Romford/
Dagenham/
A12

Hainault
Lodge

0   250   500
Metres

Hainault Forest Country Park

Redbridge Council

600ac/240ha OS Ex175/La177   GR 473 924   SSSI (part)

The area to the east and south of the ancient woodland is a country park managed by Redbridge Council. This was part of the Forest's 'plains' and therefore was treeless, but it has been invaded by birch and scrub since grazing ceased. The dense cover attracts many breeding birds including some that are scarce in Essex, such as spotted flycatchers. Nightingales were here also but have not been heard since 1992.

At the north-west corner a small area of former heathland – a rare habitat in south Essex – is being restored by removing invading birch and scrub. It still has some heather and dwarf gorse which it is hoped will spread.

The many areas of rough grassland sheltered by surrounding trees make good feeding territory for bats, which find roosting sites in the ancient trees. A number of different species can be seen feeding over the lake on warm evenings, including pipistrelles, noctules and daubenton's bats.

Visiting

The main (Foxburrows Road) entrance is off Romford Road (A1112), about one mile south of Chigwell Row. The A1112 can be entered from the south via the A12 (London – Chelmsford) and from the north via the A113 (Woodford – Chelmsford).

The nearest stations are Ilford (Liverpool St line) and Hainault (Central Line tube), from where buses run to the main entrance. Buses also run from Romford, Chadwell Heath and Barkingside.

Accessible at all times. The Foxburrows Road car park is open every day from 7.00am to dusk; the small peripheral car parks on Manor Road, Chigwell Row are always open.

May for songbirds; summer for wild flowers in the meadows and along the link to Havering Country Park; or try a misty winter day to see the fantastic tree shapes in the ancient woodland.

The Forest is heavily visited, especially on holidays. The quietest time is early morning, accessing via the car parks off Manor Road along its northern edge.

Paths in the eastern part of the Forest are often very muddy.

For details of events and activities call the country park office on 020 8500 7353.

Hainault Lodge

Redbridge Council

14ac/6ha   OS Ex175/La177   GR 476 919   LNR

Hainault Lodge is the site of an 18th-century hunting lodge, built on top of Hog Hill. It is now a Local Nature Reserve managed by Redbridge Council, supported by the Havering and Redbridge Wildlife and Countryside Group.

The former lodge and its grounds are surrounded by mature woodland including some massive oak and hornbeam pollards. New pollards of young trees are being created to eventually replace these. Woodland birds such as goldcrest and treecreeper nest in the reserve. A nature trail has been laid out.

Visiting

On the corner of Forest Road and Romford Road, on the other side from Hainault Forest Country Park.

To gain access contact the Hainault Forest Country Park office on 020 8500 7353.

Plants of the saltmarsh

Saltmarsh is a harsh and demanding habitat for plants because of the strong tidal currents and the salt water, which tends to draw water out of plants, so making it difficult for them to get enough water to survive even when surrounded by it.

The 10,000 acres or so of Essex saltmarsh are important because they represent as much as 10% of Britain's total of this habitat. Fingringhoe Wick overlooks the vast expanse of the Geedon saltmarsh on the Colne, and there are also large areas in Hamford Water, on the Blackwater Estuary and around Two-Tree Island on the Thames.

▲ Glasswort: one of the first plants to colonise the mudflats
Owen Keen

◄

Sea purslane: a widespread saltmarsh plant
Laurie Forsyth

► Sea lavender: covers the saltmarsh with colour in July
Laurie Forsyth

Hamford Water

Most of the Walton Backwaters, a shallow tidal bay between Walton-on-the Naze and Dovercourt, forms the Hamford Water National Nature Reserve, important principally (but not solely) because of its birdlife. Much of it is privately owned, but Skippers Island is an Essex Wildlife Trust nature reserve and it can also be viewed from sea wall footpaths starting from The Naze (see page 216) and from Dovercourt.

No fewer than 12 species of waterfowl winter in Hamford Water in nationally or internationally important numbers, including brent goose, teal, grey plover, black-tailed godwit and redshank. In summer it hosts one of the largest breeding colonies in Essex of little terns and a large breeding colony of black-headed gulls. In the less disturbed areas common seals breed.

The low dunes support distinctive flowering plants, including sea pea, sea holly and sea bindweed. Hamford Water is also the only place in the UK where Fisher's estuarine moth occurs, along with its foodplant, hog's fennel.

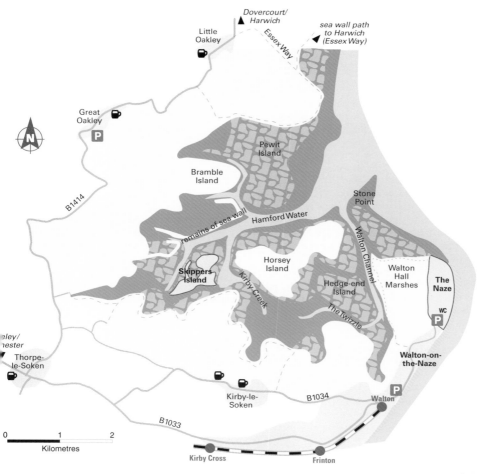

Hog's fennel
Dr Chris Gibson/English Nature

Fisher's estuarine moth
Dr Chris Gibson/English Nature

Skippers Island

233ac/93ha   OS Ex184/La169   GR 218 242   SSSI

Skippers Island is 1500m long by 800m at its widest point, and surrounded by saltmarsh. It is about 500m from the mainland, linked by two causeways built in the 19th century for the passage of livestock but now reduced to muddy pathways. It was given to the Essex Wildlife Trust by the late E.F. Williams.

The highest parts of the island, composed of London clay, are covered with vegetation, ranging from the great elms (now mostly dead) of a former heronry to extensive thorn thickets. Rides have been cut through these thickets and are mown regularly, producing fine flower-rich swards of grass.

The lower land used to be enclosed from the sea as grazing marsh but now, following breaches in the sea wall, it has reverted to saltmarsh. About one-third of the island is rough pasture and it has several pools of fresh but often brackish water.

The island has large stands of hog's-fennel, and also adderstongue fern, parsley water-dropwort, dyer's greenweed and lax-flowered sea-lavender.

Breeding birds include oystercatcher, shelduck and, in the thickets, several species of warbler and the nightingale (a recent colonist). Outside the breeding season there are good numbers of brent geese and many species of duck and wader. Birds of prey are often seen in winter,

the most regular being the short-eared owl. Common seals occur frequently.

The varied insect population includes Fisher's estuarine moth, a great rarity, large numbers of Essex skipper butterflies, feathered ranunculus and rosy wave moths, and Roesel's and short-winged conehead bush-crickets.

Visiting

Access via Birch Hall, Kirby-le-Soken. Cars can be parked next to the sea wall by the concrete shed.

No access to the reserve without prior application as the warden is required to notify the owners of the private access road of visitors in advance. Please call Essex Wildlife Trust on 01206 735456 for details. Trust members can rent the lodge for self-catering holidays.

Visitors need to be reasonably active as the saltmarsh and rough grassland can be tiring. Wellingtons or walking shoes are essential for crossing to and from the island at low tide via the causeway .

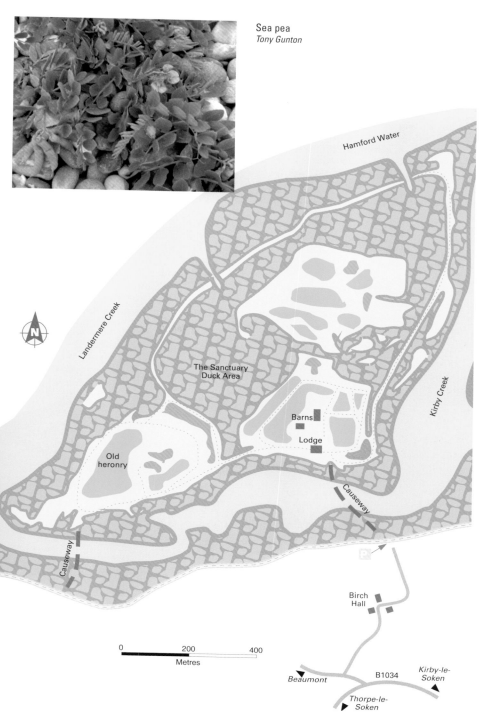

Sea pea
Tony Gunton

Hamford Water

Landermere Creek

Kirby Creek

The Sanctuary
Duck Area

Barns

Lodge

Old
heronry

Causeway

Causeway

N

Birch
Hall

Beaumont

B1034

Thorpe-le-
Soken

Kirby-le-
Soken

0   200   400
Metres

119

Hanningfield Reservoir

100ac/40ha   OS Ex175/La167   GR 725 972   SSSI

This mixed woodland at the south-eastern end of Hanningfield Reservoir is owned by Essex & Suffolk Water and managed by Essex Wildlife Trust. At least 30 acres of this, Well Wood and Hawk's Wood, are ancient in origin. Ditch and bank boundaries, dating back centuries, mark the extent of the old coppice and some remnants of the original hornbeam community survive. There is a great diversity of wildlife, with many species indicative of ancient woodland habitats. The show of spring flowers, in particular bluebells, yellow archangel and stitchworts, is not to be missed.

The reservoir is designated a Site of Special Scientific Interest (SSSI) because of its large numbers of wildfowl. The spectacle of 80,000 swifts, swallows and martins feeding over the water during peak fly hatches is just one of the delights for the summer visitor, although most people will probably associate the reservoir with large numbers of waterfowl. Gadwall, tufted duck and pochard are three of the important breeding species and year-round coot numbers are of national significance.

Much of the reservoir can be scanned from the hides, with especially good views over an island that is popular with wildfowl and a raft provided for terns to nest.

The conifer plantations are gradually being thinned, then underplanted with native broadleaved species, hazel in particular. Woodland glades are being created, linked by grassy rides, and ponds are being rejuvenated. Coppicing of neglected hornbeam stools has begun again.

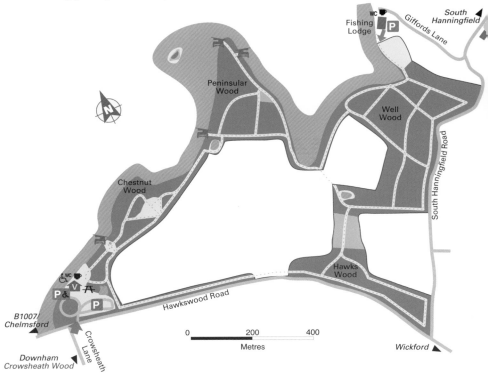

Visiting

Turn off the B1007 (Billericay–Chelmsford) on to Downham Road and turn left on to Hawkswood Road. The Visitor Centre entrance is just beyond the causeway opposite Crowsheath Lane.

Wickford to Chelmsford bus to Downham village and walk 800m down Crowsheath Lane.

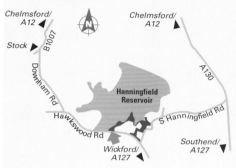

From late November 2000, Visitor Centre open daily except non-Bank Holiday Mondays from 9 am to half-hour before sunset, serving refreshments and selling a wide range of optical equipment and gifts. When Centre is closed, limited access on weekdays only from Essex & Suffolk Water's Fishing Lodge on Giffords Lane, south of South Hanningfield village.

April–July for breeding birds in woodland and on water and for wild flowers; winter and migration periods for wildfowl.

The bird hide nearest the Centre is equipped for disabled users.

Sorry, no dogs except guide dogs allowed on site, and no bicycles.

For information about events and activities call the Centre on 01268 711001.

A newly restored pond at Hanningfield Reservoir reserve
Claire Cadman

Two of the ducks that breed at
Hanningfield Reservoir…

Pochard, in nationally significant
numbers
Alan Williams

Ruddy duck, an introduction from N. America
and controversial because it threatens the
native (to Spain) white-headed duck by inter-
breeding with it
Alan Williams

*The Hanningfield Visitor Centre
is only a short walk from …*

Crowsheath Wood
20ac/8ha   OS Ex175/La178   GR 724 965

ESSEX
Wildlife Trust

This ancient coppice woodland, with 3 acres
of adjoining open land, is an Essex Wildlife
Trust nature reserve. The many mature standard
oak trees are an impressive feature of the wood.
The coppice trees are mainly hornbeam, with a
little ash, midland hawthorn, field maple and
wild service.

The ground flora is varied, and includes
bluebell, wood anemone, primrose, pignut,
ragged robin and goldilocks buttercup. Lesser
spearwort is present in the ponds near the centre
of the reserve.

Most of the bird species typical of lowland
broadleaved woodland are present. Several
species of warbler (including sedge warbler),
woodpeckers, nuthatch and nightingale have
been recorded.

Much of the western part of the wood has been
coppiced in recent years, and some broadleaved
trees have been replanted; coppicing is being
extended to enhance wildlife interest.

Routine management consists of removing
invading bramble and keeping the paths clear.
The open land is grazed by horses.

Visiting

800m south of Hanningfield
Reservoir. Access is from Crowsheath
Lane, which runs south from the road
causeway across the reservoir towards
Downham.

Buses from Ramsden Heath to
Wickford via Downham stop at the southern end of the lane.

Accessible at all times.

Spring for flowers and visiting birds;
autumn for a good selection of fungi.

Please note that the wood is marked
as Thrift Wood on many maps – the
Essex Wildlife Trust elected to adopt a
local name to avoid confusion with its
Thrift Wood reserve at Bicknacre.

Call the warden on 01268 761137 or
Essex Wildlife Trust HQ on 01206 735456.

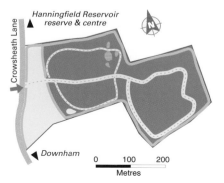

Hanningfield Reservoir
reserve & centre

Crowsheath Lane

Downham

0   100   200

Metres

Harlow Marsh

25ac/10ha   OS Ex174/La167   GR 453 115   LNR

Harlow Council

Harlow Council owns several sections of former flood meadow along the River Stort and the Stort Navigation north of Harlow. Parndon Mead is managed as hay meadow and grazed by cattle, and Harlow Town Park, also known as Maymeads Marsh, is managed more formally by cutting the grass and leaving the damper patches untouched. They are linked by the towpath footpath and crossed by other footpaths and a Green Lane.

The combination of rough grassland with plenty of water makes for good insect and bird life. In summer grassland butterflies mingle with dragonflies on the waterways, including the banded demoiselle, while moorhens and ducks look after their young families on the river and the occasional common tern flits gracefully past over the water looking for prey.

Visiting

Access via Burnt Mill Lane which turns off the A414 a short distance north of the roundabout where it meets the A1019 from Harlow town centre and the A1169.

Harlow Town station is right next to the car park at the end of Burnt Mill Lane.

Accessible at all times.

July and August for dragonflies and other insects

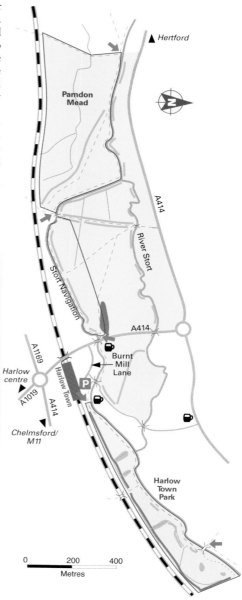

2.5ac/1ha   OS Ex209/La154   GR 557 441

ESSEX
Wildlife Trust

Named after the previous late owner, this small Essex Wildlife Trust reserve contains one of the few surviving areas of unimproved boulder clay grassland in north-west Essex, which otherwise is intensive arable farmland. Once it was part of a war-time airbase, and the old local road passes through it, now partially overgrown. It has a small wet area and also two concrete-lined brick fuel tanks. Nearly 106m above sea-level, it commands fine views over south Cambridgeshire.

Flowering plants include bee orchid, wild liquorice, twayblade, fairy flax and blue fleabane. Elsewhere on the site blackthorn and wild rose (including two uncommon species) abound.

A number of bird species inhabit the blackthorn thickets and the insect life is also of interest.

Visiting

The reserve is about three miles north of Saffron Walden, on the west side of the B1052, 800m from Hadstock. It is best identified from the road by the large hangar at its rear. Cars can be parked on the hangar entrance road.

Accessible at all times.

Late June for roses and bee orchids.

The entrance is down a 1.5m earth bank and hence is not suitable for disabled visitors.

Keep out of brick structures as there may be loose masonry.

Call the warden on 01799 525152 or Essex Wildlife Trust HQ on 01206 735456.

Bee orchid
Pat Allen

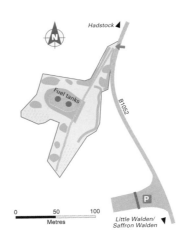

Hatfield Forest

1049ac/420ha   OS Ex195 &183/La167   GR 547 202   SSSI, NNR

Hatfield Forest is a working example of what a mediæval Forest must have been like. It is a landscape shaped by man's activities over hundreds, probably thousands, of years. There is certainly nothing as complete and well-preserved in Essex, and arguably in Europe.

Hatfield Forest is a compartmented forest. Open areas used for grazing by cattle or deer, known as 'plains', are separated from the wooded areas by means of ditches and banks, once topped by paling fences and designed to keep grazing animals out of the woods. Trees scattered across the plains are pollarded, in other words cut above head height where grazing animals cannot reach, while the wooded compartments are managed by coppicing.

Ancient trees, and particularly ancient pollard trees, are what make Hatfield Forest so special. It has about 600 pollards in total, including not only oak, hornbeam, and beech, which can be

seen elsewhere in Essex, but also many maple and hawthorn, which are rare as pollards, and just a handful of beech, lineage elm and crab apple. Nowhere else can you see such a variety of species nor such a variety of form, from gnarled, twisted old hawthorns to massive, stately oaks.

The Forest is also the stronghold in Britain of mistletoe, which is widespread on the ancient hawthorns and maples on the plains.

The coppice woods consist mainly of ash, hazel, and an unusually large number of maple. There are also some gigantic coppice stools of oak, particularly in Lodge Coppice to the west, while the west end of Street Coppice has four acres of alder on a plateau – alder is a plant of wet, flushed ground, in other words where water is moving through the soil, picking up oxygen as it goes, rather than stagnant.

The predominant woodland plant is dog's mercury but the coppice woodlands also support a very wide range of other flowers including indicators of ancient woodland such as oxlips (mainly in or near Dowsett's Coppice) and herb paris (in Long Coppice).

Hatfield Forest from the south, with part of the plains in the foreground, partly invaded by scrub. Beyond are coppice woodlands divided by broad rides.
David Corke

125

Marshy areas around Shermore Brook, which runs through the Forest from north to south and feeds the lake, are full of wetland plants and alive with insects in summer.

A range of woodland species breed in the Forest, including marsh tit and nightingale (decreasing), plus the odd woodcock and hawfinch. Look out for buzzards which are now colonising the county. Winter visitors include redwing, fieldfare and the very occasional great grey shrike.

The National Trust has been criticised for management decisions in earlier years –

particularly for grubbing out and replanting some ancient coppices, and for 'improving' the grassland – but more recently the Forest has certainly prospered in terms of wildlife, despite having to cope with growing visitor pressure.

The Trust is tackling the difficult job of preserving the pollard trees, which become top heavy and blow over easily if left for too long. Because repollarding overgrown trees is such a risky business, new young pollards are being created as well. Many can be seen in the open area around the car park and access road.

Hatfield Forest Marsh

4.5ac/2ha   OS Ex195/183/La167 GR 539 202   SSSI

The nature reserve at the centre of Hatfield Forest, managed by Essex Wildlife Trust, is a chalky fen formed by silting at the north end of the lake, together with an adjoining area of species-rich grassland containing a number of marshy hollows.

The water level of the lake was raised some years ago and as a result two-thirds of the fen area was flooded. This shallow water area provides a habitat for wildfowl, including great crested grebe, and is a rich breeding area for fish and invertebrates.

The surviving part of the fen contains many

plant species including common reed and both species of reedmace. The wet hollows contain a number of rare Essex plants, including tubular water dropwort, marsh arrow-grass, marsh willowherb, marsh pennywort and a floating liverwort *Ricciocarpus natans*.

Common snipe have nested and water rail are usually present.

Scrub is removed regularly from the grassland and it is grazed by sheep in late summer when the marsh and common spotted orchids have finished flowering.

Mistlletoe in Hatfield Forest
Geoff Gibbs

Common snipe
Alan Williams

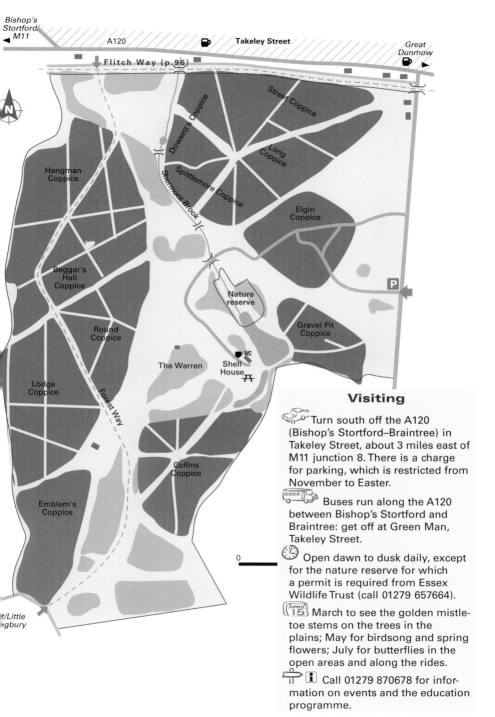

Visiting

Turn south off the A120 (Bishop's Stortford–Braintree) in Takeley Street, about 3 miles east of M11 junction 8. There is a charge for parking, which is restricted from November to Easter.

Buses run along the A120 between Bishop's Stortford and Braintree: get off at Green Man, Takeley Street.

Open dawn to dusk daily, except for the nature reserve for which a permit is required from Essex Wildlife Trust (call 01279 657664).

March to see the golden mistletoe stems on the trees in the plains; May for birdsong and spring flowers; July for butterflies in the open areas and along the rides.

Call 01279 870678 for information on events and the education programme.

Havering Ridge

The ridge that runs across the north of Havering is the site of several historic parks and some fine ancient woodlands.

Bedfords Park

90ac/36ha   OS Ex175/La177   GR 518 931

Havering Council

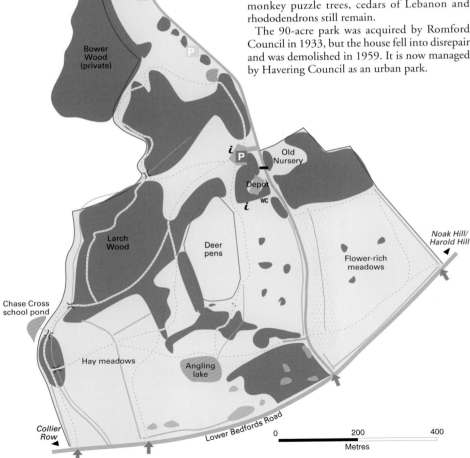

Bedfords Park was enclosed in the 15th century by Sir Thomas Cooke, one-time Lord Mayor of London, and remained in his family for almost 200 years. After a number of owners, it was acquired in 1771 by John Heaton who built the manor house of Bedfords on the crest of the hill. This was enlarged in the 19th century and gardens laid out around it – the monkey puzzle trees, cedars of Lebanon and rhododendrons still remain.

The 90-acre park was acquired by Romford Council in 1933, but the house fell into disrepair and was demolished in 1959. It is now managed by Havering Council as an urban park.

The upper section has all the scenic grandeur of landscaped parkland, with its exotic trees, its deer enclosure and its close-mown slopes. The lower section is managed for wildlife, with hay meadows and some mature woodland and scrub. The area of marsh to the east of the north-south bridleway is fed by springs seeping out at the top of the slope. Here you will find lady's smock, pignut and ragged robin flowering in spring, and later sneezewort and pepper saxifrage. Beyond it is a large meadow which is one of the finest flower-rich grasslands in Essex.

Birdlife is varied with many warbler species arriving in summer to breed, particularly in the scrub and woodland in the south of the park.

Havering Council and Essex Wildlife Trust plan to build a new visitor centre in the park, to be run by the Trust. It is expected to open in late 2001 or in 2002.

Visiting

The main entrance to the park is off Broxhill Road, which runs from the north from the junction of Lower Bedfords Road, Noak Hill Road and Straight Road up to Havering-atte-Bower village.

Frequent bus services run from Romford station (Liverpool St line) to the bottom end of the park on Lower Bedfords Road. Occasional services run to Havering-atte-Bower past the main entrance.

The vehicle entrance to the park closes 30 minutes before sunset, but pedestrian access is possible at all times.

May–June for wild flowers and bird-song, and August to September for later flowers.

For information or help phone Havering Council on 01708 433809.

Dagnam Park
150ac/60ha   OS Ex175/La177   GR 551 928

Havering Council

Dagnam Park, owned by Havering Council, was part of the former Manor of Dagnam. Across the centre is ancient parkland, sandwiched between two small ancient woodlands. It has a number of ponds in some of which great crested newts breed. The ancient grasslands in the east of the park, which are managed as hay meadows, are rich in wild flowers and insects in summer, and the many large patches of scrub and the ancient trees serve as nest sites for a variety of birds.

Visiting

Off Settle Road in the north of Harold Hill, Romford. Turn off the A12 on to Gooshays Drive east off Gallows Corner, then turn right at the roundabout on to Dagnam Park Drive. Settle Road turns off on the left.

Bus services from Romford run along Dagnam Park Drive.

Accessible at all times.

May to August for birds, wild flowers and insects.

See map over page

129

Duck Wood

24ac/10ha   OS Ex175/La177   GR 555 924

London
Wildlife Trust

This small ancient coppice woodland on the north-eastern fringe of the London Borough of Havering was once part of the Dagnam Park estate. Now it is managed as a community nature reserve by the London Wildlife Trust.

It has ten ponds, some open and surrounded by aquatic flowering plants and sedges, others shady and overhung by shrubs and trees. Wetland plants such as water-starwort and pendulous sedge can found here.

The wood has carpets of bluebells in spring, and many other wild flowers including ancient woodland specialists like wood anemones and wood violets.

Fallow deer often visit the wood and it supports many woodland birds, including hawfinches that sometimes visit in winter.

Visiting

Entry is from Sheffield Drive in Harold Hill, which leads off Dagnam Park Drive a few hundred yards north of the A12.

Bus services from Romford or Harold Wood stations (Liverpool St line) run along Dagnam Park Drive.

Accessible at all times.

April–May for flowers and birds.

For more information call London Wildlife Trust on 020 7261 0447.

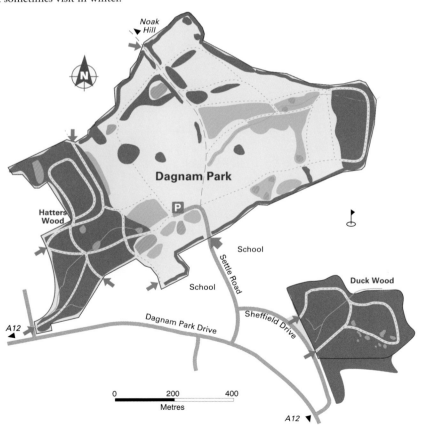

Havering Country Park
150ac/60ha   OS Ex175/La177   GR 500 924

**Havering
Council**

This country park, owned and managed by Havering Council, is mainly mature mixed woodland, including some ancient hazel coppice and one of the few established pine woodlands in this part of Essex, which attracts pine specialists such as goldcrests (which breed here) and coal tits. High on the ridge the soil is gravelly and here you find birch, gorse and bracken, while the damper, heavier clay soil of the valley to the south favours oak, hornbeam and bramble. The wildflower meadows are cut for hay in September. Agrimony, birdsfoot trefoil and ox-eye daisies grow here.

Visiting

🚗 Access via Clockhouse Lane, which runs north from the roundabout in Collier Row where Collier Row Lane (B174 from Eastern Avenue, A12) meets Chase Cross Road. Pedestrian access also from Havering-atte-Bower along Wellingtonia Avenue.

🚌 Frequent buses run from Romford and terminate at the main (Clockhouse Lane) entrance.

🕐 Accessible at all times. Car parks open from dawn to dusk.

📅15 May for migrant songbirds and early flowers in the woodland; June–July for wild flowers in the meadows; autumn for tree colours.

♿ Vehicle access to easy access trail from Wellingtonia Avenue via a radar key obtainable from Havering Council or from the Park Office (01708 720858).

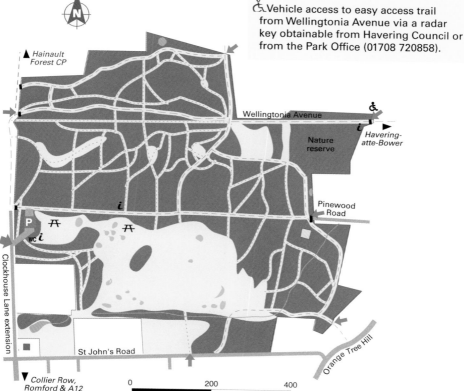

131

Hawksmere Springs

4.2ac/2ha   OS Ex175/La176   GR 508 993

ESSEX
Wildlife Trust

This small Essex Wildlife Trust reserve is mostly ancient unimproved pasture, part of it marshy, with a tiny remnant of ancient damp woodland and a boundary stream.

The reserve is extremely rich in flowers. In the meadows grow cowslip, betony, agrimony, sneezewort, fleabane and a profusion of knapweed and meadowsweet. Yellow rattle and ragged robin can also be found. In spring bluebells and ramsons carpet the small wood.

Willow warblers and other warblers join the resident birds in summer and butterflies and other insects are numerous.

The reserve is grazed in autumn-winter to keep the sward in optimum condition for wild flowers.

Visiting

Access is by right of way which leads south from the lane to the north of the reserve at a point 400m east of Little Tawney Hall, Stapleford Tawney.

Accessible at all times.

May and June for birdsong; July and August for butterflies, when the meadows are in full bloom.

For more information call Essex Wildlife Trust HQ on 01206 735456.

Agrimony
Tony Gunton

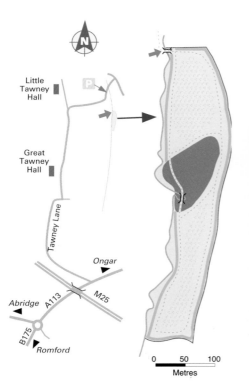

High Wood, Langley

122ac/49ha   OS Ex194/La154   GR 451 358

Forestry Commission

This Forestry Commission wood is still largely conifers but has wide rides with open wood edges which attract many butterflies in summer. It has a pond with an island which is good for dragonflies. Many deer use the wood – get there early in the morning for the best views.

Visiting

From the B1039 Royston–Saffron Walden, take a minor road south to Duddenhoe End/Langley. Park in a layby at a bend near the entrance (TL 451 358).

Occasional bus services from Newport and Clavering pass close by.

Accessible at all times.

Early morning to watch deer; summer for butterflies in the rides.

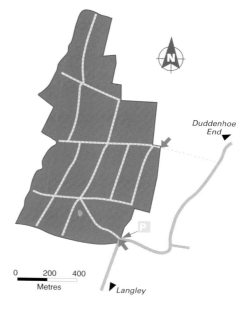

Pond in High Wood
David Corke

133

High Woods Country Park

Colchester Council

330ac/132ha OS Ex184/La168   GR 998 271

High Woods Country Park occupies land that was once part of the Royal Forest of Kingswood. Today it is a patchwork of woods, meadows, marsh and rough ground, much as our countryside must have been in the first half of the 20th century. The land was bought by Colchester Council in 1979 to save it from residential development.

The woods in the stream valley to the north, known as the Central Valley, are a remnant of Kingswood Forest. They are being coppiced and you can see the regrowth of flowering plants in the areas opened up to light. The valley floor is mainly ash and alder, with small-leaved lime and oak on the slopes. In April it is carpeted with bluebells.

The mosaic of trees, scrub and open grassland in the eastern section suits a wide variety of insects and birds, including willow warblers, whitethroats and goldfinches. In autumn it is full of berries and wild fruit.

Friars Grove is a small ancient valley wood, surrounded by its original earth bank and ditch.

Visiting

The main entrance is off Turner Road, which leaves the A134 Colchester–Sudbury road north of Colchester North station.

A footpath leads into the country park starting just south of the railway bridge over the A134, right next to Colchester North station (Liverpool St line).

Car parks open from 7 am to 10 pm in summer, and to 7 pm in winter. Visitor Centre open daily from April to September inclusive, otherwise weekends only.

April for bluebells; May/June for breeding birds in woodland and scrub; summer for wild flowers in meadow and marsh and for butterflies and dragonflies.

For more information telephone the Rangers on 01206 853588.

Goldfinch
Alan Williams

Whitethroat
Alan Williams

134

A large area of marshland has developed around the stream before it passes under the railway and this provides cover for birds such as sedge warblers and reed buntings. In summer the many insects overhead attract crowds of swifts, swallows and martins and, on warm nights, bats.

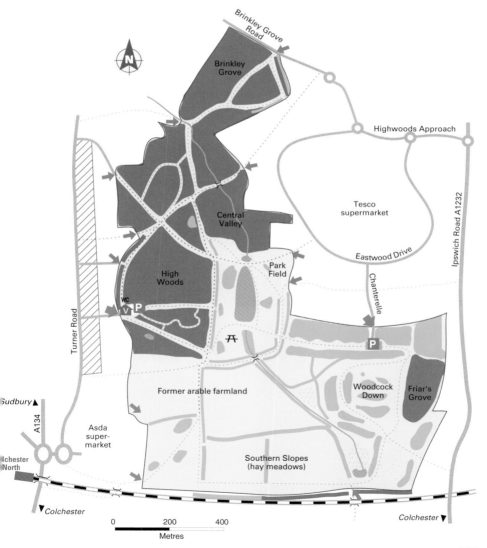

Hillhouse Wood

34ac/13.4ha   OS Ex184/La168   GR 945 280

WOODLAND TRUST

This ancient woodland in West Bergholt, near Colchester, was acquired by the Woodland Trust with help from Colchester Council and a local appeal. It is a light and open woodland with many glades and an open canopy of mainly oak and ash trees. The hazel growing beneath them is being coppiced in the traditional manner by local volunteers.

In spring the wood is carpeted with bluebells and wood anemones. Its birdlife includes all three species of woodpecker, with nightingale, blackcap and garden warbler visiting in summer. It also has a colony of white-letter hairstreak butterflies that has revived under current management.

Visiting

The wood is reached from the end of Hall Road, which runs east from the B1508 (Colchester–Sudbury) just north of West Bergholt. There is parking space for a few cars at the end of Hall Road.

Buses between Colchester and Sudbury run along the B1508.

Accessible at all times.

Spring for woodland flowers and birdsong.

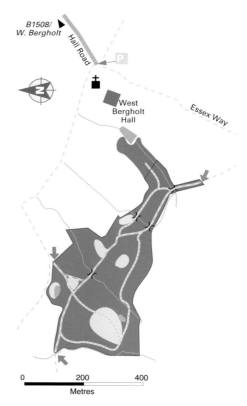

Blackcap (male)
Alan Williams

136

Coppicing

A technique known as coppicing was used to manage many ancient woodlands. Some of the trees are allowed to mature as standard trees, to be harvested when they reach the right size to build houses or ships. Beneath the standards grows an underwood of trees such as hornbeam, hazel or sweet chestnut that are cut to ground level – coppiced – on a regular cycle of between 10 and 20 years. That wood was used as fuel – both firewood and charcoal – and to provide fencing stakes, thatching spars and many other products.

After coppicing the trees regrow vigorously and live much longer than they would otherwise. Coppicing also introduces much greater diversity than nature would achieve unaided. Different parts of a coppiced wood are at different stages of regrowth and this produces a great diversity of conditions, from light to heavily shaded, which in turn support a diversity of plants and other animals. Woodland flowers like primroses have adapted to this regime and can lie dormant for years until coppicing lets in the light.

Some woods have been coppiced continuously for more than 2,000 years, but many of those fell into neglect early in the 20th century as the markets for traditional wood products declined. As a result they became dark and overgrown and lost much of their richness of wildlife. Only recently has coppicing been resumed by conservation organisations and by local authorities in many of the woods they control, as the importance of this long-established form of woodland management has been recognised. Make sure you buy British charcoal to support their efforts!

After coppicing

Three years later

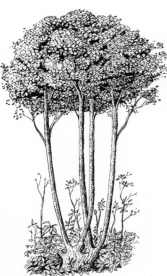

Ten years later
Richard Hull

Flowering plants respond to the extra light that coppicing allows in to the woodland floor
David Corke

Hockley Woods

270ac/108ha OS Ex175/6/La178   GR 833 924   SSSI

If you only had time to visit one ancient coppiced woodland then Hockley Woods might be the place to choose. It is the largest continuous native woodland not only in Essex, but in the whole of eastern England (unlike Epping Forest, which is divided by roads). It consists of a group of half-a-dozen ancient woods, mostly owned by Rochford Council and virtually intact except for a few bits lost around the fringes. It is not as rich in wild flowers as some of the northern Essex woods, but has a wide variety of woodland types all on one site and many ancient woodland plants.

The ground falls steeply from the car park with a variety of trees on the upper slopes including oak, sweet chestnut, ash and rowan. These give way to hornbeam on the heavier and wetter soils lower down.

The woods are criss-crossed by woodbanks dating from the Middle Ages on. Woodbanks were used both to keep grazing animals out of coppice woods and to show where ownership changed. The earliest banks show boundaries between manors and later ones those between farms as well. (The map shows only the main banks.)

Large patches of common cow-wheat are scattered through the woods. This is not a striking plant, having small yellow flowers similar to snapdragon, but it is very important as the only foodplant (in eastern England) of the heath fritillary butterfly. This butterfly is now very

Visiting

The woods lie south of the B1013 Rayleigh-to-Rochford road, just west of Hockley. The Bull Inn is right next to the entrance road. You can also reach the woods from the south, by walking through farmland and several small woods starting from the car park on Grove Road.

Hockley rail station is about 20 minutes' walk away. Bus services from Rayleigh and Southend run past the main entrance.

Accessible at all times.

May for early flowers; June–July for butterflies; October for fungi.

Call Rochford Council on 01702 546366.

Heath fritillary on common cow-wheat
David Corke

138

rare throughout Britain and had died out in Essex until it was reintroduced to these woods and to the Essex Wildlife Trust's Thrift Wood reserve. The best time to see it is from mid-June to early July.

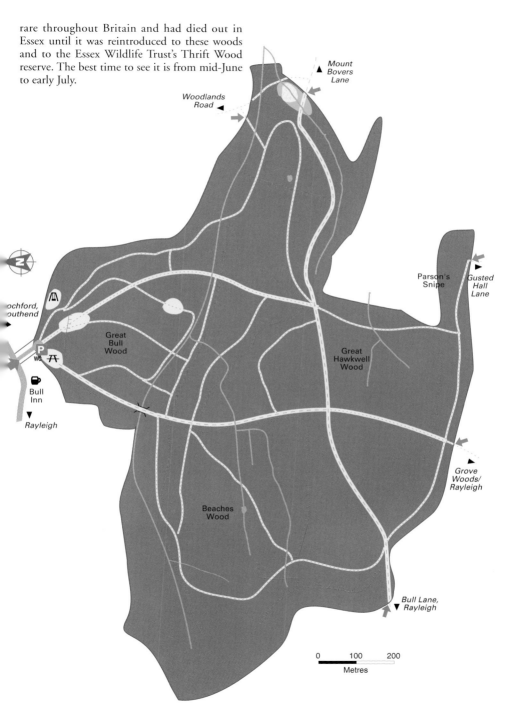

Mount Bovers Lane

Woodlands Road

Rochford, Southend

Great Bull Wood

Bull Inn

Rayleigh

Parson's Snipe

Gusted Hall Lane

Great Hawkwell Wood

Grove Woods/ Rayleigh

Beaches Wood

Bull Lane, Rayleigh

0   100   200
Metres

Hoe Wood

21.4ac/9ha   OS Ex184/La168   GR 904 263

WOODLAND
TRUST

This is a little gem of a wood a few miles west of Colchester. It is an ancient coppice wood, and coppicing has been resumed by the Woodland Trust.

The trees are mainly hornbeam coppice with oak standards, but there are also ash, field maple, hazel, sweet chestnut, wild cherry and aspen, with a few small-leaved lime and wild service thrown in for good measure. In early spring violets, primroses and wood anemones are all over the place, and it also has a couple of ponds fringed with aquatic plants.

From the northern edge of the wood and from the footpath that runs past it there are fine views across the Colne valley, with the Chappel railway viaduct in the centre of the scene.

Visiting

Turn off the A12 at Marks Tey on to the road towards Aldham. In Aldham turn left into Tey Road by the big oak. The wood is reached via a footpath on the right about 400m down Tey Road, opposite a left turn to Hoe Farm.

The nearest railway station is Marks Tey, 2 miles south-east of the wood. Colchester–Halstead buses pass: get off at Ford Street.

Accessible at all times.

Late March–May for woodland flowers and birdsong.

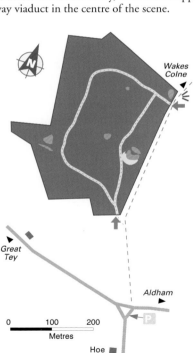

Wakes Colne

Great Tey

Aldham

0   100   200
Metres

Hoe Farm

Dog violet
David Corke

140

Visiting

Cross the River Stour into Brantham on the A137 (Colchester–Ipswich) road, parking along the Cattawade river barrage, then walk along the seawall and under the railway bridge.

Manningtree rail station is about 1200m from the reserve.

Hide accessible at all times (the reserve itself can only be entered at low tide).

Until improvements to paths are complete (2001), access will require some agility. Very soft mud surrounds most of the reserve, so wellingtons are essential.

For more information call the warden on 01206 393983 or Essex Wildlife Trust HQ on 01206 735456.

This area of saltmarsh juts out into the tidal River Stour south-east of the railway at Cattawade and opposite Manningtree, and is effectively an island. Although it is actually just over the Essex border in Suffolk, the site was donated to the Essex Wildlife Trust by Lt.-Col. C.A. Brooks in 1973.

It has plants and animals typical of Essex saltmarsh. Mute swan, canada goose and oystercatcher nest in the reserve and many other estuary bird species visit it. Good views can be gained from the bird hide that overlooks it.

The island is threatened by erosion and this is being fought by building faggot barriers and importing silt dredged from elsewhere in the river.

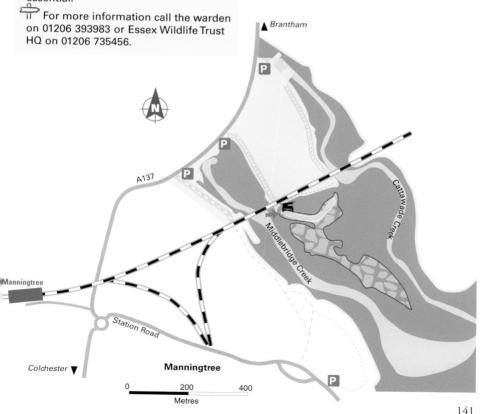

Holland Haven Country Park

200ac/80ha OS Ex184/La168   GR 220 175   SSSI (part), LNR

Tendring Council

This country park, managed by Tendring Council, consists of coastal grassland and marshland around the mouth of the Holland Brook, once the site of a small harbour called Holland Haven.

The coastal grassland is cut for hay and the inland marshes are grazed by cattle, overlooked by a bird hide. Water levels have been raised so that it attracts wildfowl and waders both to over-winter and to breed. Barn owls regularly hunt over the grassland at dusk.

It has a complex of dykes and a large brackish pond, all fringed by reeds and clubrush. All this makes for good aquatic insect life, including some rare beetles and damselflies.

Visiting

Off the B1032 to Great Holland just north of Holland-on-Sea.

Bus services between Clacton and Walton run past the entrance.

Accessible at all times.

Winter for wildfowl and waders; summer for insects.

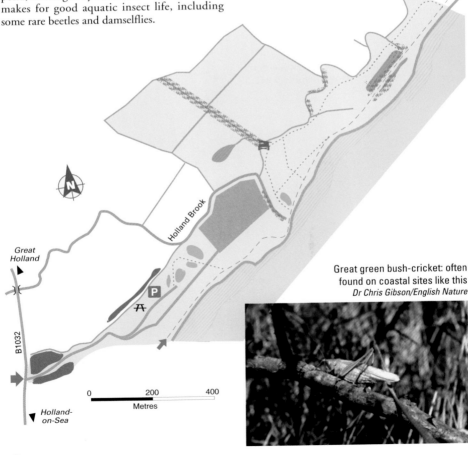

Great green bush-cricket: often found on coastal sites like this
Dr Chris Gibson/English Nature

Great Holland

B1032

Holland Brook

Holland-on-Sea

0   200   400
Metres

142

Howlands Marsh

186ac/74ha   OS Ex184/La168/9   GR 115 169   SSSI, SPA

Howlands Marsh, lying to the west of St Osyth Priory and Park, is one of the best surviving coastal grazing marshes in Essex. An Essex Wildlife Trust reserve, it consists mainly of low-lying hummocky grassland, split up by dykes and fleets. The fleets and other natural depressions in the grassland are evidence of former creeks and saltmarsh before the seawall was built. There is a narrow fringe of saltmarsh outside the seawall, widening into a large block where the two creeks meet.

The grassland contains much reed, sedge, glaucous bulrush and sea clubrush, and a variety of other plants include spiny restharrow and, particularly on the many anthills, spring whitlow grass and lady's bedstraw. Uncommon plants like slender hare's-ear, knotted parsley and sea barley grow on and near the seawall.

Among the plants in the dykes and fleets are great water dock, lesser water parsnip, tufted forget-me-not, marsh bedstraw and brackish water crowfoot. In places on the saltings, there are sea wormwood and some golden samphire as well as the more usual saltmarsh plants.

Reed warblers, lapwings, skylarks and reed buntings breed here. In winter brent geese graze among hundreds of wildfowl along with small flocks of curlews. When the tide is low, large numbers of sheldurck, dunlin and redshank feed in the exposed mud.

The reserve supports a great variety of invertebrates, including some rare species.

Howlands Marsh from the south-west
EWT library

Visiting

Reached via a public footpath which links a layby on the west side of the B1027 just south of Shangri-la caravan park (600m from the reserve) with The Quay off Mill Street (900m away). Roadside parking is usually available.

Several bus services from Clacton-on-Sea and Colchester pass the starting points for the footpath.

Accessible at all times

September to March for wildfowl and waders on and around Flag Creek.

The public path is often impassable for some time during high tides at and near The Quay.

To prevent disturbance to wildlife and grazing stock, please keep to the public footpath and the courtesy path to the hide and do not walk on the seawall. Dogs must be kept on a lead or under strict control.

Call the warden on 01255 820277 or Essex Wildlife Trust HQ on 01206 735456.

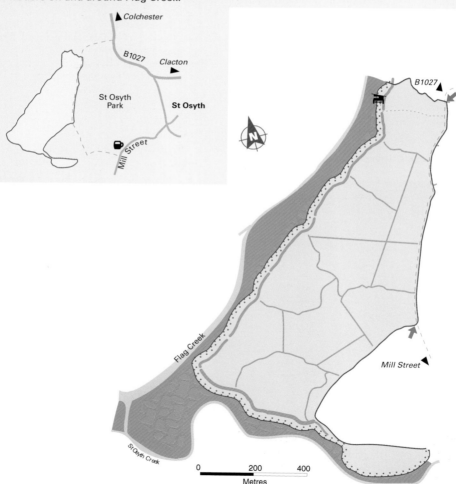

Hunsdon Mead

68ac/27ha   OS Ex174/La167   GR 421 114   SSSI

This area of common land between the River Stort and the Stort Navigation is one of the finest surviving unimproved grassland sites in eastern England. The Hertfordshire & Middlesex and Essex Wildlife Trusts acquired it jointly in 1981.

It provides a superb display of flowering plants. In April and May it is yellow with cowslips and marsh marigolds. As May gives way to June colours change continually, as plants such as yellow rattle, ragged robin, lady's smock, meadowsweet, bugle and many others flower in profusion. There are small colonies of green-winged orchid and adder's-tongue fern. Quaking grass and several uncommon sedge species are also present.

All the typical butterflies of hay meadow occur and the day-flying small yellow underwing moth is also established. Mayflies and dragonflies are much in evidence.

During the winter, when the Mead floods, large flocks of lapwing and golden plover come to feed along with other winter migrants.

For over 600 years the Mead has been managed on the ancient Lammas system under which local farmers graze their cattle in late summer after a July hay cut. If it were cut earlier some of the flowering plants would not have time to set seed for the following year. Grazing by cattle and sheep is allowed only between 14th August and 1st March, after which the vegetation is allowed to grow up. The remarkable abundance of wildlife found there is a result of that management regime, which continues today.

Visiting

Follow the Stort Navigation towpath from Roydon in the direction of Harlow – a walk of about one mile. The easiest parking is at Roydon station.

Roydon station (Liverpool St–Cambridge).

Accessible at all times.

From mid-April until the end of June for flowers, and later in the summer for dragonflies and other insects.

Between March and July please do not walk across or into the Mead itself until the hay is cut: trampling damages the plants and reduces the value of the grass as hay for the farmer. During this period please keep to the towpath or walk in single file along the permissive path beside the River Stort.

from Essex Wildlife Trust visitor centres. For more information call the warden on 01279 842775 or Essex Wildlife Trust HQ on 01206 735456.

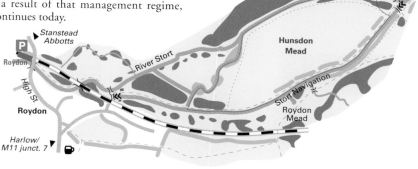

145

Flower-rich grassland

Cowslip
David Corke

The flower-rich meadows of the recent past were the result of the traditional farming regime under which a hay cut was taken in July or August, followed by grazing by cattle or sheep through the autumn and winter. Regular cutting or grazing keeps nutrient levels low and this helps a whole range of wild flowers to compete with vigorous grasses and coarse plants such as creeping thistle which otherwise would crowd them out.

Grazing is particularly good for diversity of plants because animals often graze unevenly and their trampling makes bare patches. This creates a wide range of niches which specialist plants like orchids are able to exploit. Just as in the woods, a whole range of plants and insects have adapted to conditions that prevailed for centuries.

Meadows and pastures where the gentler methods of the past are still practised look like oases in the green desert of modern farming, and serve as refuges for a range of plants and animals that are increasingly scarce elsewhere. You can find expanses of flower-rich grassland at Hunsdon Mead, Langdon, Mill Meadows, Bedfords Park and Roding Valley Meadows, and smaller examples at Danbury, Hawksmere Springs, Oxley Meadow and Sweetings Meadow.

Grass vetchling, often in ▲
coastal grassland
Tony Gunton

Ragged robin, a plant of damp
meadows
David Corke ▼

Yellow rattle, a semi-
parasite
Owen Keen ▼

Green-winged orchid
Alan Sadgrove ▼

Hutton *Country Park*

100ac/40ha   OS Ex175/La177   GR 633 959

This area of former grazing land opposite the Hutton industrial estate in Brentwood was recently acquired by Brentwood Council to form a new country park. At present it is mainly open grassland with some thick hedges and scattered patches of woodland and scrub. It has some marshy areas with tall aquatic vegetation and is bordered on its northern edge by the River Wid.

Members of the Brentwood & Billericay local group of the Essex Wildlife Trust started wildlife surveys here in 2000. Bird and insect life is already good and it will be interesting to see this develop as Brentwood's Countryside Management Service takes the site in hand.

Visiting

Entrance on Wash Road opposite the Hutton industrial estate. Enter Wash Road from the south off the A129 Brentwood–Billericay, or from the north via Lower Road which turns off the B1002 just north of the A12/A1023 junction.

Buses from the centre of Brentwood run along Wash Road up to the industrial estate.

Accessible at all times. (At present, no access under the railway to the northern section.)

For the latest information call Brentwood Countryside Management Service on 01277 261111 x503.

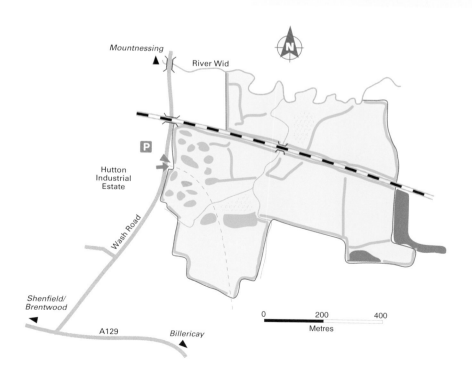

147

Ingrebourne Valley

This part of the Ingrebourne Valley, sandwiched between the built-up areas of Hornchuch and Rainham, has side-by-side a prime wildlife site, the Ingrebourne Marshes SSSI, and the developing habitats of Hornchurch country park and Berwick Woods. It is already a superb area for wildlife and can only get better.

Hornchurch Country Park

Havering Council

250ac/100ha OS Ex175/La177   GR 535 848   SSSI (part)

Hornchurch Country Park was created in the early 1980s mainly on the site of an abandoned airfield, RAF Hornchurch. The airfield was first developed during World War I and during World War II squadrons of Spitfires were based here that played a part in the Battle of Britain. Thousands of trees have been planted and are starting to create an attractive landscape.

But the highlight of the park at present is the Ingrebourne Marshes, a fine wetland next to the old airfield and further downstream alongside the River Ingrebourne. The marshes are a Site of Scientific Interest (SSSI) and about half the area lies within the park. Havering Council has raised water levels and reintroduced grazing. A marshland like this one – with a huge reed bed alongside flood meadow alongside damp grassland – is very unusual anywhere, and especially so close to London.

Redshank, lapwing and yellow wagtail breed on this kind of wet tussocky grassland. Kingfishers make their nest holes in the steep banks of the river. Many sedge and reed warblers nest here. Water rails can occasionally be seen prowling around in the tall vegetation. Teal over-winter on the ponds and bearded tits in the reedbeds.

Visiting

🚗 Main entrance off Suttons Lane, about 2km south of Hornchurch town centre (A124 from Upminster or Dagenham) via Station Lane.

🚌 About 1km walk down Suttons Lane from Hornchurch station (District Line). Frequent bus services run to both entrance roads from Rainham, Hornchurch and Romford.

🕐 Accessible at all times; car parks open daylight hours only.

📅 May–June for breeding birds; July–August for dragonflies and butterflies; migration periods for unusual birds sheltering in the marshes or plantations; winter for wildfowl on the ponds.

♿ About 4 miles of surfaced paths suitable for wheelchairs and buggies.

🚽ℹ️ Park Office phone 01708 554451.

Berwick Woods

Tarmac

50ac/20ha   OS Ex175/La177   GR 542 837   SSSI (part)

Berwick Woods is a former gravel extraction site that has been restored by the gravel company, Tarmac. As well as newly planted woods and grassland, it has some established scrub and woodland around pits and ponds. It also borders Berwick Ponds, used partly for angling but also part of the Ingrebourne Marshes SSSI and surrounded by large stands of reed, and it overlooks the flood meadows alongside the Ingrebourne. With such a mix of habitats it supports a wide range of our commoner birds and some rarities also – Cetti's warblers have nested around Berwick Ponds.

Visiting

🚗 Access from Berwick Ponds Road, which joins Hacton Lane, Hornchurch, to Warwick Lane, Rainham. Can also be reached from Hornchurch CP via the bridge across the Ingrebourne River.

🕐 Accessible at all times.

📅 May for songbirds; high summer for butterflies and other insects.

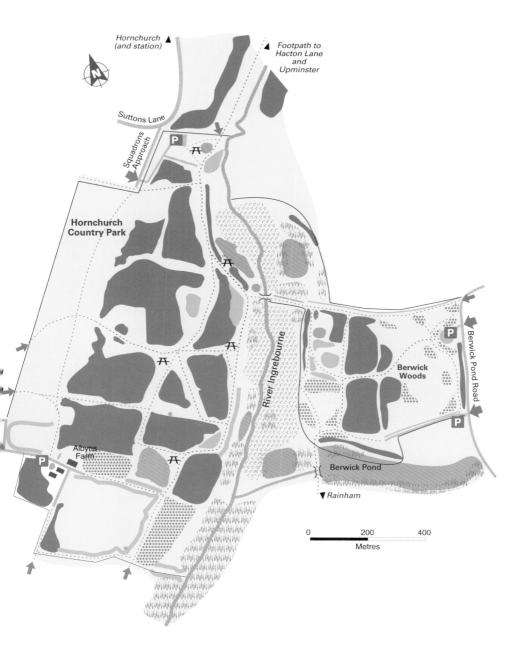

Hornchurch
(and station) ▲

Footpath to
Hacton Lane
and
Upminster ◄

Suttons Lane

Squadrons
Approach

P

**Hornchurch
Country Park**

River Ingrebourne

Berwick Pond Road

P

**Berwick
Woods**

P

Albyns
Farm

P

Berwick Pond

▼ Rainham

0   200   400
Metres

Iron Latch

10.5ac/4ha   OS Ex184/La168   GR 951 261

ESSEX
Wildlife Trust

This Essex Wildlife Trust nature reserve consists of a flower-rich meadow, plus four acres of woodland, long established and possibly ancient. It is quite wet in parts with a good selection of timber, especially ash.

Scrub has been cleared from the meadow and this has resulted in an increase in common spotted orchids and has consolidated a small population of green-winged orchid, which had almost died out, and other flowering plants such as field scabious and wild and barren strawberries.

The meadow attracts impressive numbers of the commoner butterfly species in late summer, and purple hairstreaks can be seen around the hedgerow oaks.

Nightingales have been attracted to nest in the new coppice and others nest nearby. Sparrowhawks are seen regularly and hobby occasionally.

Following initial scrub clearance the meadow is managed by mowing and sheep grazing. The woodland is managed on a five-year coppice cycle.

Visiting

The reserve is three miles west of Colchester town centre at Eight Ash Green. It is reached by way of the unmade Iron Latch Lane which runs from the old Halstead road at GR 955 254. Cross over the railway bridge and continue along the lane with woodland on your left. The reserve lies to the right of the footpath at the end of the field on your right.

Accessible at all times

May for grassland flowers, and late summer for butterflies.

Call the warden on 01206 768771 or Essex Wildlife Trust HQ on 01206 735456.

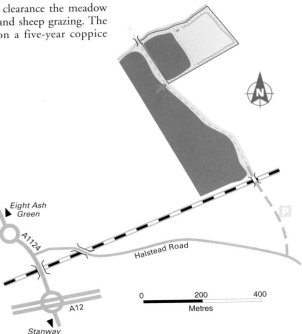

Langdon

Just south of Basildon lies a crescent-shaped hilly ridge more than 100m high, extending from the former plotland township of Dunton in the west to Vange in the east and giving tremendous views over the Thames estuary and into east London. Its name, Langdon, means 'long hill' and much of its land is set aside for wildlife and for recreation, with Essex Wildlife Trust's Langdon nature reserve to the north and west, partnered by Langdon Hills country park, managed by Thurrock Council, to the south and east. Horndon Meadow, a small wildflower meadow managed by Essex Wildlife Trust, lies nearby.

Langdon *Nature Reserve*

461ac/184ha   OS Ex175/La177 & 178   GR 659 874

Just to the south-west of Basildon New Town lies Essex Wildlife Trust's largest inland reserve. Its 461 acres contain a mosaic of habitats: flower-rich meadows, ponds, ancient and secondary woodland, and hundreds of former plotland gardens. Its importance lies not in its rarities but in the abundance of wildlife once common in our countryside but now threatened by intensive farming and urban spread. To date 29 species of butterfly and over 350 flowering plants have been recorded, and the list still grows. Badgers, foxes and weasels thrive in 'unimproved' meadows and orchids can be counted in their thousands.

Langdon Visitor Centre is the gateway to people's understanding of the social and natural history of this fascinating reserve, enabling thousands of visitors each year to explore what lies on their doorstep.

The reserve consists of four sections: from west to east these are Dunton, Lincewood, Marks Hill and Willow Park.

Dunton

Dunton today consists of the remains of plotland homes and gardens; wide grassy avenues bordered by hawthorn scrub and glades where wild grassland species compete with garden perennials. This patchwork of habitats is superb for butterflies, and a valuable resource for visiting school groups. Old orchards with pear, apple, plum and damson trees attract people and animals alike in autumn and the plotland ruins offer many basking sites for snakes and lizards. The Visitor Centre and the adjacent picnic area make Dunton an ideal starting point for your visit to the reserve.

The Dunton Plotlands

The 'Plotlands' represent a unique period in the social history of Basildon. During the early 1900s agricultural land was auctioned off in small plots to people mainly from the east end of London. These little pieces of countryside allowed many families to enjoy weekends and holidays away from the city, gradually blossoming into a bustling estate of around 200 homes. Despite unmade roads and poor services, this close-knit community enjoyed fresh fruit and vegetables from their own gardens and the freedom of owning their own place in the countryside.

After the Second World War the drive for higher standards of living led to the designation of Basildon New Town in 1949 and many plotlanders saw their homes compulsorily purchased. The area that was once the Dunton Hills Estate was designated as an open space for recreation, acknowledging the wildlife interest of the abandoned plotland gardens.

Following its purchase by Essex Wildlife Trust in 1989, the estate is now managed for its social history as well as its wildlife. Stroll along the old avenues and capture the fragrance of garden plants now growing wild. And visit The Haven, home to the Mills family for two generations, now restored to its original condition and furnished in the style of the 1930s and 1940s, allowing visitors to step back in time.

151

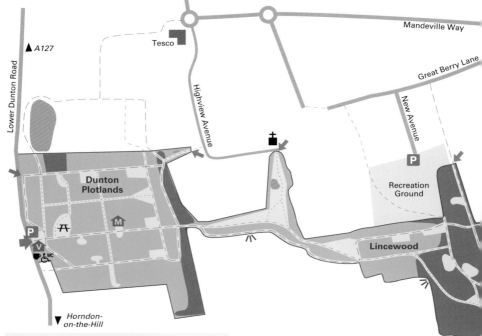

Visiting

4.5 miles east of M25 junction 29 between the A127 and the A13. Routes are signposted from the north from the B148 turning off the A127 and from the south from the A13 – follow the brown-and-white duck signs.

Laindon station on the Fenchurch Street–Southend line is less than 800m from the reserve. Frequent bus services run from Basildon town centre to Laindon station, to Langdon Hills and to Highview Avenue.

Reserve accessible at all times. Visitor Centre open 9 am–5 pm except Mondays.

Something of interest all the year round: spring for breeding birds and early flowers such as primroses; summer for orchids and other flowers, and for birdsong, autumn for fruit and berries and for late butterflies; winter to see huge flocks of migrant thrushes and perhaps a long-eared owl.

Call the Centre on 01268 419095 for more information and details of events and activities for young and old.

Lincewood

The derelict plotland roads in Lincewood are accompanied by ancient and secondary woodland on higher ground, making it a good spot to look out for all three woodpecker species. Bluebells carpet the woodland floor in spring and a riot of garden escapes flower throughout the summer - goats rue, old roses and many others. An adjacent recreation ground has thousands of green-winged orchids in May.

Marks Hill

Marks Hill, managed for the Trust by the Basildon Natural History Society, is a patchwork of ancient and secondary woodland, meadows and deserted plotlands. Stands of oak, ash and hornbeam are being brought back in to a coppice cycle to enhance the rich diversity of flowering plants. In spring there is an impressive display of bluebells, wood anemones and primrose. The grassland supports a large number of common spotted orchids. Several warbler species breed and in some years the nightingale. The boundary oaks are home to a colony of purple hairstreak butterflies and the locally rare cave spider lives in an old well.

Willow Park

Willow Park is the largest section of the reserve and was once a mediæval deer park. The unimproved hay meadows are bordered by ancient hedgerows and more recent mixed plantations, planted by the Commission for New Towns in the 1980s. The meadows and rough grassland are home to many flowering plants, including several species of orchid, some interesting sedges and the grizzled skipper butterfly, this being its last remaining site in Essex. Seven ponds of varying sizes attract a wide range of dragonflies and damselflies.

153

▲ Ancient coppice woodland in Marks Hill
Gordon Reid

On your way to or from Langdon in May, why not go and admire the orchids in ...

Horndon Meadow
2ac/1ha   OS Ex175/La177   GR 672 851

This small Essex Wildlife Trust reserve consists mostly of unimproved hay meadow on clay soil, which has probably never been ploughed. It is important primarily for its wild flowers, the hay meadow alone containing about 80 species. The highlight is a fine display of several hundred spikes of green-winged orchid, at their best in early May, when patches of adder's-tongue fern can also be seen. These are followed by yellow rattle in profusion, several patches of musk mallow, and the prominent spikes of black knapweed, which attract the reserve's butterflies.

An annual hay cut is taken in July, followed by light grazing by sheep.

Visiting

South-east of the B1007 from Horndon-on-the-Hill to Basildon, about 2km from Horndon village. The entrance is at Tyelands Farm, where a stony area to the right of the farm track provides parking for a few cars. There is further parking on Council-owned land just to the north. A track leads south from the stony area to a gate on the right opening into the meadow.

Accessible at all times

April to July for wild flowers (early May for orchids in particular).

154

Plants of ancient woods

Bluebell ▲
David Corke

Woodlands are described as ancient if they date from before 1600. They are sometimes known to be ancient from historical records, but they can also be identified because they contain plant and insect communities that are rarely found elsewhere. Some of the plants typical of ancient woods are shown here.

Butcher's broom
Owen Keen ▼

Herb Paris ▲
David Corke

Yellow archangel
Claire Cadman
▶

Wood anemone
Tony Gunton ▼

Langdon Hills Country Park

400ac/160ha OS Ex175/La177/8   GR 697 861   SSSI (part)

This mixture of ancient and more recent woodland and flower-rich meadows was bought by Essex County Council in the 1930s under the Green Belt scheme and designated a country park in 1973. It is managed now by Thurrock Council.

Northlands, Martinhole and Hall Wood are all ancient in origin, and dominated by oak,

hornbeam and ash trees. Northlands Wood also has a large number of wild service trees, a reliable sign of an ancient wood, while Hall Wood to the west has an unusual concentration of wild cherry along its western and southern fringes. Coombe Wood and The Park are former parkland, while the others are secondary woods that have grown up on former farmland.

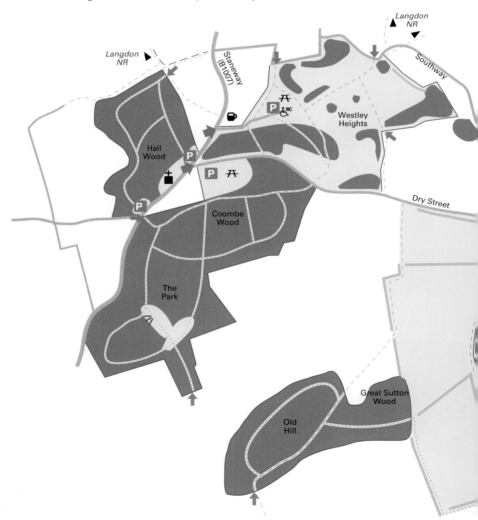

The meadows around One Tree Hill are either cut for hay or grazed to keep their diversity of plants. Two of them, east of One Tree Hill, are good enough to qualify as Sites of Special Scientific Interest: be sure to visit before the hay cut, usually in July.

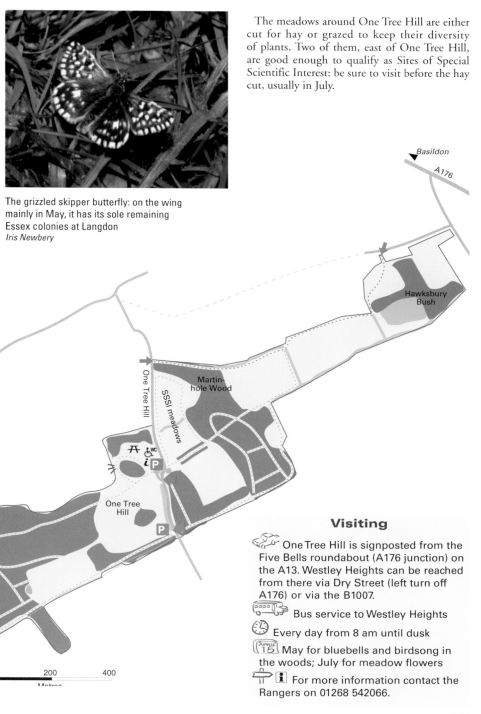

The grizzled skipper butterfly: on the wing mainly in May, it has its sole remaining Essex colonies at Langdon
Iris Newbery

Basildon

A176

Hawksbury Bush

One Tree Hill

SSSI meadows

Martin-hole Wood

One Tree Hill

Visiting

One Tree Hill is signposted from the Five Bells roundabout (A176 junction) on the A13. Westley Heights can be reached from there via Dry Street (left turn off A176) or via the B1007.

Bus service to Westley Heights

Every day from 8 am until dusk

May for bluebells and birdsong in the woods; July for meadow flowers

For more information contact the Rangers on 01268 542066.

200   400

Metres

157

Larks Wood

43ac/17ha   OS Ex174/La177   GR 382 925

Waltham Forest Council owns and manages this ancient, former coppice woodland. It covers two adjacent hills and has many hornbeam and mature oaks, plus wild cherry and rowan and a good number of wild service trees. Bluebells and wood anemones flower near the woodland edge in spring.

Visiting

Between Chingford and Walthamstow. Access to Larks Wood from Inks Green, New Road and Larkshall Road and to Ainslie Wood from Royston Avenue, Woodside Gardens or Ropers Road.

Highams Park station is about 600m away. Buses run along New Road and Winchester Road.

Accessible at all times.

Spring for bluebells and other early flowers.

Ainslie Wood

5ac/2ha   OS Ex174/La177   GR 377 921

London
Wildlife Trust

This small ancient woodland, managed by London Wildlife Trust, was once part of Epping Forest. The canopy is dominated by ancient oaks and it also has many wild service trees. Parts of the wood have carpets of bluebells in spring, along with wood anemones and lesser celandine. It has a good selection of woodland birds, including treecreepers.

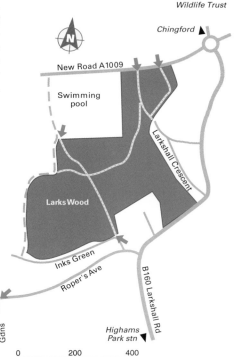

Uncommon damselflies

Red-eyed damselfly
Andy McGeeney

White-legged damselfly (f)
Andy McGeeney

Banded demoiselle (m)
Ken King

Scarce emerald damselfly (f)
Ted Benton

Lee Valley Park

4000ac/1600ha   OS Ex174/La166   GR 377 033

The Lee Valley Regional Park extends some 25 miles down the valley of the River Lee, from Ware in the north deep into London as far as the Thames in the south, straddling the borders of Hertfordshire and Essex.

The gravel beds of the valley were left behind by retreating ice at the end of the last Ice Age 10,000 years ago. There has been massive extraction since the 1920s and this has created a huge complex of lakes and marshes in the northern half of the park, while in the south there are a number of large water supply reservoirs. Together these provide an area of open water to rival even the Norfolk Broads.

It is a spectacular place to watch birds, both on the open waters of the gravel pits and reservoirs, on the many channels and streams, and in the surrounding marshes and meadows. But you do not need to be especially interested in birds to enjoy wandering around in this tremendous (in both senses) wetland.

We begin with the River Lee Country Park, an area of unbroken countryside stretching from Waltham Abbey just north of the M25 to Broxbourne, then cover other places further south.

There are a number of other good wildlife sites within the Regional Park. For birdwatchers, the most interesting of these are the Thames Water Authority's reservoirs at Chingford and Walthamstow, for which permits can be obtained from Thames Water. There are also nature reserves in Hertfordshire at Rye House Marsh and Amwell Quarry. Full details can be obtained from the Lee Valley Park Information Centre near Waltham Abbey.

Visiting

Four car parks serve the country park on the Essex side. All can be reached by leaving the M25 at junction 26 and following the signs to the Lea Valley Park, which bring you to the Information Centre. Highbridge car park is just north of the A121 between Waltham Cross and Waltham Abbey. Cornmill Meadows, Hooks Marsh and Fishers Green car parks are all sign-posted from the B194 to Nazeing.

Train to Cheshunt station from Liverpool St for River Lee Country Park or to Waltham Cross for Cornmill Meadows (bicycles welcome). Many bus services serve the area: leaflet available from the Information Centre tel. 01992 702200, email info@leevalleypark.org.uk or web www.leevalleypark.org.uk.

Accessible at all times. Information Centre at Waltham Abbey open daily 9.30am–5pm Easter to end October; Tuesday–Sunday 10am–4pm November to Easter.

Winter and migration periods for birds; late spring through the summer for wetland wildlife.

Many paths are shared-use paths, intended for pedestrians and cyclists: most of these are also suitable for wheel-chair users.

Lee Valley Park Information Centre open daily 9.30am–5pm Easter to end October, otherwise 9.30am–4.30pm Tuesday to Sunday only. tel. 01992 702200, email info@leevalleypark.org.uk or web www.leevalleypark.org.uk.

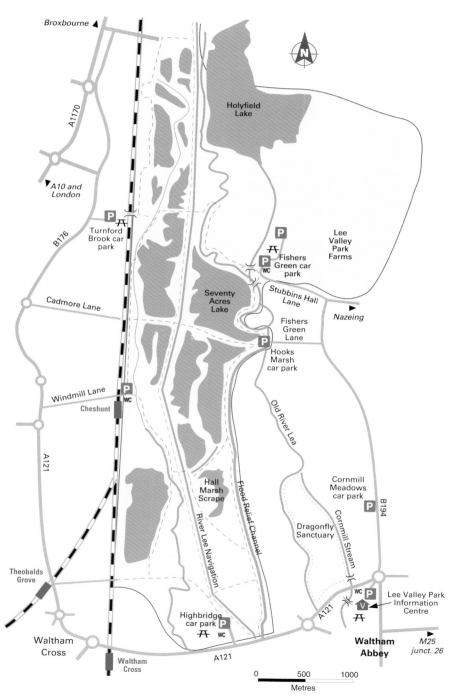

Broxbourne ◄

A1170

Holyfield Lake

A10 and London

B176

Turnford Brook car park

P

Fishers Green car park

P

P
WC

Lee Valley Park Farms

Cadmore Lane

Seventy Acres Lake

Stubbins Hall Lane

Fishers Green Lane

Nazeing ►

Windmill Lane

Cheshunt

P
WC

Hooks Marsh car park

P

Old River Lea

A121

Hall Marsh Scrape

Flood Relief Channel

River Lee Navigation

Cornmill Meadows car park

P

B194

Dragonfly Sanctuary

Cornmill Stream

Theobalds Grove

Highbridge car park

P
WC

WC

P

V

Lee Valley Park Information Centre

Waltham Cross

Waltham Cross

A121

Waltham Abbey

M25 junct. 26

0   500   1000
Metres

161

River Lee Country Park

Holyfield Lake

Holyfield Lake is the largest of the gravel pits in the Lee Valley and has many wooded islands where birds breed and among which they shelter while sailing is in progress on the lake. Goldeneye, goosander and smew visit in winter; yellow wagtail and sedge warbler join residents like great crested grebe and kingfisher in summer, when terns, swallows, martins and swifts feed over the lake.

Cormorants roost on the wooded islands. The tangle of wet alder and willow woodland on the margins and islands also suits breeding warblers and nightingales. Grasshopper warblers, finches and green woodpeckers may be seen or heard in the marshy scrub and woodland in the centre of the island.

The Grand Weir Hide gives different views of Holyfield Lake. The path to it crosses open farmland where golden plovers, lapwing and canada geese may be seen in winter. There are also several shallow pools which attract waders in summer and in migration periods.

Cheshunt Gravel Pits

The lakes of Turnford Marsh Gravel Pit and North Metropolitan Pit are the oldest in the valley - up to 50 years old. With their varying depths of water and many spits and islands they have developed a very varied wetland vegetation, showing all the stages between reed bed, carr and wet woodland. Near Cheshunt Lock thousands of orchids (flowering May-July) grow on fly ash dumped from local power stations a couple of decades ago and, a few hundred yards further you come to wild flower meadows near Aqueduct Lock. Cowslips flower here in spring, followed in early summer by bee orchids.

Seventy Acres Lake is another long-established lake with many islands covered with scrub, and is a wintering site for gadwall, shoveler, coot and bittern. The bittern is one of Britain's rarest birds, with only around 20 males breeding here. In winter the resident birds are joined by visitors from Europe and up to seven birds have previously wintered in the Lee Valley, attracted by the reedbeds and a good food supply. A special Bittern Watchpoint has been set up overlooking Seventy Acres Lake. This is reached via Fishers Green car park and is open every day from mid-October to mid-March, with a small charge to non-permit holders on weekdays.

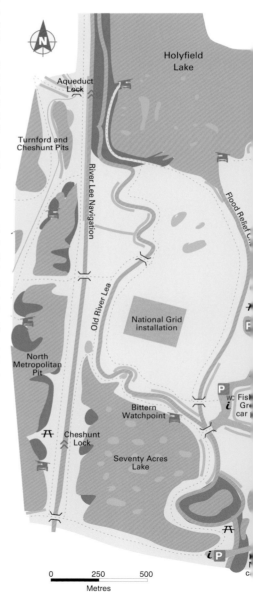

Spits and islands on Turnford Marsh Pit
Tim Hill

Marsh orchids near Cheshunt Lock
Tim Hill

Gravel pit birdlife

We think of the Broads as a natural habitat, but in fact they were formed by peat-cutting in the Middle Ages. Just as mediæval man created the Broads, so modern man has created new wetlands by digging out gravel and by building water supply reservoirs. The prime example here is the Lee Valley Regional Park, whose string of lakes and reservoirs rivals even the Broads.

Disused gravel pits often need to be modified initially to maximise their value for wildlife, and they certainly need to be managed carefully in the longer term if they are to maintain their value. Fingringhoe Wick near Colchester, the flagship reserve of the Essex Wildlife Trust, shows what can be achieved after 40 years of careful management. Other nature reserves that were once gravel pits can be found at Asheldham Pits, Berwick Woods, Chigborough Lakes, Great Holland Pits and Stanford Warren.

To suit many birds, for example, gravel pits need to have shelving banks and an irregular shoreline that provides good cover. Islands are important too, especially for breeding gulls and terns. Common terns nest on small islands and coastal saltmarsh, and have difficulty finding safe and undisturbed sites on our crowded coast. Many have moved inland to shingle-covered islets provided in gravel pits as substitutes.

▲ Little ringed plovers returned to breed in the 1940s and nest beside gravel pits
Alan Williams

▲ Sand martins nest mostly in the banks of sand pits
David Harrison

Great crested grebe numbers have doubled because of water-filled gravel pits
David Harrison ▼

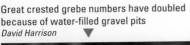

▲ Common terns take readily to islets in gravel pit lakes
Alan Williams

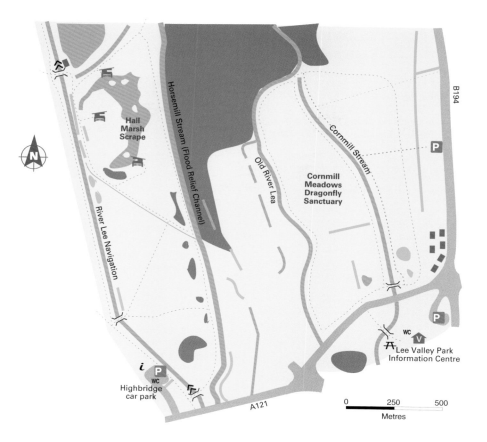

Hall Marsh Scrape

Hall Marsh Scrape (scrape meaning an area of shallow water) was created on land backfilled with refuse after gravel extraction. Shallow pools had formed there and were attracting ducks and waders. Shallow water like this is an increasingly rare habitat, so the pools were enlarged and sluice gates were installed to control the water level. Now redshank, little ringed plover and lapwing breed regularly, and teal, shoveler, wigeon and snipe visit in winter.

Cornmill Meadows

The man-made Cornmill Stream used to power the corn mills of Waltham Abbey. Most of the Lee Valley waterways have been canalised, but the Cornmill Stream and the Old River Lea meander in natural channels. Consequently they have a much wider range of waterside plants including some scarce ones like flowering rush (bright pink, July-August). It is also rich in aquatic insect life - more than half of all Britain's dragonfly and damselfly species have been seen here including the banded demoiselle (the best place to see them is the fast-moving water near the weir where the Cornmill Stream leaves the River Lee) and the hairy dragonfly.

Comfrey, branched bur-reed and purple loosestrife grow alongside the Old River Lea.

Walthamstow Marsh

95ac/38ha   OS Ex174/La177   GR 354 871   SSSI

One of the last surviving marshlands in London, declared a Site of Special Scientific Interest (SSSI) in 1985. Formerly grazed as common land under the Lammas system (under which the grass was left uncut until late summer), part of it is now cut annually for hay. These regimes encourage wild flowers and over 160 species have been recorded here. Reed and sedge warblers nest in the reed beds and snipe and stonechat visit in winter.

Middlesex Filter Beds

10ac/4ha   OS Ex174/La177   GR 359 865

Until they were closed in 1969 these filter beds were used to clean water taken from the River Lee for supply all over north-east London. Since then nature has taken over and created, in a relatively small area, a mosaic of different habitats, including open water, reed bed, scrub, wet woodland and, last but not least, old brickwork that provides many crevices for toads, frogs, lizards and other animals. In 1988 the Lee Valley Regional Park Authority took the site in hand as a nature reserve.

Reed buntings, coot and moorhen nest in the reeds and the reedmace, and the area hosts a spectacular range of dragonflies, including species like red-eyed damselfly that are unusual in Essex, let alone in the heart of east London.

Visiting

Park at Lee Valley Ice Centre on Lea Bridge Road (A104). Follow the signs from the car park over the bridge and along the towpath.

Regular bus services into London from Walthamstow and Leyton run along Lea Bridge Road.

Filter Beds open at weekends and on Bank Holidays, 10am–6pm Easter to end September, 10am–4pm otherwise. Also Monday–Friday 10am–5pm during school summer holidays and summer half-term.

Summer for wild flowers, dragonflies and other insects.

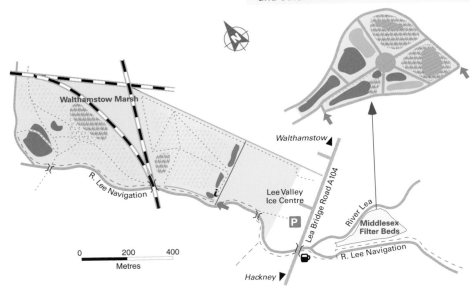

166

Cornmill Stream looking towards Waltham Abbey
Tim Hill

Linnets Wood

12ac/5ha   OS Ex195/La167   GR 516 273

WOODLAND
TRUST

This small plantation in the village of Ugley Green, consisting of conifers with oak, cherry and hornbeam, was given to the Woodland Trust in 1992 by Rosalind 'Linnet' Latham. An additional area to the west was planted up to local residents' design in 1997 as one of the Trust's 'Woods on your doorstep' projects.

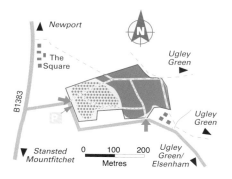

Visiting

 A public footpath running from the B1383 north of Stansted Mountfitchet to the minor road from the B1383 to Ugley Green passes through the wood.

Accessible at all times.

THE
wildlife
TRUSTS
ESSEX
Wildlife Trust

Lion Creek

16ac/6ha   *OS Ex176/La168*   *GR 923 948*   *SSSI, SPA*

This former creek on the southern shore of the Crouch Estuary has been cut off from the estuary by a new sea wall. As well as the creek it has rough grassland with scrub, bounded on three sides by the old sea wall. The original 12 acres were bought by Essex Wildlife Trust from Anglian Water in 1986 for a nominal sum. A further four acres, bought by the Trust as part of its acquisition of Lower Raypits Farm, have since been added to the reserve and the meadow and saltmarsh to the south were acquired in 1998.

The creek contains brackish water and in late summer has an attractive border of saltmarsh plants such as sea lavender, golden samphire and sea spurrey.

Above the zone affected by salt water, sea couch and false oat are the dominant grasses, with a mixture of tall herbs. Where the grass is shorter, smaller plants can be found, including the localised slender birdsfoot trefoil and, on the sea wall, sea clover.

Among the insects there are Essex skipper and brown argus butterflies, and Roesel's and short-winged conehead bush-crickets.

The water margins attract a variety of wading birds in due season, and birds of prey such as hen harrier and short-eared owl hunt over the grassland in winter. Barn owls can be seen at any time of the year.

Visiting

Entry is from the Canewdon–Wallasea Island road, 1.5 miles east of Canewdon village.

Buses run hourly from Southend to Canewdon (Loftman's Corner).

Lion Creek is accessible at all times. Access to Lower Raypits is limited to the public footpath along the seawall except by prior permission from the warden (call 01702 258492).

For more information call the wardens on 01702 258324 (Lion Creek) or 01702 258492 (Lower Raypits), or Essex Wildlife Trust HQ on 01206 735456.

Lion Creek from the south with the meadow in front of it on the right and the seawall path and the Crouch Estuary beyond
David Corke

Lower Raypits

143ac/57ha   OS Ex176/La168   GR 923 948   SSSI, SPA

This area of saltmarsh, permanent pasture and seawalls on the Crouch estuary was purchased by the Essex Wildlife Trust in 1991 following an appeal. Most of the reserve lies within the Crouch & Roach Estuaries SSSI, an important complex of saltmarsh, intertidal and grazing habitats that serves as a notable feeding and roosting area for wildfowl and waders. Wigeon, teal and pintail often use the area in winter in nationally important numbers, with up to 5,000 birds on the Crouch.

Dykes and seawalls support nationally scarce plants, including sea barley and curved hard-grass. The scarce emerald damselfly breeds in the borrowdyke, and Roesel's bush-cricket and a wealth of insects and other invertebrates are present.

The pasture and grassy seawall support populations of small mammals which attract hen harrier and short-eared owl in winter.

Work has been carried out to raise the water table on the marsh pastures to attract brent geese and other wildfowl and waders. Sheep grazing will continue to improve the grass sward for visiting birds.

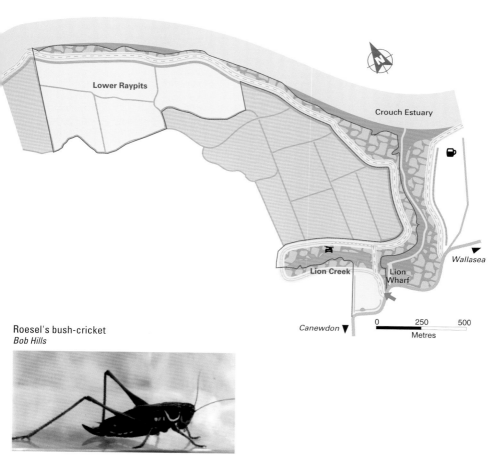

Roesel's bush-cricket
Bob Hills

169

Loshes Meadow

17ac/7ha   OS Ex196/La155   GR 873 369

ESSEX
Wildlife Trust

This Essex Wildlife Trust nature reserve lies on the side of an attractive valley in low hills rising from the River Stour flood plain. It was farmed until the mid-1950s then left to 'go wild' until leased by the Essex Wildlife Trust in 1974.

Its main part, east of the road and south of Loshes Brook, contains grassland, woodland, new plantations of hardwood trees, thick hedgerows and a marsh. The higher ground is on a considerable depth of coarse sand; the lower on chalky boulder clay, with a high water table. As often happens, this situation gives rise to spring flushes.

It has a variety of flowering plants including ramsons, opposite-leaved golden saxifrage, yellow archangel, nettle-leaved bell-flower and common spotted orchid.

The Hop Ground over the road has mature oaks at the top but is mostly swamp covered by hazel, alder and willow thickets. It has guelder rose, lady's smock and hemp agrimony.

Birdlife is plentiful with nightingale, grasshopper warbler and (formerly) willow tit among the nesting species. Insects include the ringlet and white-letter hairstreak butterflies.

Visiting

The reserve is three miles from Sudbury and six from Halstead. Take the Sudbury road from Halstead and, shortly after passing the Fox inn, take a turning signposted to Henny. After a mile this road descends a steep hill to a T-junction. Turn left and continue along a winding lane to a signpost to Alphamstone and Twinstead and turn right. The reserve is on the left at the bottom of the hill, where there is a large barn with the Trust sign outside.

Accessible at all times

Spring and early summer

Please keep dogs on leads at all times. Children must be supervised by stream and ponds, which have steep banks.

Call the warden on 01787 269613 or Essex Wildlife Trust HQ on 01206 735456.

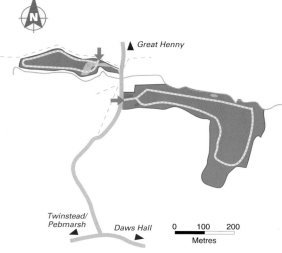

Great Henny

Twinstead/
Pebmarsh

Daws Hall

0   100   200
Metres

Hemp agrimony: a plant of damp grassland and waterside, flowering July/August
Tony Gunton

170

Lower Wyburns, Land at

10ac/4ha   OS Ex175/La178   GR 813 897

WOODLAND
TRUST

This young woodland in Rayleigh, just north of the A127, was planted up as a broadleaved woodland by Rochford District Council in 1992/93, and given by them to the Woodland Trust in 1995. The Trust is now completing the planting. Mature oaks grow along the northern boundary, bordering a small stream. A wide grassy ride allows visitors to access the whole of the site.

Visiting

Between Daws Heath Road and the A127, about 1 km east of the Rayleigh Weir roundabout. Access is via a path that leaves Daws Heath Road westwards by the stream at the north end of Lower Wyburns Farm.

Accessible at all times.

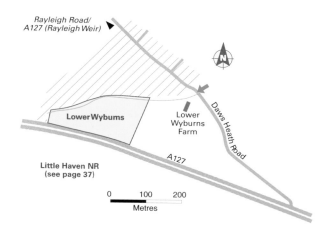

Rayleigh Road/
A127 (Rayleigh Weir)

N

Lower Wyburns

Lower
Wyburns
Farm

Daws Heath Road

Little Haven NR
(see page 37)

A127

0   100   200
Metres

Guelder rose in fruit (NB the berries are poisonous!)
David Corke

Ancient oak in Loshes Meadow
Robin Hart

Maldon Wick

15ac/6ha   OS Ex183/176/La168 GR 842 057

THE
wildlife
TRUSTS
ESSEX
Wildlife Trust

This Essex Wildlife Trust nature reserve consists of one-and-a-half miles of the former Maldon–Woodham Ferrers railway line, most of it on embankment. The northern 250m has been isolated by the Maldon southern link road.

The reserve has earned a reputation for its butterflies, 28 different species having been recorded since it was established. They include purple, green and white-letter hairstreaks, and large numbers of speckled wood and ringlet.

The central trackway is kept open and additionally the Trust has created small clearings on the slopes, felled some trees and coppiced others. As a result flowering plants have increased dramatically. These include primrose, moschatel, sweet violet, wild strawberry, field scabious and St John's-worts. Spindle and wild service trees can also be found.

It has many breeding birds, sometimes including nightingales.

Visiting

Just over a mile south of the centre of Maldon, bisected by the southern link road. A small car park is sited behind steel gates immediately east of the embankment on the south side of the link road. Return to the road and climb the steps leading to the reserve.

Close to the Maldon–Chelmsford bus which runs along the A414.

Accessible at all times.

May to July for flowers and butterflies.

Call the warden on 01621 858260 or Essex Wildlife Trust HQ on 01206 735456.

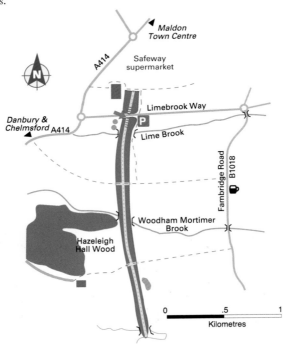

Marks Hall Estate
450ac/180ha OS Ex195/La168   GR 841 255

The Mark's Hall Estate is an ancient estate set in attractive countryside north of Coggeshall. It runs to some 2,000 acres, of which 150 are enclosed and hold an arboretum and formal gardens and a further 300 acres are accessible via footpaths. The estate was left to the nation by its last owner, Thomas Phillips Price, and is managed now by the Thomas Phillips Price Trust. It had been neglected for many years until the Trust set about the work of restoration in 1971.

Great wildlife interest can be found in the old deer park, which sadly has lost all but one of its massive ancient oaks, and in a large area of

Visiting

Reached via a turning off the B1024 to Earls Colne north of Coggeshall: follow the brown-and-white signs from the A120. Pay-and-display car park.

Accessible via public footpaths at all times, but permissive paths are closed on Thursdays from November to February inclusive. The Visitor Centre – housed in a 15th-century barn – is normally open from Easter until 31st October except non-Bank Holiday Mondays, 10.30 am to 4.30 pm on weekdays and to 6 pm on weekends and Bank Holidays.

Call the visitor centre on 01376 563040. Waymarked walks of varying lengths start from the Centre.

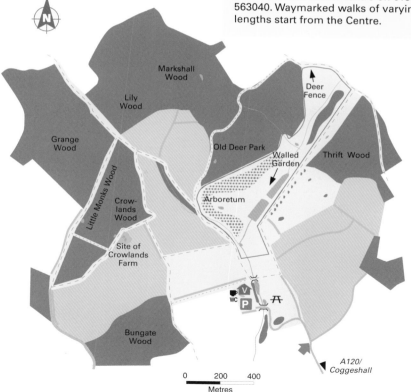

ancient woodland. Some of these woods have been planted with conifers but a great amount of the original woodland remains, containing large areas of small-leaved lime – a tree that once dominated the woods of East Anglia but now, because of long term climate change, confined to just a few ancient woods – and a number of wild service trees. The woods are being coppiced and this encourages flowering plants such as lily-of-the-valley, sweet woodruff, wood sorrel and early purple orchid. The woods are frequented by deer and a wide range of woodland birds, including nightingales.

Wild service tree
Pat Allen

Spring flowers at Marks Hall
Gianetta Nosworthy

Mill Meadows

90ac/36ha   OS Ex175/La177   GR 678 943   SSSI (part), LNR

This large area of old meadows not far from the centre of Billericay was acquired by Basildon Council in 1991 and is now a Local Nature Reserve. The meadows lie in rolling countryside cut by streams and ditches with occasional marshy areas. Scrub and young woodland has encroached in places but grazing by cattle is keeping much of the area open.

Stoats and foxes and many birds frequent the meadows, but it is the plant life that makes them special. There is a succession of colour from bluebells and cuckoo flower in spring through to devilsbit scabious in late summer, including some plants that are scarce locally like harebell, ragged robin and sneezewort. Such a range of nectar sources also attracts a wealth of butterflies and other insects.

A group of local volunteers help Basildon's Countryside Service team to manage the site.

Visiting

Stretches between Southend Road (A129) and Greens Farm Lane just south of Billericay Centre. Limited parking close by: use car parks in Billericay.

About 600m from Billericay station. A number of bus services run along the A129.

Accessible at all times.

Late spring to late summer for wild flowers and insects.

Call 01268 550088.

Cuckoo flower, also known as lady's smock and by many other names: flowers in spring
Jeremy Dagley

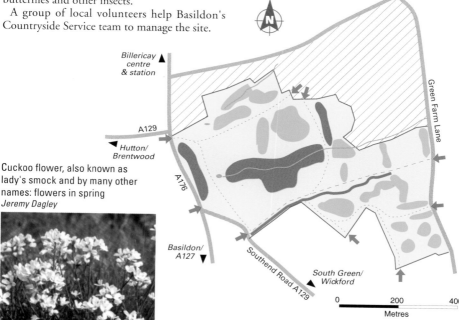

175

Norsey Wood

165ac/66ha   OS Ex175/La177   GR 691 955   SSSI, LNR

Norsey Wood, just east of Billericay, has had an eventful history: Iron Age and Roman remains have been found there and it is believed to have been used as a last refuge by the rebels who took part in the Peasants' Revolt of 1381, led by Wat Tyler, before they were destroyed by the forces of the Crown.

It also has one of the greatest concentrations of bluebells in the world. It consists of 165 acres of mixed coppice woodland, at least part of it continuously wooded since Roman times, and managed now by Basildon Council. It is criss-crossed by ancient woodbanks and ditches, marking former ownership boundaries.

Like a number of woods in southern Essex it lies on gravelly deposits on top of London Clay, so the vegetation varies greatly from a well-drained plateau down to the damper and heavier soils in the southern valleys. There is mainly sweet chestnut coppice on the higher and better-drained soils, with occasional colonies of heather. Not far from the visitor centre are some massive stools of coppiced hornbeam, which must be at least 500 years old.

Descending into the marshy valleys you find different trees and plants from the higher gravelly parts. Alder, ash and willow coppice grow here with areas of pendulous sedge, buckler fern and sphagnum moss (from which peat bogs are formed).

Visiting

Norsey Road turns off the B1007 just north of Billericay centre.

About ten minutes' walk from Billericay rail station.

Site and car park open at all times; Visitor Centre weekends only.

April–May for bluebells and song-birds; October for fungi.

Call the Information Centre on **01277 624553**.

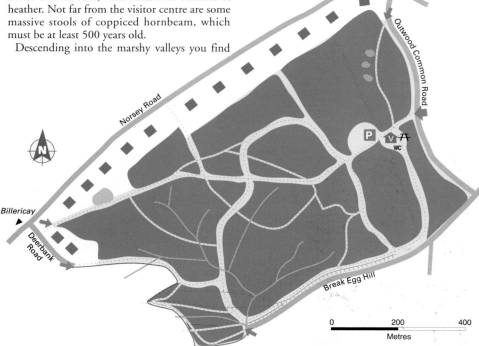

Northey Island

286ac/114ha   OS Ex183/La167   GR 872 058   SSSI, SPA

Northey Island lies near the head of the Blackwater Estuary east of the port of Maldon, and is managed as a nature reserve by the National Trust. It is reached via a causeway (probably Roman in origin) that is covered for several hours every high tide.

Its large areas of undisturbed saltmarsh are important for overwintering wildfowl and the pasture is managed to be the right height when the brent geese arrive in the autumn. The geese commute on and off the island to bathe in Heybridge pits and in the tidal creeks and up to 5,000 can be present from January to March.

In summer birds such as oystercatcher and shelduck nest.

The island has also been used as a testing ground for managed retreat, by breaching parts of the seawall in order to recreate saltmarsh.

Visiting

Reached from Mundon Road, Maldon, via South House Farm.

Access by permit only, available from the resident warden at a minimum of 24 hours notice either in writing to *The National Trust, Northey Cottage, Northey Island, Maldon, Essex* or by telephoning 01621 854142. A fee is payable for non-members of the National Trust.

Winter for large numbers of wildfowl; summer for saltmarsh flowers and insects.

No dogs allowed.

Northey Island from the south. Grazing marsh, enclosed by the inner seawall, is in the foreground, with the causeway entering bottom left. Beyond is saltmarsh enclosed by the outer seawall which has been breached in places. The managed retreat area can be seen bottom right
David Corke

Old Ford Island

2.5ac/1ha   OS Ex162/La177   GR 374 839

London
Wildlife Trust

Old Ford Island is a small island on the River Lee near Stratford, managed by London Wildlife Trust. Field vole, hedgehog and many butterflies take advantage of the flower-rich grassland and scrub. Dwarf elder, which is characteristic of this part of London, is a special feature.

Visiting

⏱ Open for events and workdays only: call 020 7261 0447 for details.

Onslow Green

2.5ac/1ha   OS Ex183/La167   GR 654 183

ESSEX
Wildlife Trust

This attractive village green, made up of about 1.5 acres of grassland with a wide marginal hedge and two ponds, is managed by Essex Wildlife Trust.

Most of the grassland is on light, loamy soil. It supports some interesting late spring/early summer flowers, including dyer's greenweed, tormentil and a small quantity of sulphur clover.

On its margins the larger pond has yellow flag, water forget-me-not and fine-leaved water dropwort. It attracts damselflies, dragonflies and great diving beetles, and common newts and occasional great crested newts have been seen.

The grassland is cut at least once annually in order to preserve its floral diversity. The margins are kept short by mowing for amenity reasons.

The spread of reedmace in the ponds is controlled and the banks are cleared on a rotational basis.

Visiting

🚗 About one mile south of Barnston village. Approach along the A130 Chelmsford–Great Dunmow road and take the turning to Onslow Green. The reserve is clearly visible on the left past a sharp left-hand bend.

🚌 Buses from Chelmsford to Bishops Stortford go through Barnston.

⏱ Accessible at all times.

🛈 Call the warden on 01371 820268 or Essex Wildlife Trust HQ on 01206 735456.

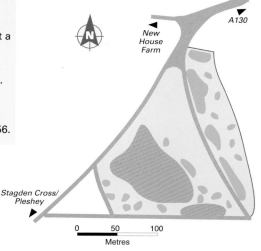

Oxley Meadow

8ac/3ha   OS Ex184/La168   GR 918 149

ESSEX
Wildlife Trust

Despite its name, this Essex Wildlife Trust reserve consists of *two* flower-rich meadows. The larger one extends to 6.5 acres and is almost completely surrounded by wide luxuriant hedgerows with a number of mature oaks and other trees.

A large colony of green-winged orchids is scattered across both meadows, and adderstongue fern is perhaps more numerous here than anywhere else in Essex.

The meadows support the commoner grassland butterflies, and the hedgerows provide nesting sites for a variety of birds, and notably the lesser whitethroat.

To maintain the diversity of grasses and wild flowers, the meadows are managed by taking a hay cut in mid-July and then by grazing from August until October or November.

Visiting

Leave the A12 at the Kelvedon exit and take the B1023 towards Tiptree. Continue on the B1023 through Tiptree village and down Factory Hill to a Y-junction, where you take the left fork (Brook Road, becoming Barnhall Road) towards Mersea. Turn down Park Lane (first turning on left after telephone box) and reserve entrance is second opening on left. There is limited parking for about six cars on the grassed area at the front of the reserve when conditions allow.

Regular Colchester-Maldon buses to Tiptree: the reserve is about 1 mile distant along footpaths.

Accessible at all times.

From late March up to the hay cut in mid-July – the orchids are usually in flower in April/May.

Call the warden on 01621 816659 or Essex Wildlife Trust HQ on 01206 735456.

Paternoster Heath

Tiptree Parish Field

Park Lane

Tiptree

Barnhall Road

Mersea

Tolleshunt Knights

0   50   100

The larger pond at Onslow Green
Lloyd Rankin

179

Oxlip woods

Oxlips, looking something like a cross between primroses and cowslips, are very unusual in that they grow almost exclusively in ancient woods, and what is more only in ancient woods in an area where the counties of Cambridgeshire, Suffolk and Essex meet. This is an area of boulder clay soils, which are very chalky and produce woods that are unusually complex, with a wide range of different plants.

Bendysh Woods

Forestry Commission

224ac/90ha OS Ex195 & 209/La154   *GR 619 398*

David Corke

These two Forestry Commission woods are ancient deciduous woods planted up with conifers which are now being removed. They have wide rides which are good for flowers: oxlips and wood anemones in March/April and later on many orchids.

They are a good place to see deer: both the native species red and roe, and the introduced fallow and muntjac.

Visiting

Where the B1053 (Saffron Walden–Great Sampford) meets the B1054 at The Plough PH, take the unclassified road to Ashdon. After about 1200m turn right on to Golden Lane, then turn first left to Radwinter End, parking on the roadside just before Swan's Farm and following the footpath on the left. Footpaths also lead into the woods from other directions.

Accessible at all times.

Call 01394 450164.

Pond in Gt Bendysh Wood
David Corke

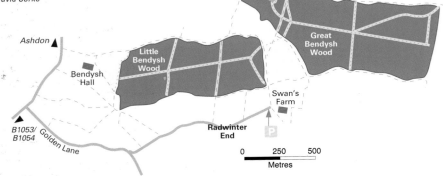

Shadwell Wood

17.5ac/7ha   OS Ex209/La154   GR 573 412   SSSI

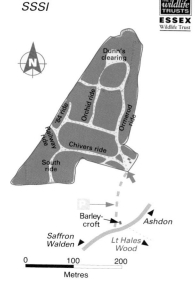

This oxlip woodland is owned and managed by the Essex Wildlife Trust. The dominant trees in the wood are oak and ash, with coppiced hazel and maple growing beneath them. The wood also has midland hawthorns, and rare trees like lineage elm and bird cherry. It also has *Daphne mezereum*, popular for the garden but rare in the wild.

A host of flowering plants grow on the woodland floor. Early spring brings oxlips, wood violets and wood anemones. These slowly give way to early purple orchids, bluebells, bugle and herb Paris. Summer brings common spotted orchids, meadowsweet and sanicle.

The wood is managed in the traditional manner by coppicing. This encourages many summer-visiting birds to nest, including the occasional nightingale. Fencing is used to exclude deer from the wood. Otherwise they browse the tender coppice regrowth, killing or stunting the trees, and eat the heads off the flowers.

Little Hales Wood

45ac/18ha   OS Ex209/La154   GR 575 406

Forestry Commission

It is interesting to compare this Forestry Commission wood with Shadwell Wood just a short distance away. This wood has been planted up with conifers, a fate that Shadwell Wood has escaped. Both woods have many deer present, although in Shadwell they are fenced out of newly coppiced areas, and both have oxlips, although in this wood rather stunted. The new small ponds just inside the wood have frogs breeding.

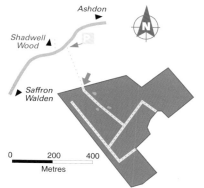

Visiting

The woods are either side of the main road from Saffron Walden about one mile before the village of Ashdon. Entrance to Shadwell Wood is by a gravel track at the side of 'Barleycroft' bungalow and entrance to Lt Hales Wood is on the other side of the road. Please do not park so as to block access to the bungalow or interfere with farming operations.

Occasional bus service from Saffron Walden.

Accessible at all times.

Spring through to early summer. Birdsong is at its height in May and early June.

Please keep deer gates shut. Please keep your dog on a lead.

Shadwell Wood: **i** at the interpretation board or call 01440 786423.

Hales Wood

20ac/8ha   OS Ex195 & 209//LA154   GR 572 400   SSSI, NNR

ENGLISH
NATURE

Hales Wood is one of only two inland National Nature Reserves in Essex. It is a small oxlip woodland on chalky boulder clay with a long history of coppicing.

Visiting

🚗 On Ashdon Road about 1 mile south of Shadwell and Lt Hales woods (see previous page).

🕐 By permit from English Nature's Colchester office: call 01206 796666.

Rowney Woods

204ac/82ha   OS Ex195/La154   GR 574 338

Forestry Commission

This large ancient oxlip wood was planted up with conifers in the 1950s but has now to a large degree been returned to native deciduous by the Forestry Commission. It has good ground flora (including ragged robin), white-letter hairstreak butterflies and many deer.

Visiting

🚗 Turn south off the B184 Thaxted–Saffron Walden just west of Rowney Corner and park in the layby near Carver Barracks.

🚌 Buses run from Saffron Walden to Rowney Corner and Debden.

🕐 Accessible at all times.

♿ Circular route made up with compacted gravel usable by wheelchairs in all but the worst weather conditions.

📋 Some of the tracks are very muddy when forestry work is under way and parallel temporary footpaths are provided.

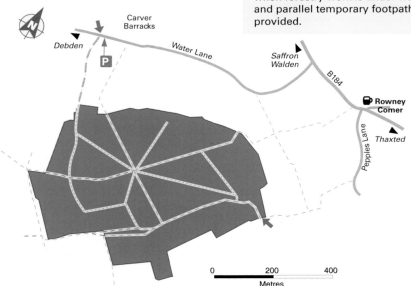

West Wood, **Uttlesford**

58ac/23ha   OS Ex195/La167   GR 624 332   SSSI

This ancient woodland on the chalky boulder clay is owned by Essex Wildlife Trust. As well as oxlips it has early purple and greater butterfly orchids, and also wood barley, a rarity in Essex. Another feature is the pendulous sedge along the rides which grows to a considerable size.

The wood has a good selection of nesting birds among which are goldcrest, redpoll, several species of warbler, and stock dove.

It has a population of dormice and supports a wide variety of butterflies including speckled wood, brimstone and ringlet.

The wood is gradually being returned to a coppice cycle and areas of Norway spruce are being thinned. Fallow and muntjac deer frequent the wood and various methods are used to discourage them from browsing the young coppice regrowth and thus stunting or killing the trees.

Visiting

The reserve is midway between Thaxted and Great Sampford, set back from the B1051. A track leads to the reserve entrance from the left-hand side of the road, one mile north-east of Thaxted. Or you can walk in along the bridleway from Tindon End.

Accessible at all times.

Early spring through to mid-summer for flowers and breeding birds; mid-spring through to early autumn for butterflies.

Call the warden on 01376 321271 or Essex Wildlife Trust HQ on 01206 735456.

Coppicing encourages a flush of flowers by letting light in to the woodland floor
David Corke

Great
Sampford

B1051

Thaxted

Tindon
End

0   100   200
Metres

183

Fallow deer: first introduced by the
Normans and now widespread
Alan Williams

Muntjac deer, introduced from China
and no bigger than a Labrador dog
Alan Williams

Parndon Wood

Harlow Council

30ac/12ha   OS Ex174/La167   GR 444 070   SSSI, LNR

This ancient woodland on the fringes of Harlow was bought by Harlow Council in 1968. It consists mainly of hornbeam coppice with oak standards. Coppicing lapsed after World War II but has now been resumed and this has encouraged woodland plants and animals.

There is a small visitor centre.

Visiting

On Parndon Wood Road, on the southern fringe of Harlow. Turn off the A414 on to the A1169 and follow signs to Parndon Wood Crematorium. The entrance to the nature reserve is just before the crematorium.

Sundays 9 am–1 pm and 2 pm–6 pm throughout the year; Tuesday evenings 7 pm–9 pm April to September inclusive. Education and group visits by arrangement with the warden (01279 430005).

A1169/
Harlow
Parsloe Road
Paringdon Road
Parndon Wood Road
P
Cemetery
Nature reserve

0   100   200
Metres

Pelham

40ac/16ha   OS Ex194/La167   GR 457 286

ESSEX
Wildlife Trust

Pelham straddles the Essex/Hertfordshire border between the villages of Berden and Stocking Pelham. The reserve surrounds one of the National Grid Company's major sub-stations and is an educational reserve with a well-equipped Field Centre running daily courses for school groups and occasional courses for adults. The Centre is staffed and supported by the Essex and Hertfordshire County Councils and the National Grid Company.

Pelham has extensive meadows supporting cowslips, adderstongue fern and five species of orchids. Along the northern edge lies an ancient moat, now broken into a series of ponds. It has mixed deciduous woodland planted in the early 1970s as screens to the sub-station and also two areas of old secondary woodland. The western edge of the site consists of an ancient hedge: the parish boundary between Stocking Pelham and Berden.

The meadows on the west of the site (Dove House Green and Dove House Field – approx. 10 acres) are cut once yearly in late summer and the hay crop composted for tree mulch. Other meadows are left as rank grassland and open scrub. Old Orchard Wood, an area of old secondary woodland to the north is coppiced

as is a small area of hazel to the south. The deciduous plantations are thinned rather than coppiced in order to maintain the screen to the sub-station.

Visiting

From Saffron Walden or Bishop's Stortford head towards Newport. Take the B1038 to Clavering then turn left to Berden. From Berden head for Stocking Pelham. The reserve is down an access road on the left before you reach Stocking Pelham. Look out for the National Grid sign.

Visits by appointment only: call 01279 777 680 or richard.wren@essexcc.gov.uk. During non-school times the access gate is locked but there is a footpath and stile from Crabbs Green.

June for bee, spotted and marsh orchids; July/August for meadow and pondside insects.

A free visitors' guide to the site is available from the Field Centre. A nature trail of about one mile has been laid out: available from Essex Wildlife Trust visitor centres.

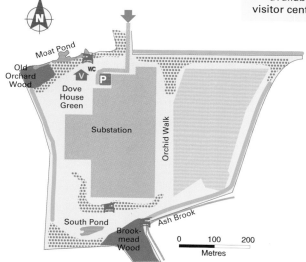

185

This nature reserve sloping down to a tributary of the River Ter was left to the Essex Wildlife Trust by Mrs Phyllis Currie.

It is an attractive and varied landscape in its own right but what adds interest is to see how the Trust's management is increasing its value, both as a wildlife site and as a piece of the countryside.

The reserve is home to a wide variety of plants, birds and insects. The most attractive single feature is a lake, created in the stream valley in the 1960s. The lake, streams and ditches are important breeding sites for dragonflies and damselflies, 13 species having been recorded. The grassland and sheltered glades and rides provide breeding sites for butterflies (23 species recorded). Tufted duck nest and kingfisher and grey heron are regular visitors.

In 1999 a reedbed was created, a shallow pool excavated and dams installed to raise the water level in the main stream. The Scots pine plantation is being thinned to favour broadleaved trees. A plantation of hybrid poplar and sycamore is being felled in blocks and replanted with native tree species grown from local seed.

To help wild flowers to increase a hay crop is taken from the meadows and then they are grazed by sheep.

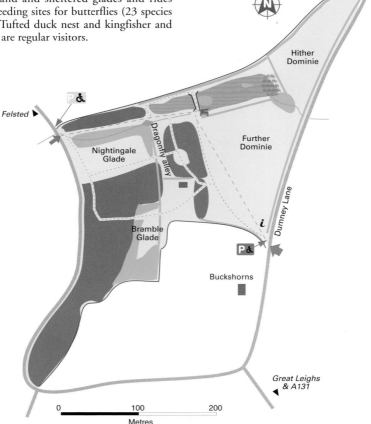

Visiting

The reserve entrance is in Dumney Lane, Great Leighs. Take the road to Felsted from the A131 at the St Anne's Castle PH. Dumney Lane is the first right turning.

Regular buses run to St Anne's Castle PH from Braintree and Chelmsford.

Accessible at all times.

Interesting all the year round. A succession of flowers from blackthorn in February through to the last of the water-side plants in autumn is followed by the lovely colours of leaves and fruits at the end of the year, with the extra attraction of butterflies and dragonflies in summer.

The path from the car park at the Dumney lane entrance to the other entrance on the Felsted road is designed for wheelchairs.

Please keep dogs on leads at all times.

Call the warden on 01376 324311 or Essex Wildlife Trust HQ on 01206 735456.

Tufted duck pair (male on left)
Owen Keen

Phyllis Currie lake in winter
Sylvia Jiggins

Rainham

The complex of grazing marshes alongside the Thames near Rainham has been the centre of controversy for years, because it is an important SSSI threatened by development. Now that the RSPB has bought a large part of it from the MoD its prospects look much brighter. Nearby, Havering Council has developed a riverside path.

Inner Thames Marshes

1250ac/500ha   OS Ex162/La177   GR 535 800   SSSI

As this book went to press the RSPB had just acquired Aveley and Wennington Marshes, formerly used by the MoD as a firing range and a substantial part of the Inner Thames Marshes SSSI. The remainder of the SSSI consists of silt lagoons owned by the Port of London Authority, also to be taken over by RSPB, plus Rainham Marsh to the west. Rainham Marsh is owned by Havering Council which has been attempting for many years to develop the site and still hopes to do so.

This area is very important in wildlife terms particularly for its birds. It also has a large population of water voles and many unusual plants and invertebrates.

As soon as RSPB has got to grips with the job of making it ready it will be essential visiting for anyone interested in wild birds.

Visiting

No visiting arrangements in force as yet: contact RSPB (phone 01767 680551 or web www.rspb.org.uk) for the latest news.

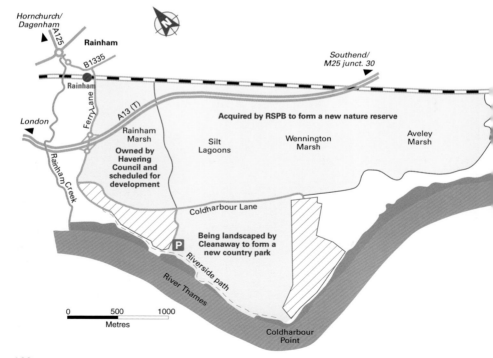

Rainham Riverside Path

2ac/1ha   OS Ex162/La177   GR 517 803

Havering Council is developing this riverside walk alongside the Thames at Rainham. At present it finishes at Coldharbour Point but eventually it will extend to Purfleet further east.

It provides good views of the Thames foreshore and of the new habitats developing on the former landfill site inland. Some unusual birds, such as short-eared owl, water pipit and rock pipit, can be seen along here in winter, while in summer it is a good hunting ground for the insect and flower enthusiasts.

Visiting

Take Ferry Lane south from Rainham Village or from the A13 and turn left on to Coldharbour Lane. A parking area is signposted on the right.

Rainham station is about 15 minutes' walk via Ferry Lane from the western end of the path.

Accessible at all times.

Rat Island

35ac/14ha   OS Ex184/La168   GR 055 171   SSSI, SPA

This low-lying island consisting of saltmarsh is managed as a nature reserve by Essex Wildlife Trust. It lies in the mouth of Geedon Creek on the west side of the Colne Estuary and is distantly visible from the Fingringhoe Wick Visitor Centre.

It is the site of one of the county's largest nesting colonies of black-headed gulls. Common terns nest intermittently and sandwich terns visit occasionally.

Visiting

Visiting only by arrangement with the warden: call 01206 729338 or Trust HQ on 01206 735456.

Black-headed gull in summer plumage
Alan Williams

Short-eared owl: visits Rainham Marsh in winter
Alan Williams

189

Ray Island

100ac/40ha   OS Ex184/La168   GR 011 154   SSSI, SPA

This large sandy mound rising out of the surrounding saltings is owned by the National Trust and managed by Essex Wildlife Trust. It has a shingly foreshore/beach area on its northern side, with a sizeable freshwater pond nearby, and extensive areas of rough grassland. On higher ground, there are blackthorn thickets and some spectacular old hawthorns.

The southern edge of the island has some of the finest natural transition areas of saltmarsh–grassland–scrub to be found on the Essex coast. The wide range of saltmarsh plants includes lax-flowered sea lavender, golden samphire and sea rush.

An experimental grazing scheme is running on the island using Soay sheep, a primitive rare breed.

Among the breeding birds are redshank (in some numbers), oystercatcher and shelduck. Large numbers of wildfowl and waders over-winter – flocks of more than 2,000 brent geese are not unusual. All the common finches can be seen throughout the year, but numbers increase dramatically in winter when large flocks feed on the seed heads of sea aster and other saltmarsh plants. Birds of prey are commonly seen, including long-eared and short-eared owl, hen harrier, merlin and barn owl.

A number of the commoner butterflies are abundant in normal summers and mammals, particularly voles, are plentiful.

Bonners Saltings

Thes saltings lying between the Strood causeway and Ray Island are private property, but the owners have kindly agreed to Essex Wildlife Trust members having access to study the natural history and to cross to Ray Island. Plant enthusiasts will find a large patch of dittander by the Strood causeway.

Ray Island view
David Nicholls

Visiting

The reserve lies to the west of the Strood – the causeway which carries the main road (B1025) from Colchester across to Mersea Island. A pathway starts at the north end of the Strood and runs across Bonner's Saltings to Ray Island. Alternative access is by boat, leaving Mersea moorings at high tide and sailing up Ray Channel.

Regular bus services (half-hourly on weekdays, hourly on Sundays) run between Colchester and West Mersea and will drop off and pick up at Strood Villa.

There is general public access to the reserve as part of the management agreement with the National Trust. It is a popular picnic venue for the local boating community during July and August.

For more information call the warden on 01206 384341 or Essex Wildlife Trust HQ on 01206 735456.

Birdwatchers will find plenty to interest them from late September all the way through to May (in summer, holiday activity in the surrounding creeks often creates too much disturbance); in July flowering sea lavender covers several acres of saltings.

Take great care to check the state and times of the tide before crossing the saltings as both the pathway and saltings are often flooded to a depth of several feet. For general safety do not attempt to cross in the two hours preceding high water. The pathway is approximately one mile long and visitors have to negotiate a number of single-plank bridges without handrails. Care must be taken as these can be very slippery. Wellington boots and weatherproof clothing are essential.

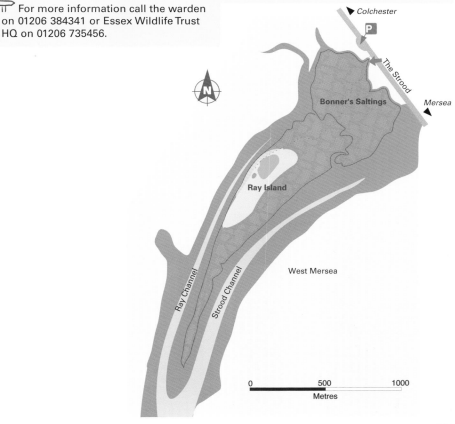

Roding Valley Meadows

158ac/63ha   OS Ex174/La177   GR 430 943   LNR, SSSI (part)

ESSEX
Wildlife Trust

This Essex Wildlife Trust reserve comprises the largest surviving area of traditionally managed river-valley habitat in Essex. It consists of flower-rich unimproved hay meadows, both wet and dry, bounded by thick hedgerows, together with a small amount of scrub, secondary woodland and tree plantation. It follows the River Roding for some 1.5 miles between Chigwell Lane and Roding Lane, Buckhurst Hill, as it meanders across this ancient landscape.

The meadows are rich in flowers, including sneezewort and pepper saxifrage, with southern marsh orchid, ragged robin, marsh marigold and several rare sedge species in the wetter areas. The impressive green lane which runs from near the river to the M11 motorway by Grange Farm has many woodland flowers.

Sedge warbler and reed bunting frequent the marshy areas, while kingfisher and sand martin occasionally nest in the river bank and a small number of meadow pipits nest on the meadows. In winter grey heron, little grebe, snipe, green and common sandpiper are regular visitors.

The meadows are managed in the traditional way by taking a hay cut in summer, followed by cattle grazing. A total length of almost ten miles of hedgerow is managed by laying and coppicing.

Southern marsh orchid, flowering in June
Tony Gunton

Visiting

Part of the Roding Valley recreation ground and accessible via a number of entrances on the Loughton side of the river. The car park is next to the David Lloyd Centre off Roding Lane.

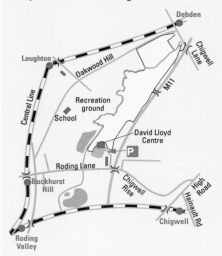

Buckhurst Hill, Loughton and Debden tube stations on the Central Line are all within a few minutes' walk of the reserve. Many bus services run to Debden and Loughton stations.

Accessible at all times.

For meadow flowers, any time from late spring up to mid-July when the hay is cut.

One-mile linear surfaced track for wheelchairs; all kissing gates adapted to accommodate wheelchairs and scooters.

from the warden (020 8508 1593), Epping Forest DC (01992 564222) and Essex Wildlife Trust visitor centres. For help call the warden on 020 8508 1593.

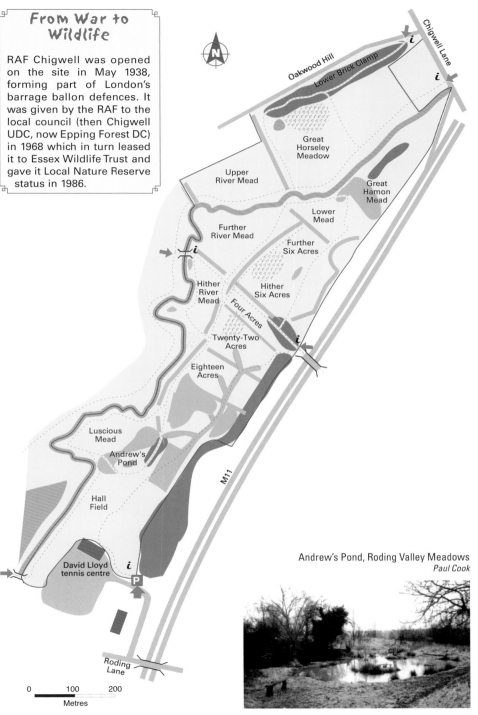

From War to Wildlife

RAF Chigwell was opened on the site in May 1938, forming part of London's barrage balloon defences. It was given by the RAF to the local council (then Chigwell UDC, now Epping Forest DC) in 1968 which in turn leased it to Essex Wildlife Trust and gave it Local Nature Reserve status in 1986.

Chigwell Lane

Oakwood Hill

Lower Brick Clamp

Great Horseley Meadow

Upper River Mead

Great Hamon Mead

Lower Mead

Further River Mead

Further Six Acres

Hither River Mead

Hither Six Acres

Four Acres

Twenty-Two Acres

Eighteen Acres

Luscious Mead

Andrew's Pond

Hall Field

M11

David Lloyd tennis centre

P

Roding Lane

Andrew's Pond, Roding Valley Meadows
Paul Cook

0   100   200

Metres

193

Roman River Valley

The Roman River is a tributary of the Colne and its valley, running to the south of Colchester, is extremely rich in wildlife, and particularly plants and insects. This is because it has a varied mosaic of habitats with a long and continuous history – ancient and more recent woodland, scrub, grassland, heath and fen. It has remained like this while all around these habitats have been disappearing mainly because the Ministry of Defence owns much of the land and uses it for military training. The Essex Wildlife Trust has a nature reserve in the valley also.

Friday Wood

225ac/90ha   OS Ex184/La168   GR 986 209   SSSI

Ministry of Defence

Friday Wood is an ancient woodland owned by the Ministry of Defence. It has a good range of woodland plants but is particularly important for its butterflies and moths. White admirals, now restricted to only a few Essex woods, were 'rediscovered' there in 1995 and it also has white-letter hairstreaks, whose caterpillars feed on elm. Both butterflies fly from July onwards but, unfortunately, spend much of their time in the tree canopy, so you need to work quite hard to spot them.

It is also a good place to hear nightingales.

Visiting

The main parking area is on a minor road that runs south from Berechurch Hall Road to Layer, parallel to the B1026 (Colchester–Maldon).

Bus services run along Berechurch Hall Road.

Accessible at all times.

Spring for woodland flowers and birdsong; July–August for butterflies and other insects.

Please keep to the waymarked rights of way and obey Army warning notices.

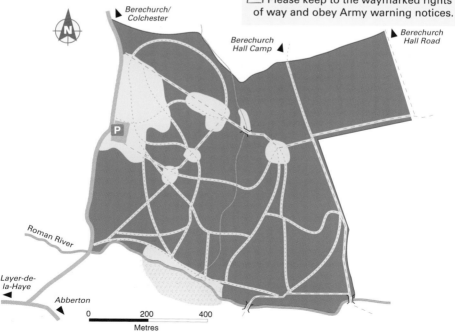

Roman River Valley *nature reserve*
44ac/18ha   OS Ex184/La168   GR 975 211

ESSEX
Wildlife Trust

This fragment of traditional river valley landscape is an Essex Wildlife Trust nature reserve. The Roman River is a narrow stream at this point, and meanders through marsh and woodland, mostly old.

The marsh is fed by springs filtering out of glacial gravels, and is full of aquatic plants including one that is unusual – the small teasel, which has globular white flowers in late summer.

The woodland is part of Needle Eye Wood, and has a variety of trees including standard oaks, coppiced hornbeam and several old yews. Its flowering plants include yellow archangel and moschatel.

Birdlife includes most of the common woodland species, nightingales, and one that has almost disappeared from Essex – the willow tit. Like most wetland sites it has a rich insect life as well.

Visiting

Entrance on the west side of the B1026 (Colchester–Layer) just north of Kingsford Bridge, north of Layer-de-la-Haye.

Bus services from Colchester to Layer and Maldon pass the reserve entrance.

Accessible at all times.

April–May for birdsong and early flowers; July for dragonflies and other insects.

For more information call the warden on 01206 734496 or Essex Wildlife Trust HQ on 01206 735456.

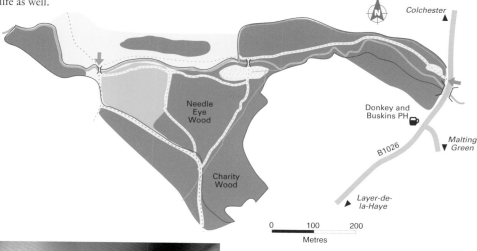

Colchester

Needle Eye Wood

Donkey and Buskins PH

Malting Green

B1026

Charity Wood

Layer-de-la-Haye

0   100   200
Metres

Willow tit: almost lost from Essex
David Harrison

195

Rushy Mead

11.5ac/5ha   OS Ex194/La167   GR 497 197

The name *Rushy Mead* comes from an old tithe map showing the site as riverside meadows. More recently it has been occupied by a pumping station for a sewage works. Pumping ceased in the 1950s and the site started to revert to nature. A nature reserve was created through an agreement between the site owners, Thames Water plc, Wimpey Homes who made a generous contribution towards running costs, and Essex Wildlife Trust that manages the site.

The low ground has water near the surface all year, and there are good areas of sedge and reed. These produce tall, dense growth that provides cover for sedge and reed warbler in summer, and for snipe and water rail in winter.

The northern end of the site has developed into mature alder woodland with ash and willow and is a particularly good area for birds. Yellow iris and wild angelica are just two of the many plants that flower here in summer.

A network of drainage ditches supports a rich variety of water-loving wildlife including marsh marigolds, water beetles and dragonflies.

The drier ground has areas of scrubby woodland and chalky grassland. The latter supports a good variety of wild flowers including bee orchid and wild carrot.

The Trust's main management aims are to maintain open water in ditches and ponds and to control the spread of invasive plants such as Russian comfrey.

Visiting

One mile south of Bishop's Stortford, lying between the A1060 road to Hatfield Heath and the River Stort. It can be entered from the A1060 or from the towpath running alongside the Stort Navigation.

Only half-a-mile walk from Bishop's Stortford station (Liverpool St–Cambridge): head south along the towpath.

Accessible at all times.

Spring and summer for flowers, birds and insect life.

Call the warden on 01279 757428 or Essex Wildlife Trust HQ on 01206 735456.

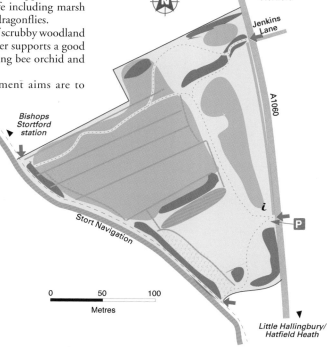

Saint Peter's Marsh
0.5ac/0.2ha OS Ex195/La167   GR 757 237

ESSEX
Wildlife Trust

This is the one of the smallest nature reserves in Essex. It comprises fresh marsh, fed by springs, and was planted with poplars, most of which have been felled to let in more light.

The reserve is a traditional frog breeding site and for this reason Essex Wildlife Trust acquired it from Essex County Council for a nominal sum. An adjoining strip of land was donated later by Messrs G. Tanner and P. O. Wicks.

Visiting

To the north of St Peter's church, Bocking (close to Braintree Council offices). Entrance off St-Peter's-in-the-Fields (unadopted road).

Train or bus to Braintree town centre.

Accessible at all times.

Dress for nettles and soft wet ground.

Call the warden on 01376 347255 or Essex Wildlife Trust HQ on 01206 735456.

Common frog
Tony Gunton

Wild angelica: a plant of damp grassland, flowering in late summer
Tony Gunton

... not to be confused with the common toad, which has a dry, warty skin, and walks, rather than hops.
David Corke

The price of intensive farming?

The price we seem to be paying for intensive farming is clear from the British Trust for Ornithology (BTO) statistics on the decline in farmland birds in the 25 years ending 1996. These show declines in 20 farmland species of between 24% and 85%. This is the result of changing practices such as, for example, autumn sowing of cereal crops, which has eliminated the seedy stubble fields in which many birds used to find winter food. It is also the result of widespread use of pesticides that have all but eliminated the insect food on which most birds feed their young.

Is modern farming simply inconsistent with a countryside rich in wildlife? A small but determined minority of farmers with a commitment to wildlife, supported by the Farming & Wildlife Advisory Group (FWAG), try to demonstrate that it is not.

Recently they have been joined by the Essex Wildlife Trust at Abbotts Hall Farm and the RSPB at Hope Farm in Cambridgeshire, while for its part the Government is introducing new incentives for wildlife-friendly farming, such as the Arable Stewardship Scheme.

Turtle dove: down 85% ▲
David Harrison

▲ Bullfinch: down 62%
David Harrison

▲ Skylark: down 75%
Alan Williams

Corn bunting: down 74%
David Harrison ▼

Grey partridge: down 75%
Alan Williams ▼

Salary Brook

50ac/20ha   OS Ex184/La168   GR 027 250

This secluded area of marsh, wet grassland and ponds lies alongside Salary Brook on the eastern fringe of Colchester. It is owned by Colchester Council, who are working with local volunteers to improve access and encourage the fine wetland vegetation, which includes hemlock water dropwort and devilsbit scabious. The Council also plans to reintroduce grazing.

Visiting

In the north-east of Colchester. Salary Brook can be reached via footpaths off Avon Road, which runs from the Tesco roundabout on the A133 to Bromley Road, near the Beehive PH. Welsh Wood is between the Roach Vale, Woodlands and Salary Close estates.

Bus services from Colchester run along the A133.

Accessible at all times.

May for birdsong. High to late summer for wetland flowers and insects

Call 01206 853588.

Welsh Wood

7ac/2.68ha   OS Ex184/La168   GR 025 263

A small fragment of ancient woodland with a wide variety of trees, including small-leaved lime, a tree characteristic of very old woodlands that used to be widespread but, probably because of climate change, is now very localised. It lies in a stream valley and is very wet, which makes for a wide variety of woodland flowers.

199

These two attractive small woods next to one another were donated to the Essex Wildlife Trust in 1982 by the late Mr Roland Adams and Mrs Adams. They contain a quantity of coppiced small-leaved lime, growing on boulder clay. One lime, in the middle of a ride in Sandylay Wood, is of great size and age. Sycamore and planted poplars are now being reduced in favour of other species, including small-leaved lime for coppicing; and conifer plantations are being reduced in favour of broadleaved trees.

The woods are rich in flowering plants. In spring wood anemones are abundant by the small stream and primroses alongside the paths and rides. Other species include sweet violet, spurge laurel, early purple orchid, twayblade and gladdon. Wood sedge is widespread, and the localised thin-spiked wood sedge also occurs.

The reserve has many typical woodland birds, notably goldcrest around a plantation of Norway spruce, and a rich insect life.

Visiting

The reserve is in Great Leighs. Mill Lane passes to its east and a public footpath leads to the main entrance from the west side of this lane, a distance of about 400m. Cars can be parked on the wide grass verge along the lane, but please do not obstruct the gateway providing access to the footpath.

Buses stop on the A131 near the Dog and Partridge PH, from where a public footpath runs west from the road to another entrance.

Accessible at all times.

Late March to May for flowering plants and breeding birds.

Call the warden on 01245 443639 or Essex Wildlife Trust HQ on 01206 735456.

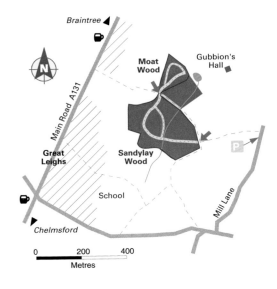

Sawbridgeworth Marsh

22ac/9ha   OS Ex194/La167   GR 493 158   SSSI

ESSEX
Wildlife Trust

This reserve lies in the valley of the River Stort and consists of three distinct areas: ten acres of waterlogged marsh, normally under an inch or two of water for most of the year; six acres of peaty meadow sloping up from the marsh to the eastern boundary; and a low-lying willow plantation to the south of both these areas. Most of it is in Hertfordshire and a small part in Essex, so it was acquired jointly by the Essex and Hertfordshire & Middlesex Trusts when the site became available in 1970.

It contains plants which were once quite common but are now found on only a few sites in the county, such as marsh willowherb and marsh valerian. Other uncommon plants include marsh arrow-grass, southern marsh orchid and blunt-flowered rush.

It has several open drainage ditches and two ponds rich in aquatic life, including the rare slender amber snail. The areas of sedge, reeds and tall fen vegetation provide a valuable nesting habitat for reed warbler, sedge warbler and grasshopper warbler. Other breeding birds include snipe and water rail. The reserve is rich in insect life.

The management regime is designed to encourage diversity of species. Enclosures are grazed by horses and parts of the marsh are cut on an annual or biennial basis. To prevent it from smothering smaller plants, the dead material is raked off and either burnt on permanent fire sites or gathered into permanent stacks which provide a valuable habitat for grass snakes and invertebrates. Additionally the willows which fringe the marsh are pollarded periodically.

Visiting

To the west of the unclassified road from Sawbridgeworth to Gaston Green and Little Hallingbury. There is no car park, but there are two small lay-bys on the opposite side of the road about 200m north of the reserve entrance. Care should be taken since the road is narrow and traffic travels at high speeds.

About 800m north-east of Sawbridgeworth station (BR Liverpool Street to Cambridge).

Accessible at all times.

Worth a visit at all times of the year but the spring and summer months are usually the most interesting.

Not suitable for wheelchair access due to the wet nature of the ground, and narrow paths and plank bridges.

Wellingtons usually necessary.

Call the warden on 01279 725017 or Essex Wildlife Trust HQ on 01206 735456.

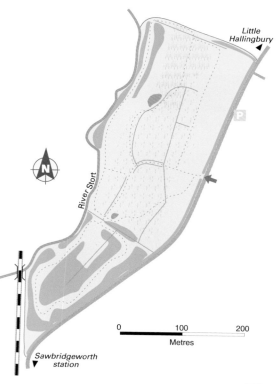

Little Hallingbury

River Stort

0   100   200
Metres

Sawbridgeworth station

Sergeant's Orchard

8ac/3ha   *OS Ex196/La168*   *GR 907 308*

THE
wildlife
TRUSTS
ESSEX
Wildlife Trust

Left to the Essex Wildlife Trust in 1996 by the owner of Sergeant's Farm, this site comprises two ex-arable fields and a 19th century orchard. Within the orchard area a wide range of old varieties of fruit trees remain, together with an old pond and the remnants of the hedges.

The Trust plans to restore the old orchard, the hedges and the ponds, and to establish a new orchard on the western field using stock taken from the old varieties in the existing orchard, and to manage the eastern field as a spring-sown arable field for the benefit of arable weed species. The western meadow has been reseeded with a suitable grass and wildflower mix prior to being fenced and replanted with cuttings taken from the old trees. The whole orchard will then be managed with sheep or pigs feeding beneath the fruit trees in the traditional manner.

Visiting

Between Aldham and Chappel turn off the A1124 into Vernons Road. Follow signs for Bures/Sudbury and at the T-junction turn right. There is a small pull-in at the entrance to the bridle path with a chain attached to two metal posts.

Accessible at all times.

Call the warden on 01206 231517 or Essex Wildlife Trust HQ on 01206 735456.

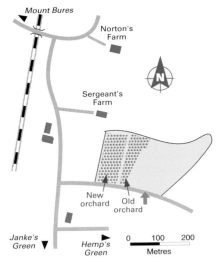

Corncockle, once a widespread weed of arable fields but now very scarce
Owen Keen

Shotgate Thickets

8ac/3ha   OS Ex183/La178   GR 765 939

ESSEX
Wildlife Trust

This Essex Wildlife Trust nature reserve is situated on both sides of the tidal River Crouch which is narrow at this point. It consists of a remnant of old oak woodland on the south side, and thorn thickets, rough grassland and large ponds on the north side. With the adjoining river banks and railway embankment this small area has a surprising diversity of habitats and, consequently, of wildlife.

Well over 100 plant species can be found, including golden dock and dyer's greenweed. More than 70 species of bird have been recorded, about half of which breed on or near the reserve. This includes all three species of woodpecker, and a good selection of finches and warblers.

The ponds teem with life and eleven species of dragonfly have been identified, including the emerald damselfly and black-tailed skimmer. Butterflies are numerous. Among the other insects Roesel's bush-cricket is found in good numbers.

Management work is aimed at maintaining a mosaic of scrub, glades and ponds.

Visiting

800m north-east of Wickford. A railway bridge spans the river separating the two parts of the reserve, but cannot be used to cross it. The southern part can be reached via Beauchamps Drive and Royal Oak Drive, or by walking through the Memorial Park, following the river. Access to the northern part is either through Southlands farm (parking at far end of the farm road) or west along the river bank from Battlesbridge, starting close to the Hawk public house.

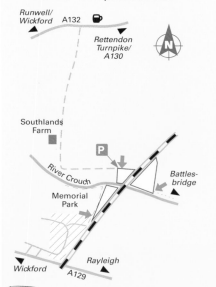

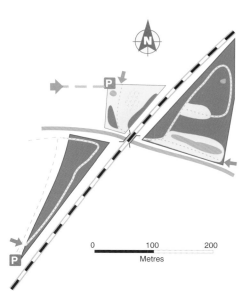

Frequent buses along the A129 or train to Battlesbridge.

Accessible at all times. For a single visit the north side is recommended.

At its best in mid-to-late spring when scrub and wood resound with birdsong.

The large pond on the north side has steep banks and deep water.

Call the warden on 01268 765872 or Essex Wildlife Trust HQ on 01206 735456.

Shut Heath Wood

50ac/20ha   OS Ex183/La168   GR 853 133

This Essex Wildlife Trust reserve, just below the crest of the Great Totham Ridge, includes 23 acres of ancient woodland forming part of the Chantry Wood complex. The remaining 27 acres are arable land managed by a tenant farmer.

The wood comprises large oak standards with sections of sweet chestnut and hornbeam coppice, and ash, elder and hazel understorey. The eastern edge is wet, with an open glade and thick scrub areas, while the southern edge consists of secondary woodland of silver birch and hawthorn that has colonised the adjacent field edges. The Trust has resumed coppicing and created some open areas to rejuvenate the wood.

In spring bugle, cuckoo flower, wood sorrel, bluebells, wood anemone, primrose and dog violet flower, followed in summer by willowherb, yellow pimpernel, red bartsia, greater birdsfoot trefoil and wood sage.

Dragonflies and damselflies may be seen in the glade and purple hairstreak butterflies in the oak canopy. Large amounts of standing dead wood in the site make it excellent for invertebrates, including wood ants which are numerous in summer. Glow-worms can be seen in the glade in July.

Visiting

Leave the B1022 Maldon Road at Roundbush Corner, Great Totham, taking Mountains Road. After about 1200m take the first turning on the right (Tiptree Road), and the entrance is about 400m down on the left with double gates at the entrance. Take care when leaving as visibility is restricted.

Bus to Great Totham from Maldon or Colchester and get off at Great Totham post office. The reserve is 800m north.

Accessible at all times.

March and April for spring flowers.

Call the warden on 01621 891302 or Essex Wildlife Trust HQ on 01206 735456.

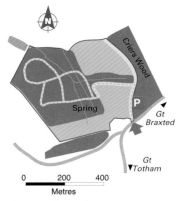

Bluebells in Shut Heath Wood
Suzy Torino

South Woodham

On the Crouch Estuary, right next to South Woodham Ferrers new town, is a large area of coastal marshland that has been set aside as Marsh Farm Country Park. A mile or so north of the country park via a walk along the seawall is Woodham Fen, an Essex Wildlife Trust nature reserve. Part of the country park also is managed as a nature reserve.

The area has something to suit most tastes – a long-established grazing marsh that is rich in wildlife, farm animals to interest children; and some relics of the eventful history of the Essex coast. Finally, Woodham Fen is one of the few places where you can still see the natural transition from saltmarsh to dry grassland. Elsewhere, seawalls force an abrupt change from one to the other.

Marsh Farm Country Park
350ac/140ha OS Ex175/La168   GR 810 961   SSSI, SPA
Essex County Council

The country park is centred on Marsh Farm, which is operated by Essex County Council on a semi-commercial basis. Both the farm itself, which raises cattle, sheep and other animals, and the surrounding grazing marsh are open to the public, with a small charge for entry to the farm. The grazing marsh has a long history going back to when the first seawall was built in the 18th century.

The land was purchased originally to build the new town, but it was decided that land below the 5-metre contour was not suitable for building because of the risk of flooding, and for that reason it became a country park. Part of the seawall surrounding Marsh Farm was in fact breached in 1953 and the remains are still visible from the present wall built further back.

At the eastern end of the park is a nature reserve consisting of rough grassland, saltmarsh and a scrape – a shallow water lagoon. Hares are often about in the grassland and reed buntings nest along the dykes. The scrape, which is overlooked by a hide, attracts many wildfowl in winter and at migration periods, and especially wigeon and teal.

Shelduck, dunlin and redshank feed in Clementsgreen Creek when the mud is exposed.

Woodham Fen
20ac/8ha   OS Ex175/6/La168   GR 798 975   SSSI, SPA
ESSEX
Wildlife Trust

This Essex Wildlife Trust reserve lies between and near the tidal limits of two small creeks running north from the River Crouch. It was common land given c. 1140 by the Lords of the Manor to the poor of the community to graze animals. The southern part is saltmarsh and the northern rough grassland with a transitional zone between the two – of special interest to naturalists because this natural transition is now very unusual in Essex. It has a wide range of saltmarsh plants, including sea wormwood, and the grassland is full of wild flowers, including unusual ones like slender birdsfoot trefoil, grass vetchling, wild carrot and crested hair-grass.

It also attracts many birds. Reed bunting, yellow wagtail and meadow pipit breed here, and a variety of small waders occur on passage. Teal, common and jack snipe, and rock pipit are to be found in winter, when kingfishers hunt along the creekss.

The harvest mouse occurs here and field voles are abundant, regularly attracting barn owls and other birds of prey to hunt over the grassland.

Bush-crickets and saltmarsh moths are notable among the insects. Essex skipper and a number of the other common butterflies are abundant.

The reserve lies within a much larger area of common land owned by South Woodham Ferrers Town Council. This area is managed on advice from the Trust and in all includes about 85 acres of grassland, scrub, ditches and ponds.

205

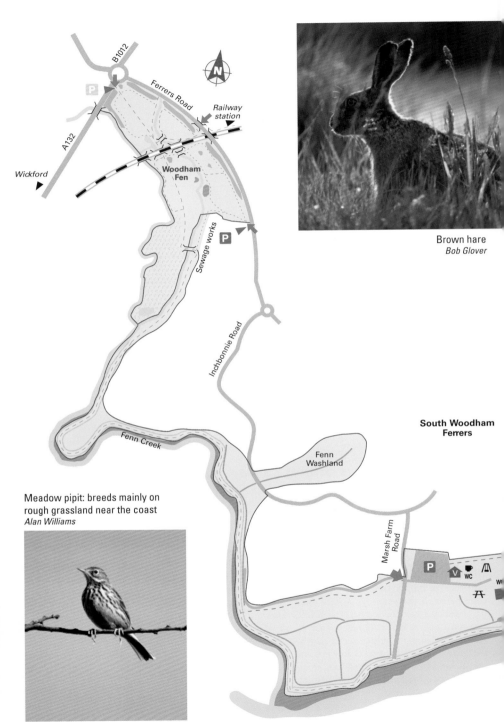

B1012

Ferrers Road

Railway station

A132

Wickford

Woodham Fen

Sewage works

Inchbonnie Road

Fenn Creek

Fenn Washland

South Woodham Ferrers

Marsh Farm Road

Brown hare
Bob Glover

Meadow pipit: breeds mainly on rough grassland near the coast
Alan Williams

Visiting

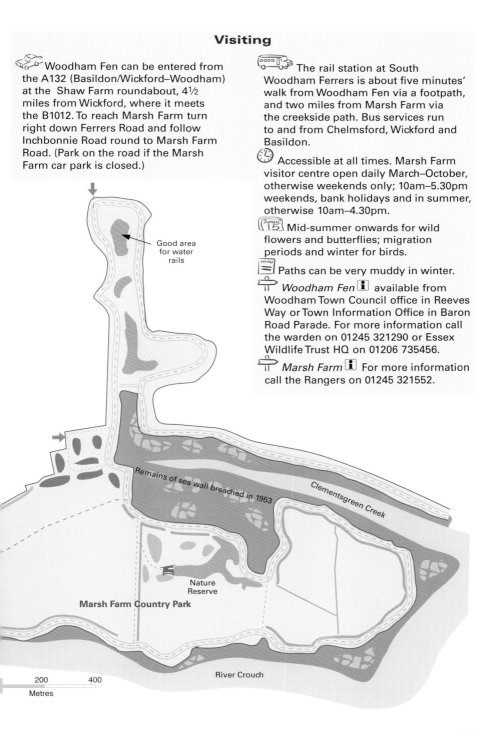

Woodham Fen can be entered from the A132 (Basildon/Wickford–Woodham) at the Shaw Farm roundabout, 4½ miles from Wickford, where it meets the B1012. To reach Marsh Farm turn right down Ferrers Road and follow Inchbonnie Road round to Marsh Farm Road. (Park on the road if the Marsh Farm car park is closed.)

The rail station at South Woodham Ferrers is about five minutes' walk from Woodham Fen via a footpath, and two miles from Marsh Farm via the creekside path. Bus services run to and from Chelmsford, Wickford and Basildon.

Accessible at all times. Marsh Farm visitor centre open daily March–October, otherwise weekends only; 10am–5.30pm weekends, bank holidays and in summer, otherwise 10am–4.30pm.

Mid-summer onwards for wild flowers and butterflies; migration periods and winter for birds.

Paths can be very muddy in winter.

Woodham Fen ℹ available from Woodham Town Council office in Reeves Way or Town Information Office in Baron Road Parade. For more information call the warden on 01245 321290 or Essex Wildlife Trust HQ on 01206 735456.

Marsh Farm ℹ For more information call the Rangers on 01245 321552.

Good area for water rails

Remains of sea wall breached in 1953

Clementsgreen Creek

Nature Reserve

Marsh Farm Country Park

200   400

Metres

River Crouch

Stanford Warren

30ac/12ha   OS Ex175/La177   GR 687 812   SSSI, SPA (part)

This Essex Wildlife Trust reserve beside the Thames consists of one of the largest reed (*Phragmites*) beds in Essex, created by gravel extraction in the 1920s, together with areas of marsh and rough grassland. Recently an additional area to the east has been leased to the Trust by Cory Environmental.

In spring and summer the reed beds are full of birds fussing around, including reed buntings, reed warblers and sedge warblers, all of which breed. Cuckoos regularly use the warblers as hosts for their eggs. Water rail breed here too, but you will be lucky to see them because they are very shy, creeping quietly around in the reeds – dusk is the best time.

Winter brings in bearded tits, grey wagtail and snipe – best seen along the Hassenbrooke, a small river that bisects the reserve and crosses under the footpath.

Visiting

Access to the reserve is from London Road in Stanford-le-Hope – off the A1013, which runs alongside the A13. Turn south down Butts Lane then left into Mucking Wharf Road. Please park considerately by the former church at the start of footpath no. 38.

Accessible at all times.

Late spring and summer for breeding birds and flowering plants; winter for visiting birds such as bearded tits.

Please keep to the footpath that crosses the reserve on a low embankment, providing good views over the whole area.

Call the warden on 01708 470241 or Essex Wildlife Trust HQ on 01206 735456.

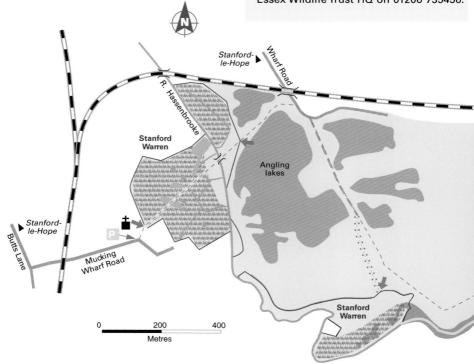

Common lizard, grass snake and adder frequent the rough grassland, and harvest mice nest among the reeds.

Management consists in the main of rotational cutting of reed in the winter months and raking to clear reed litter. This encourages stronger stem growth and slows up the drying process.

Stanford Marsh

A large area of rough ground to the east of Stanford Warren has been set aside as public open space by Thurrock Council. The Thames Estuary is about a mile wide at this point and is bordered by Mucking Flats, a large area of intertidal mudflats that serves as a feeding ground for many wading birds. Inland of the flats is the Earl's Hope saltmarsh.

This is a good birdwatching area at most times of the year, with many small songbirds using the rough grassland and scrub for nesting, in addition to the waders and water birds that feed on the mudflats and roost or nest on the saltmarsh.

River Hassenbrooke
at Stanford Warren
Tony Gunton

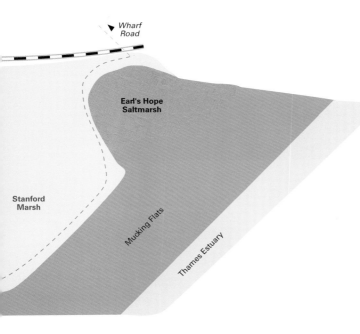

Wharf Road

Earl's Hope Saltmarsh

Stanford Marsh

Mucking Flats

Thames Estuary

Stour Estuary

This section of the estuary of the River Stour to the west of Harwich has saltmarsh and intertidal mudflats adjoining ancient woodland and is the only place in Essex where you can see the one close alongside the other. The saltmarsh and mudflats of Copperas Bay are nationally important for wading birds such as black-tailed godwit, dunlin and redshank and, together with Stour Wood, form the RSPB's Stour Estuary reserve. Another ancient woodland alongside the bay, Copperas Wood, is also a nature reserve, owned by the Essex Wildlife Trust, while a short way to the west lies Wrabness nature reserve and Oakfield Wood, a 'green burial ground'.

Stour Wood

135ac/54ha   OS Ex184/La169   GR 192 311   SSSI

Stour Wood is one of the best ancient sweet chestnut woods in Essex. It was worked as coppice until the 1970s and coppicing has since been resumed by the RSPB, to whom the Woodland Trust has leased the wood. The sweet chestnut is being coppiced on a long (20-year) cycle. It has a mixture of trees apart from sweet chestnut, including a few surviving small-leaved lime and many field maple on the edge of the wood. Some unusual flowers characteristic of ancient woodland are sweet woodruff and early purple orchid.

It is full of birdsong in spring and early summer. Among the butterflies look out for white admiral, flying in July, a woodland butterfly that is common in woods further south and west but rare in East Anglia.

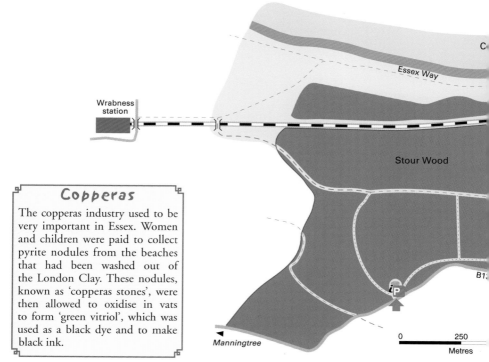

Copperas

The copperas industry used to be very important in Essex. Women and children were paid to collect pyrite nodules from the beaches that had been washed out of the London Clay. These nodules, known as 'copperas stones', were then allowed to oxidise in vats to form 'green vitriol', which was used as a black dye and to make black ink.

Copperas Bay

717ac/287ha OS Ex184/La169   GR 195 318   SSSI, SPA

Copperas Bay has large areas of mudflats fringed by saltmarsh and reedbed, lying immediately west of the port facilities of Parkeston. It is reached by crossing the bridge over the railway and walking down the Essex Way to the public hide. This hide is best for birdwatching at low and half tide when many waders come to feed on the mudflats.

From there a path runs along in a narrow strip of woodland between railway and estuary to two hides (reserved for RSPB members), which give good views of birds at their high-tide roost. It is unusual in Essex for a wood to run right down to the waterside as it does here and this makes it an enjoyable walk in its own right. From the path there are occasional views through the screen of trees over Copperas Bay, which is

Visiting

🚗 North of the B1352 from Ramsey to Manningtree, between the villages of Wrabness and Ramsey. Turn off the A120 Colchester-Harwich road on to the B1352. The main entrance to Stour Wood, with car park, is signposted from the road; Copperas Wood is 300 yards down a public footpath (the route of the Essex Way) beside a large white flat-roofed house, with parking for one or two cars on the verge. Copperas Bay and its bird hides can be reached via either.

🚌 Stour Wood is about 800m walk from Wrabness station via a public foot-path, and the public hide by the estuary is about as far again. A bus service from

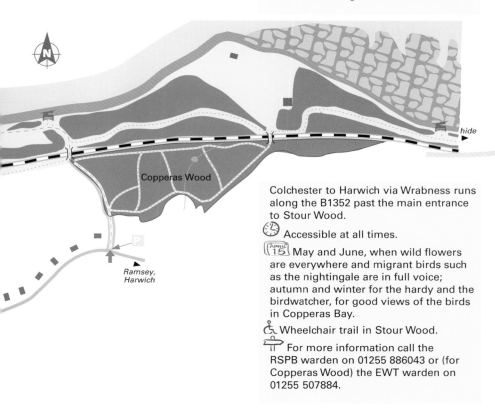

Colchester to Harwich via Wrabness runs along the B1352 past the main entrance to Stour Wood.

🕐 Accessible at all times.

📅 May and June, when wild flowers are everywhere and migrant birds such as the nightingale are in full voice; autumn and winter for the hardy and the birdwatcher, for good views of the birds in Copperas Bay.

♿ Wheelchair trail in Stour Wood.

🪧 For more information call the RSPB warden on 01255 886043 or (for Copperas Wood) the EWT warden on 01255 507884.

used by a variety of birds in autumn and winter including brent geese, many ducks and a large flock of black-tailed godwits.

The Stour estuary is the second most important UK wintering site for this bird after the Wash, with more than 2,000 present most winters. They are part of the population that breeds in Iceland.

Copperas Wood
34.3ac/14ha   OS Ex184/La169   GR 199 312   SSSI

This ancient wood, owned by the Essex Wildlife Trust, consists mainly of coppiced sweet chestnut and hornbeam. It was severely damaged in the great storm of 1987 and sections of the wood have been left in their devastated state for wildlife value and for scientific study.

After the Trust bought the wood in 1980 coppicing was re-introduced, and this has produced carpets of bluebell, yellow archangel and red campion. Among other flowering plants are moschatel, climbing corydalis, and a few sweet woodruff and vervain. The wood is rich in ferns, soft shield-fern being particularly well represented.

100 species of bird (43 of which have nested) have been seen, including all three species of woodpecker and the nightingale.

Purple hairstreak is notable among the 23 species of butterfly and over 300 species of moth that have been recorded.

Oakfield Wood
7ac/3ha   OS Ex184/La169   GR 167 315

Oakfield Wood is a 'green burial ground' overlooking the Stour Estuary at Wrabness, a natural alternative to traditional graveyard or crematorium burials. It was one of the first in the UK and has been visited by Church and other organisers who have since set up sites throughout the country.

For each burial a native broadleaved tree is planted with a wooden plaque at its base, thus each burial contributes towards creating a new woodland on what used to be arable farmland. When the burial ground is full it will be managed as a nature reserve by Essex Wildlife Trust.

Black-tailed godwit
Alan Williams

Yellowhammer
David Harrison

Wrabness Nature Reserve

54ac/22ha   OS Ex184/La169   GR 167 315   LNR

**Wrabness
NR Trust**

Visiting

Reached via Wheatsheaf Lane, which turns off the B1352 (Ramsey–Manningtree) at the Wheatsheaf PH. A turning half-left just beyond the railway bridge leads to the Wrabness NR car park and the Oakfield Wood car park is on the left further on. From there a path takes you past the burial ground and joins the Essex Way public footpath.

About a mile walk from Wrabness rail station via a public footpath. A bus service from Colchester to Harwich runs along the B1352.

Accessible at all times.

Good wheelchair access because of the pre-existing road infra-structure, since improved by the Trust.

For information about Wrabness NR contact the warden on 01255 870056. For information about burials at Oakfield Wood, contact Peter Kincaid on 01255 503456.

This area served as a mine depot until its demolition in 1963. Attempts to develop the site ran into public opposition and in 1992 it became a nature reserve under the care of the Wrabness Nature Reserve Charitable Trust.

It is mainly open grassland and scrub, with a pond, a bog, a wooded fringe and a bird hide overlooking the Stour Estuary. It attracts open country birds such as yellowhammers (increasingly scarce elsewhere) and whitethroats to nest, and has large numbers of grassland butterflies and other insects in summer.

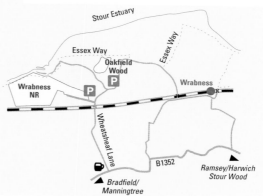

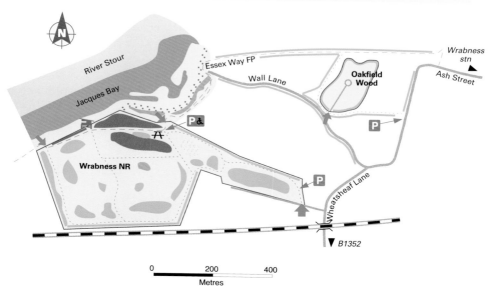

213

Stow Maries Halt

5.5ac/2ha   OS Ex175/La168   GR 835 991

ESSEX
Wildlife Trust

This Essex Wildlife Trust nature reserve consists of the former Stow Maries Halt on the disused Maldon–Woodham Ferrers railway line, along with an adjoining four-acre meadow acquired later.

The remains of the platform are still visible by the reserve entrance and four species of fern – wall-rue, maidenhair spleenwort, black spleenwort and harts-tongue – grow in the mortar of the bridge here. This part of the reserve grades from cutting to shallow embankment and consists largely of hawthorn and blackthorn scrub with occasional privet and a scattering of young oak and ash.

The lower part of the reserve has benefited from scrub clearance, and a pond has been excavated in marshy ground in its north-west corner. In late spring there are many common spotted orchids and a number of adderstongue ferns, followed in summer by common fleabane (in profusion), wild carrot and St John's worts.

The reserve has a good selection of butterflies, including purple and white-letter hairstreaks, and dragonflies. Glow-worms reliably put on a show in July every year, scattered throughout the reserve.

Visiting

Reached via Church Lane, which connects the lower Burnham road between South Woodham Ferrers and North Fambridge with the road through Stow Maries village (junction opposite the Yugo garage). Cars can be parked on the wide grass verge of the bridge over the dismantled railway.

Accessible at all times.

Late spring for orchids; summer for wild flowers and insects (glow-worms in July).

Call the warden on 01621 828191 or Essex Wildlife Trust HQ on 01206 735456.

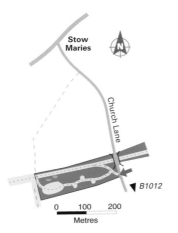

Stow Maries

Church Lane

B1012

0   100   200
Metres

Glowworm (female): she uses her light to attract a mate
Phil Luke

Swan Wood

32ac/13ha   OS Ex175/La167   GR 688 993

WOODLAND
TRUST

This ancient woodland, owned by the Woodland Trust, has a mix of broadleaved trees, including sweet chestnut and hornbeam coppice. Remnants of its mediæval wood banks can still be seen. An attractive stream runs through the wood, with alder trees along its banks. It is a bluebell wood, and yellow archangel, wood sorrel and wood anemone can also be found.

It has a good range of woodland birds, including hawfinches.

The traditional practice of coppicing has been reintroduced for the hornbeam and sweet chestnut. Sycamore invading the wood is being felled.

Visiting

From Chelmsford or from the A12 take the B1007 south towards Billericay. In Stock turn right by The Cock PH into Swan Lane. Swan Wood is on the right after 400m. Park in the layby on the left.

Buses from Chelmsford to Billericay pass through Stock.

Accessible at all times.

Sweetings Meadow

1.6ac/1ha   OS Ex195/La167   GR 632 285

ESSEX
Wildlife Trust

This small traditional hay meadow, also containing a number of fruit trees, is a tiny oasis in an intensively cultivated countryside. It is owned and managed by the Essex Wildlife Trust.

On chalky boulder clay, it boasts impressive populations of cowslip and pyramidal orchid. The many other plants include bee orchids, common spotted orchids and pepper saxifrage.

Visiting

Take the lane from Lindsell that meets the B184 north of Monk Street. The entrance is on the left side of the lane a short way past Holder's Green.

Accessible at all times.

Call the warden on 01371 830422.

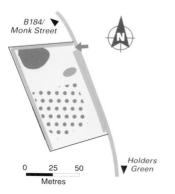

215

The Naze

Tendring Council

100ac/40ha   OS Ex184/La169   GR 264 235   SSSI (part)

The Naze is from the Old English *naes*, meaning a nose. It is a headland roughly three miles long and one mile wide, stretching northwards from the town of Walton-on-the-Naze. Behind it is Hamford Water, which it shelters from the North Sea. At its southern end is a hill that is being eroded (see box right), with the result that 70 foot high cliffs rise directly from the beach – unique on the Essex coastline.

Originally the Naze was farmland, then a golf course, then was requisitioned at the beginning of World War II. In the late 1950s permission was sought to develop the area but, following a public enquiry in 1961, it was decided that the Naze should become a public regional open space. Tendring Council owns it now.

In summer the cliffs provide secure sites for the nesting holes of sand martins. The large gorse bushes and elder scrub on top of the cliff provide cover for small birds such as linnets and goldfinches, as do the taller plants growing on the fallen cliff material at its foot. Waders, gulls and terns can be seen along the shore.

During migration periods it is a prime birdwatching site. Curlew sandpipers are regularly seen along the beach, with gannets and arctic skuas passing offshore. With east winds blowing, small birds such as firecrest and black redstart may be found sheltering in the bushes on the clifftop.

A mile-long shingle beach stretches forwards from the tip of the Naze, ending at Stone Point. This is an important nesting site for little terns and other shorebirds like oystercatchers and ringed plovers. (It is cordoned off in the breeding season to prevent disturbance.)

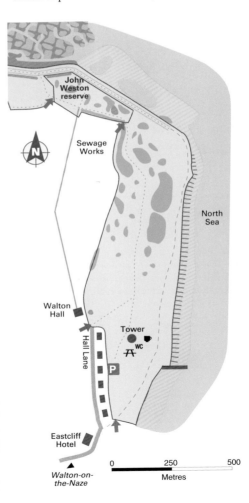

Visiting

🚗 Head northwards along the coast road in Walton with the sea on your right. By the Eastcliffe Hotel take the left fork and follow Hall Lane and Naze Park Road for about a mile. This will bring you to the public car park on the cliff top.

🚌 Regular buses run from Clacton and Frinton via Walton station (train link to Colchester) and from the bus station on the front.

🕓 Accessible at all times.

📅 April–June for early flowers and birdsong; spring and autumn for migrating birds.

🚏 A waymarked nature trail about 2km long runs around the Naze Open Space, starting from the tower.

216

Cream-spot tiger moth ▲
Dr Chris Gibson/English Nature

Lapwing
Alan Williams

John Weston

9ac/4ha   OS Ex184/La169   GR 266 245   SSSI

ESSEX
Wildlife Trust

This Essex Wildlife Trust reserve lies within the Naze public open space. It consists of blackthorn and bramble thickets, rough grassland and four ponds or 'scrapes', three of them excavated since the reserve was established. It is named after the late John Weston, a leading Essex naturalist who was warden of the reserve until his death in 1984.

Its nesting birds include lapwing, redshank, and sedge and reed warblers, the latter having colonised the reeds that were introduced to one of the new pools. It is an important landfall for migrants – for example the firecrest occurs regularly and red-backed shrike and barred warbler occasionally – and also attracts a good variety of winter visitors.

Notable among its flowering plants and grasses are parsley water-dropwort, slender thistle, pepper saxifrage, fenugreek and bush grass.

Being so close to the shore, it inevitably attracts shore-loving insects, including emperor, cream-spot tiger and saltern ear moths.

Visiting

The John Weston reserve forms the north-western part of the public open space and can be reached via a nature trail established by the Trust which runs through it.

Several bus services run to The Naze via Walton station.

This reserve acts mainly as a sanctuary although organised and casual visits are possible.

For more information call Essex Wildlife Trust HQ on 01206 735456.

Winter erosion at The Naze
Geoff Gibbs

Barnes Spinney

2ac/1ha   *OS Ex184/La169*   *GR 258 277*

This small garden site at Walton-on-the-Naze was left to the Essex Wildlife Trust in 1984 by the late Mrs L. Barnes and named in memory of her husband, the late Rt Hon. Alfred Barnes PC.

It contains fine displays both of cultivated plants, especially daffodils, fritillaries and primroses in spring, and also of wild flowers, including twayblade and good numbers of common spotted orchid.

Visiting

 On arriving in Walton, follow the main road north-east through High Street into Hall Lane, then on for about 800m. Turn sharp left into lane beyond Brenalwood nursing home, which leads down to the reserve.

Buses run every half hour from Walton church and from the bus station on the front and stop just past Brenalwood.

Can normally be visited only on open days. These are announced and publicised locally, or dates can be obtained from the warden on 01255 673452 or Essex Wildlife Trust HQ on 01206 735456.

Walton-on-the-Naze
High Street and station

218

The Paddock

3ac/1ha   OS Ex175/La168   GR 905 946

WOODLAND
TRUST

The Paddock is a small Woodland Trust 'Woods-on-your-Doorstep' site near Canewdon in Rochford.

Visiting

Access via a path that runs north from Lambourne Hall Road at the east side of *The Paddock* about 200m east of Canewdon.

Accessible at all times.

The Ripple

25ac/10ha   OS Ex162/La177   GR 467 824

London
Wildlife Trust

Set among the industrial landscape of Barking Reach, the Ripple was once a dumping area for pulverised fuel ash, and shows how nature can reclaim industrial wasteland. It is now a London Wildlife Trust nature reserve. Hundreds of southern marsh and common spotted orchids can be seen dotted throughout the birch woodland in May and June, and the new meadow nearby has swathes of native wildflowers, attracting a wide range of butterflies and other insects in summer.

Visiting

Next to Thamesmead Park City Farm at the junction of Thames Road and Renwick Road in Barking.

District or Fenchurch St. lines to Barking, then bus to end of its route in Thames View estate.

May to June for orchids.

Call London Wildlife Trust on 020 7261 0447 for details of events.

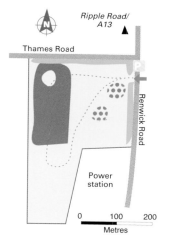

Common spotted orchid
Alan Sadgrove

Thorndon

Few areas offer such variety as Thorndon Park and its surroundings. Ancient woodland and historic deer parks lie close alongside new woodland planted by the Woodland Trust and a landscape of small pastures recreated by Essex County Council's Ranger Service, while nearby is the high forest of Hartswood and former common land.

Thorndon Country Park

300ac/120ha OS Ex175/La177   *GR 716 108*   *SSSI (part)*   Essex County Council

Thorndon Country Park is in two parts, the northern section on a gravel ridge and the southern part lower down. The two parts are now linked by Old Thorndon Pastures, which is farmland that has been restored to a traditional farming landscape with small hedged fields, grazed by English White cattle, a rare breed.

It has ancient woodland and parkland, ponds, a marsh and meadow. Ancient trees are an outstanding feature. Giant oak and hornbeam pollards with towering canopies remind us that this was once a deer park.

The park attracts a large number of woodland birds and sees more than its fair share of passage migrants and winter visitors. For example, large flocks of siskins and redpolls often gather in the birches, and bramblings can be seen near to the Centre feeding on beech mast.

It also hosts an unusually wide variety of butterflies, including rarities like purple and white-letter hairstreaks, brown argus and ringlet.

The park is managed by Essex County Council's Ranger Service. Conifer plantations are gradually being returned to grassland or broadleaved woodland as mature trees are harvested. The storms of 1987 and 1990 have lent a powerful hand here – where windblown conifers have been cleared a new woodland of native trees is regenerating naturally, while in other areas new native trees have been planted to speed the process.

The Countryside Centre in Thorndon Park North is managed by Essex Wildlife Trust in a joint venture with Essex County Council. It was built just after the 1987 hurricane and some of the storm-fallen timber was used in its construction. It is the Trust's most popular centre with over 100,000 visitors per year. The interpretation provided here is enhanced with many hands-on displays to get you thinking.

Visiting

The park lies south of Brentwood, just west of the A128, which runs from Ongar through Brentwood to Halfway House on the A127 Southend Arterial. The main entrance to Thorndon North is off The Avenue, which links the A128 and the B186 (Brentwood–South Ockendon). The entrance to Thorndon South is off the A128 just north of Halfway House.

Brentwood rail station is about 1.5 miles (via Hartswood and Little Warley Common) from the Countryside Centre in Thorndon North. Buses from Brentwood Town Centre run to Eagle Way, Warley.

Open all year from 8 am to dusk. The Countryside Centre is open every day except Mondays, Christmas and Boxing Days from 10 am to 5 pm (spring and summer) or to 3.30 pm (autumn and winter).

May for spring flowers and birdsong in the woods; July for butterflies in the open grassland; October for fungi.

The Countryside Centre has wheelchair access and a disabled person's toilet. A battery-powered scooter can be provided on request.

For more information about the park or about events and activities call the Countryside Centre on 01277 232944 or the Rangers on 01277 211250.

Ancient parkland, Thorndon Park North
Thorndon Rangers

220

The Old Park

135ac/54ha   OS Ex175/La177   GR 620 906

A large section of Hatch Farm lying between the two halves of Thorndon Country Park has been acquired by the Woodland Trust as one of its Plant-a-Wood sites. Oak, ash, sweet chestnut and hornbeam have been planted and 84 acres have been sown with grass and wildflower seed, to recreate a parkland atmosphere.

Hatch Farm (still privately owned) was built as a 'model farm' in 1777 to raise deer and cattle. The ancient oaks on the edge probably date from a mediæval deer park.

The grassland is grazed by a herd of British White cattle, a rare breed.

Ceps *Boletus edulis*: Thorndon is famous for its fungi
Tony Gunton

Ancient oak in Thorndon Park
Thorndon Rangers

Hartswood

In the 17th century this ancient woodland was owned by diarist John Evelyn. A Site of Special Scientific Interest (SSSI), it has towering oaks and sweet chestnut trees and small streams lined with ferns. It is managed by Brentwood Council.

Brentwood

Brentwood

Thorndon Hall

Harts Wood

Hartswood Road

The Avenue

Warley/ Ford HO

Little Warley Common

Childerditch Lane

Thorndon North

Priva Lan

Childer ditch Pond

Childer

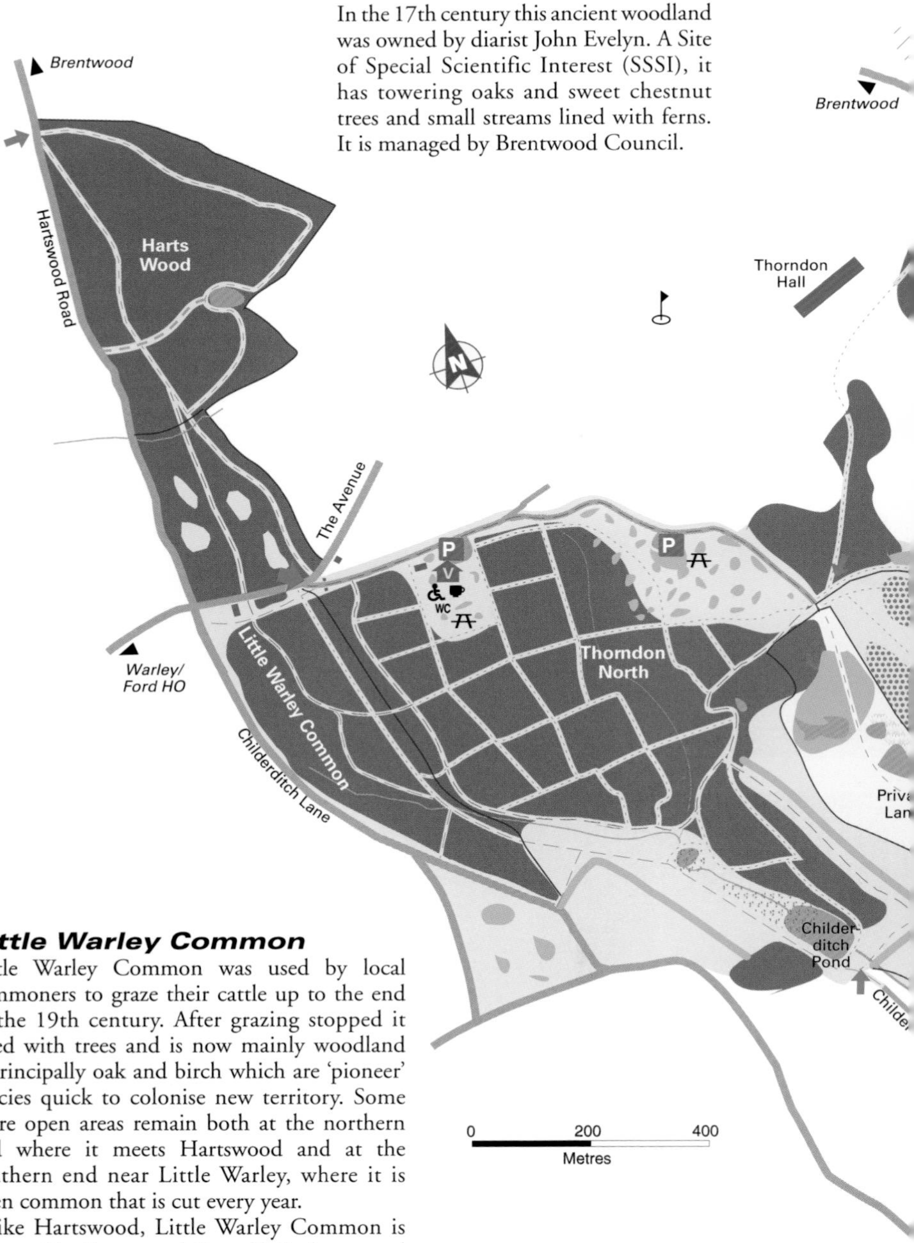

Little Warley Common

Little Warley Common was used by local commoners to graze their cattle up to the end of the 19th century. After grazing stopped it filled with trees and is now mainly woodland – principally oak and birch which are 'pioneer' species quick to colonise new territory. Some more open areas remain both at the northern end where it meets Hartswood and at the southern end near Little Warley, where it is open common that is cut every year.

Like Hartswood, Little Warley Common is managed by Brentwood Council. Both are good places to head for on busy summer weekends if you want to avoid the crowds in Thorndon Country Park.

| 0 | 200 | 400 |

Metres

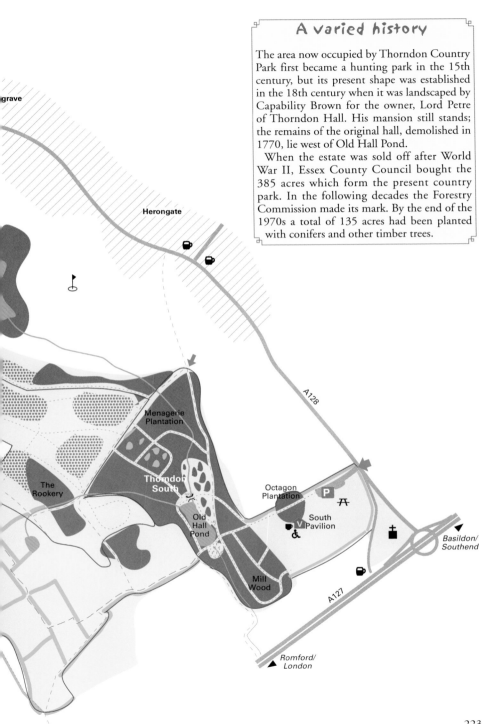

The area now occupied by Thorndon Country Park first became a hunting park in the 15th century, but its present shape was established in the 18th century when it was landscaped by Capability Brown for the owner, Lord Petre of Thorndon Hall. His mansion still stands; the remains of the original hall, demolished in 1770, lie west of Old Hall Pond.

When the estate was sold off after World War II, Essex County Council bought the 385 acres which form the present country park. In the following decades the Forestry Commission made its mark. By the end of the 1970s a total of 135 acres had been planted with conifers and other timber trees.

grave

Herongate

Menagerie
Plantation

The
Rookery

Thorndon
South

Old
Hall
Pond

Octagon
Plantation

South
Pavilion

A128

Mill
Wood

A127

Basildon/
Southend

Romford/
London

Thrift Wood

48ac/19ha   *OS Ex183/La167*   **GR 790 017**   *SSSI*

ESSEX
Wildlife Trust

This ancient wood, owned and managed by Essex Wildlife Trust, consists of hornbeam coppice with many oak standards, some birch, ash and coppiced sweet chestnut, and a number of wild service trees.

It is one of the principal Essex sites of the common cow-wheat, food plant of the heath fritillary butterfly. After becoming extinct in Essex, this butterfly was re-established in the reserve in 1984. It also has lots of slender St John's wort, heath wood-rush and pale and pill sedges.

There is a sizable pool with a raised bog, thought to have been formed many years ago from clay-digging for brickmaking. Here can be found greater spearwort, hop sedge and other aquatic plants, three species of sphagnum moss and the hair-moss *Polytrichum commune.*

Birds include woodpeckers and a good population of woodland warblers. The wood teems with wood ants and has a wide range of other insects.

Coppicing has been reintroduced, resulting in a marked increase in both resident and summer migrant birds and also in plantlife. The pond with its raised bog is cleared annually of rank vegetation.

Visiting

The entrance is on the B1418 road 400m south of the Brewer's Arms PH in Bicknacre. There is parking for a few cars at the main gate, with overflow parking on the verge opposite.

Buses run every half-hour between Chelmsford and South Woodham Ferrers, stopping at the main gate to the wood.

Accessible at all times.

May for spring flowers and bird-song; late May on for heath fritillary and other butterflies.

Do not attempt to cross the pool's raised bog as conditions are dangerous..

Call the warden on 01245 320630 or Essex Wildlife Trust HQ on 01206 735456.

Common cow-wheat
EWT library

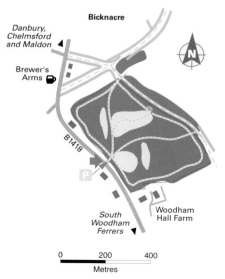

0   200   400

Metres

Tilbury Power Station

20ac/8ha   OS Ex163/La177   GR 655 764

ESSEX
Wildlife Trust

This educational nature reserve is associated with the Energy and Environment Centre, a joint venture between National Power, Thurrock Council and Essex Wildlife Trust that opened in 1990. It consists of former Thames-side grazing marsh and the remnants of ditch systems, complete with reedbeds, ponds and disused railway sidings. Some of the grassland is 'unimproved' in agricultural terms, but the whole reserve has been greatly modified by the construction of the neighbouring power station, and is dissected by access roads.

The grassland areas provide a good display of commoner wild flowers, and haresfoot clover is found on the disused railway sidings. There are small areas of thorn scrub and other areas have been planted up with a mixture of broadleaved trees.

The dry ditches of the reserve are dominated by false fox sedge and hard rush, the wetter ones by common reed. Their plants include brackish water-crowfoot and tubular water-dropwort.

One of the two ponds is fringed by reedmace and the other is brackish and fringed with sea club-rush. They hold populations of ten-spined sticklebacks and smooth newts. Great silver diving beetles are also present.

Breeding birds include sedge warblers and stonechats. Black redstarts are seen occasionally. Kestrels and barn owls hunt over the reserve and kingfishers and snipe visit in winter.

Butterflies include gatekeepers, common blues and small heaths. The emperor dragonfly is seen every year. Foxes and hares are often seen. Adders and lizards occur in good numbers.

Visiting

Details supplied when visits are confirmed.

Open for group visits only, with a minimum of ten people per visit. Non-school group visits should be arranged with the Trust's Field Officer (01375 844281), who has organised visits for a wide range of groups, with many coming back for a second visit. The Teacher Warden, from Thurrock Council, takes school groups for environmental studies related to the National Curriculum, using the adjacent grassland and freshwater habitats (01375 844217). Guides are available to take groups around the power station itself, by arrangement: call 01375 852704. The visit includes an audio-visual display in the lecture theatre. For safety reasons, nine is the minimum age for group members.

Leaflet available detailing events and opportunities at the centre: call any of the above numbers.

Centre equipped for disabled visitors.

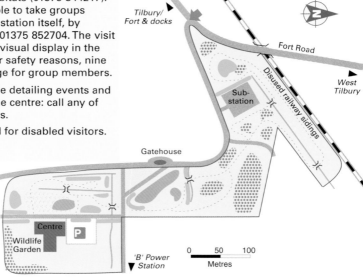

225

Tiptree Heath

60ac/24ha   OS Ex184/La168   GR 883 14   SSSI

Tiptree Heath is a small fragment of a huge heathland that used to stretch from Maldon to Messing, covering thousands of acres. It is the finest and largest area of heath in Essex, and the only place you will find all three heather species growing together.

The heath had been nibbled away by enclosure for centuries before it received what seemed like a death blow during World War II, when the common land laws were suspended and it was ploughed up for agriculture. But it produced only poor crops, and in 1955 was sown with grass seed and left to look after itself. The result was that some of it turned into light woodland and scrub, but on large areas the heathland plants re-appeared.

In 1973 the present heath was designated a Site of Special Scientific Interest (SSSI). It is owned by the Lord of the Manor and managed by Tiptree Parish Council, supported by local conservation groups.

Ling heather, which is tall and vigorous enough to survive in gorse, covers large areas, and there are areas of bell heather and a small amount of cross-leaved heath that prefers the wetter parts. In late summer harebells can be seen with their dainty blue bell-shaped flowers. The heath also has a number of other unusual wild plants, including heath dog-violet, allseed and chaffweed.

Heathland is very difficult to recreate once scrub and trees have taken over. Radical measures have had to be taken to restore Tiptree Heath, including bulldozing down to the mineral soil. Routinely, areas are flailed on rotation, so you can see ling heather at all stages of growth. Without this management the whole heath would quickly turn into impenetrable thickets of gorse and birch.

Visiting

The heath straddles the B1022 (Colchester–Maldon) 800m on the Maldon side of Tiptree.

A regular bus service between Maldon and Colchester runs along the B1022 past the heath.

Accessible at all times.

April to see acres of gorse in flower; July–September for late flowers, including the heather, and grassland butterflies.

Call the warden on 01621 815016

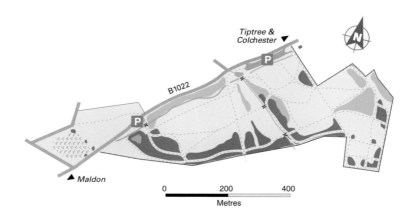

Tiptree & Colchester ▼

B1022

▲ Maldon

0   200   400

Metres

Three kinds of heather growing
together on Tiptree Heath
Fred Boot

Tiptree Parish Field

6ac/2.4ha   OS Ex/La184   GR 913 159   LNR

**Tiptree
Council**

Tiptree Parish Field is an area of wet grassland that has probably never been ploughed. It is rich in flowers including a number of heathland species. A stream runs across the bottom (southern) edge of the field, where a pond has been dug out attached to the stream.

It was declared a Local Nature Reserve in 1999 and is managed by Tiptree Council.

Visiting

About 500m down Park Lane, an ancient highway. Park Lane is an unmade road leaving Newbridge Road between a factory and a house opposite the end of Grove Road, about 1 km from the junction with the B1023. Newbridge Road leaves the B1023 (Kelvedon–Tolleshunt d'Arcy) opposite the jam factory.

Accessible at all times.

Call the warden on 01621 815016.

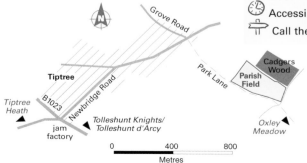

Commons and heaths

A common is land where people other than the owner have rights to use the land, such as to graze their cattle. The 'commoners' are people who live in designated houses nearby and hold those rights.

It was mainly grazing, both by domesticated cattle and wild rabbits, that shaped the commons, but other rights gave rise to a whole range of uses. Gorse, ling (the commonest type of heather) and dried turf were used for fuel; bracken was used for animal bedding and for thatching; and heather was also used to stuff mattresses and as a walling material. Often gravel was extracted too, and consequently many commons are full of pits and depressions.

It was the use of land as commons that created heaths. Grazing on free-draining soils creates a poor, acid soil that favours gorse, heathers or bracken. Conversely, as soon as grazing stops they revert to scrub and then to woodland as birch and oak invade, shading out the gorse and heather.

For centuries heathland was regarded as a valueless wasteland. Most of the extensive Essex heaths outside Epping Forest vanished in the early 19th century. They were enclosed as common rights were bought or stolen, and ploughed up as innovations in farming practice and machinery made it possible to cultivate them.

Heathland is only found in Western Europe and everywhere only small pockets remain, but it has its own increasingly unusual plants and animals. In Essex, heathland is concentrated on gravelly soils in the south of the county, on top of ridges such as at Epping, Danbury and Tiptree, and there are also fragments at Galleywood and Thundersley (see *Daws Heath*).

Cross-leaved heath (above) and bell heather
Fred Boot

Gorse
Laurie Forsyth

Reptiles like this common lizard thrive in the dry, sunny conditions found on heathland
Tony Gunton

Turner's Spring

8ac/3ha   OS Ex195/La167   GR 529 243

ESSEX
Wildlife Trust

Turner's Spring is a mixed deciduous woodland, including a strip running alongside the Bourne Brook, plus a meadow with a central wet area of sedge beds. It was given to Essex Wildlife Trust by the Cawkell trustees in 1975.

The main wood contains oak, beech, ash and sycamore, with areas of hazel and hornbeam coppice. Spring brings a fine display of oxlips, violets, dog's mercury and herb paris, with naturalised daffodils in profusion on either side of the central path.

The meadow has a wide range of flowering plants including cowslip, bugle, salad burnet, agrimony and meadowsweet.

The woodland strip along the Bourne Brook has carpets of violets in the spring, with some oxlips and scattered wood anemones. Where the water from the sedge beds drains into a deep depression a tufa pile has formed – pendulous sedge grows here.

Over 60 species of bird have been recorded on the reserve. Butterflies are mostly limited to the commoner species but including the ringlet.

The meadow is mown annually to maintain its diversity of plants and the insects that they support.

Visiting

Reached via a footpath from the Stansted–Burton End road. The footpath is on the left about 600m beyond the bridge over the M11, marked by a footpath sign beside a black-painted village pump. Cars may be parked on the road nearby.

Accessible at all times.

Spring for wild flowers.

Call the warden on 01799 550378 or Essex Wildlife Trust HQ on 01206 735456.

Pendulous sedge
Tony Gunton

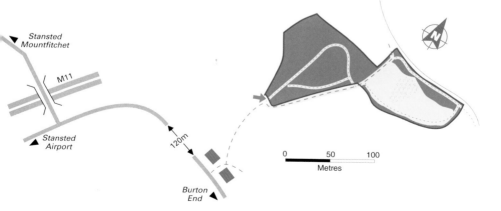

Stansted Mountfitchet

M11

Stansted Airport

120m

Burton End

0   50   100
Metres

Tylers Common, now owned by Havering Council, is the last remaining sizeable piece of common land left in Havering. Its name derives from the brick and tile industry that exploited the clay deposits around here from Saxon times onwards.

Parts are kept open by grazing by horses and parts have been invaded by scrub and trees. In summer the grassland is full of wild flowers including (in the damp south-east corner) unusual plants like sneezewort, and supports large numbers of grassland butterflies. The mix of scrub, tall hedges and open grassland attracts birds like yellowhammers, linnets and bullfinches.

Visiting

Between Nags Head Lane and Warley Road, within the triangle formed by the A127, A12 and M25 near Upminster.

Accessible at all times.

High summer for wild flowers and insects.

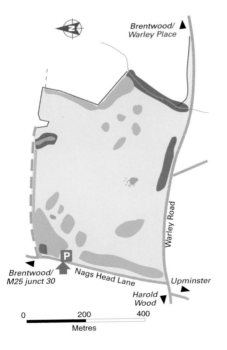

River Chelmer at Little Waltham Meadows
Janet Spencer

Upper Chelmer valley
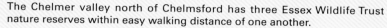

The Chelmer valley north of Chelmsford has three Essex Wildlife Trust
nature reserves within easy walking distance of one another.

Little Waltham Meadows
22ac/9ha   OS Ex183/La167   GR 713 119

Acquired by Essex Wildlife Trust in December 1996 with the help of a local appeal and a grant from the National Heritage Lottery fund, this reserve comprises a chain of old flood meadows, dry meadows and alder carr woodland on the east bank of the river Chelmer, just south of Little Waltham.

A range of grassland plants and animals can be found, including meadow saxifrage, bee orchid and yellow oat grass. The interconnecting network of old hedgerows contain many pollards and coppice stools of elm, common hawthorn and midland hawthorn (together with hybrid) and hazel, willow, alder and oak. Green woodpecker, tawny owl, sparrowhawk and kestrel all use the hedgerows and wood or hunt over the meadows.

The meandering River Chelmer has a good range of marginal and aquatic plants and animals, including water vole, kingfisher, water cress, water lilies, brooklime, iris and rushes. Emperor dragonfly, common darter, ruddy darter and black-tailed skimmer occur in the summer.

The alder spinney is a good example of mature

alders over wet ground conditions, providing a fine show of marsh marigolds in spring, together with yellow iris, fool's watercress and flote grass throughout the summer.

The meadows are grazed by cattle in the traditional way. Old hedges are being restored by planting up gaps and by coppicing or pollarding mature trees. The ditch system in the southern meadows is being restored and water control devices have been installed to maintain water levels.

Visiting

The reserve is 400m west of the A130 Essex Regiment Way, just south of Little Waltham. Access is via Back Lane, Little Waltham, parking on the wide verge at the end of the bridleway. The reserve can also by reached from Broomfield from the other end of that bridleway to Croxton's Mill.

Bus services from Chelmsford run to Little Waltham via Broomfield to the west and via Essex Regiment Way to the east.

Accessible at all times.

Call the warden on 01245 362316 or Essex Wildlife Trust HQ on 01206 735456.

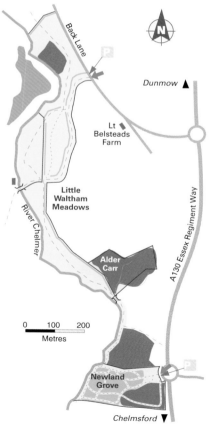

231

Newland Grove & Alder Carr

8ac/3ha   OS Ex183/La167   GR 716 108

Newland Grove is an Essex Wildlife Trust reserve consisting of rough grassland with thorn thickets and a small wood. The River Chelmer flows along its western boundary.

Such a mixture of habitats makes for a variety of plants – over 230 species have been recorded. The grassland is flower-rich: cowslips and hairy violet are among the spring flowers, and in midsummer the area sloping down to the river in particular is a riot of colour, with common St John's wort, knapweed, musk mallow and a number of other species growing in profusion. Twayblade, wood spurge and pale wood violet can be found in the wood.

Because of the abundance of flowers the reserve is also rich in butterflies – 23 species have been recorded.

Among the birds, good numbers of warblers of several species nest in the thickets and wood, while mallard, kingfisher and sedge warbler are often seen by the river.

Alder Carr is a three-acre alder swamp a short distance to the north of Newland Grove. It has marsh marigold and common valerian, and an interesting insect population.

Visiting

Adjoins the A130 north of Chelmsford about 1200m from the North Springfield housing estate. Entry is from the west side of a roundabout on the A130 east of Broomfield, opposite the turning to the Channels Golf Club and Windsurfing Centre. Parking for 2–3 cars at the entrance.

Accessible at all times

Midsummer for wild flowers and butterflies.

Call the warden on 01245 269453 or Essex Wildlife Trust HQ on 01206 735456.

Vange Marsh

3.2ac/1ha   OS Ex175/La177   GR 728 872   SSSI

This small Essex Wildlife Trust reserve consists of over 800m of sea-wall and a narrow belt of saltmarsh.

The estuarine plants along the sea wall include sea and strawberry clovers and sea barley; wild celery is found in a freshwater pond at the northern end; and there is a typical saltmarsh flora.

Two species of seaslug and a rare shellfish, *Assiminea grayana*, are found on the saltmarsh mud.

Shelduck, redshank, oystercatcher and curlew feed on the saltmarsh and mudflats along with many other waders and wildfowl.

Oystercatchers
Gerald Downey

Visiting

Because of the fragility of this reserve no visiting is permitted.

Warley Place

15ac/6ha   OS Ex175/La177   GR 583 906

ESSEX
Wildlife Trust

Warley Place is the site of a house (demolished in the 1930s) and once-famous gardens said to have been laid out by the diarist John Evelyn in the 17th century. The last occupant of the house was Miss Ellen Willmott, who died in 1934. She re-modelled the gardens and introduced into them a vast assortment of new plants from all over the world. It is now a nature reserve managed by Essex Wildlife Trust.

The site had been neglected but is now being restored by an enthusiastic team of volunteers, although not in the form of the original gardens. Parts of their remains can still be seen, along with parts of the old house and a number of the surviving plants. Daffodils, snowdrops, winter aconites, anemones, cranesbills and ferns grow in profusion again, mingling with indigenous species. Among a variety of trees, some exotic, is a line of huge sweet chestnuts.

The reserve attracts a wide variety of birds, including the nuthatch, and has a good selection of invertebrates, including stag beetles.

Visiting

The reserve is on the B186 (Brentwood–S. Ockendon) just south of Brentwood. The reserve gate is next to the Thatcher's Arms PH, from where a short track leads to the car park. From there a path leads to the main part of the reserve through one of the famous early purple crocus meadows (not part of the reserve).

Infrequent buses from Brentwood to Romford and Grays run past the entrance; ask for Thatchers Arms.

Except as indicated below, Trust members and holders of day permits only. Permits can be obtained from Trust HQ: call 01206 735456.

Weekends from end February to early April when the gates are manned by volunteers and several thousand visitors come to see the daffodils and other spring flowers.

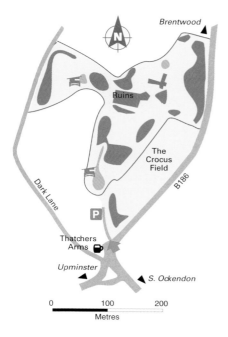

Brentwood

Ruins

The Crocus Field

B186

Dark Lane

P

Thatchers Arms

Upminster

S. Ockendon

0   100   200
Metres

Crocus field next to Warley Place
EWT library

233

Wat Tyler *Country Park*
125ac/50ha OS Ex175/La178   GR 739 867

Wat Tyler Country Park, managed by Basildon Council, is named after the leader of the Peasants' Revolt of 1381 against the poll tax, and does indeed have a chequered past. Despite this, and in fact partly because of it, it now has some exceptional wildlife habitats.

Views from the hides over the nearby fleet, saltmarsh and creek give a feel for what the largely vanished marshland habitats of the past must have been like, while past industrial use of the site has created some strikingly unusual habitats – nowhere else in Essex can you see mature woodland consisting almost entirely of hawthorn, for example, which normally plays second fiddle to larger trees like oaks.

The hawthorn hedges planted many years ago have spread to dominate the site, crowding other shrubs such as blackthorn, dogwood, elder and wild rose out to the margins. In places it has formed a dense canopy under which very little else grows except for fungi in autumn. Elsewhere it has been coppiced to ground level, and in other parts forms impenetrable cover that is good for many songbirds. This kind of patchwork of scrub of different ages supports a great diversity of wildlife.

There are many ponds, ditches and creeks both within and around the park and consequently in summer dragonflies are everywhere. The clearings and the broad rides are rich in wild flowers including birdsfoot trefoil, lady's bedstraw, blue fleabane and agrimony. Because of the poor soil they are able to compete with more aggressive grasses. On sunny days these open areas are crowded with grassland butterflies like the skippers and the common blue, and day-flying moths like the six-spot burnet.

Three hides overlook the saltmarsh and mudflats of Timbermans Creek. Wading birds and ducks often feed on the mudflats, especially when driven off the estuary by the rising tide. Sparrowhawks and other birds of prey can sometimes be seen hunting over the rough ground beyond.

Six-spot burnet moth: its bright colours are a warning to potential predators that it is poisonous
Dr Chris Gibson/English Nature

Visiting

🚗 From the roundabout in Pitsea where the A132 joins the A13 follow Wat Tyler Way south across the railway and into the country park.

🚌 Pitsea station (Fenchurch St line), then walk south down Wat Tyler Way.

🕐 9am to dusk all the year round.

📅 May–June for birdsong and early flowers; July for butterflies and dragonflies and saltmarsh colours; migration periods and winter for visiting birds.

🚻 For more information call the Country Park office on 01268 550088.

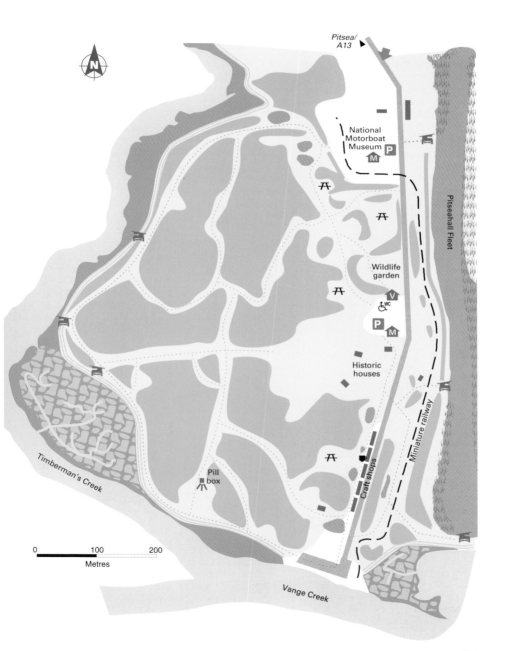

Pitsea/
A13

National
Motorboat
Museum

Wildlife
garden

Historic
houses

Pitseahall Fleet

Miniature railway

Craft shops

Timberman's Creek

Pill
box

Vange Creek

0   100   200
Metres

235

Weald Country Park

424ac/170ha OS Ex175/La177 GR 570 939

Essex County Council

Weald Country Park, which lies just north-west of Brentwood, is an attractive mix of semi-formal parkland with large areas of woodland and the remnants of the 'tree pasture' of a deer park. Its south-eastern quarter, called The Park, is scattered with massive oak and hornbeam pollards, some of which are probably more than 500 years old. It was bought by Essex County Council in 1953 and became a country park.

The woodland to the north positively shimmers with bluebells in spring, particularly where conifers have recently been removed. Golden saxifage, an unusual ancient woodland plant, grows in Foxdown Wood, which escaped conifer planting.

Visiting

From M25 junction 28 (where the M25 crosses the A12) take the A1023 towards Brentwood and turn left on to Wigley Bush Lane. This meets Weald Road in South Weald village. The main entrance is a short way down Weald Road to the left.

Regular bus services from Brentwood to Pilgrims Hatch. Occasional services to South Weald village.

Accessible at all times. Car parks open from dawn to dusk. Visitor centre open daily except Mondays 10am–5pm from April–October, otherwise weekends only 10am–4pm.

April–May for bluebells and bird-song; July for butterflies, dragonflies and wild flowers in the damper parts.

For more information call the Rangers on 01277 261343.

Recovering from past abuse

Weald Park was originally a mediæval deer park and would certainly have much greater wildlife value but for the damage it suffered during and shortly after World War II, when it was requisitioned and its plantations of conifers were cleared for pit props. As a result parts of the woodland became overrun with birch and sycamore. Towards the end of the war the fence was breached and the deer escaped.

Abuse in wartime is understandable, but the ancient grassland of the deer park suffered to no good purpose at all. The entire south-eastern quarter was ploughed up in great haste in 1948 when a false rumour got about that the ploughing subsidy was about to be lifted. Rich plant and insect communities that had taken centuries to develop were destroyed virtually overnight. Later, much of the grassland was reseeded with a mix of vigorous grasses that still exclude most wild flowers.

The woodland is gradually being rehabilitated. In the 1950s and 1960s the areas cleared during the war were replanted with a mixture of conifers and native hardwood trees such as beech and oak. At first the faster-growing conifers shelter the young hardwood trees so that, when the conifers are harvested, they can grow through and take over. This promises to create some fine woodland for the 21st century and beyond.

Ancient hedgerow trees at Weald Park
Tony Gunton

236

Such a variety of habitats attracts a wide variety of birds. Great crested grebes and moorhens breed on the lakes. Nuthatches and woodpeckers are often seen in and around the woods. Flocks of seed-eating birds such as goldfinches and siskins can sometimes be seen feeding on the ground or in the lakeside alders. Little owls can often be seen hunting in the early evening.

237

The Mores

38.8ac/16ha OS Ex175/La177   **GR 565 967**

WOODLAND
TRUST

This wood near Brentwood is long established and parts of it possibly ancient, although the eastern part was once part of Weald Common and is now overrun by birch and holly. Many of the oaks in the western part of the wood were cleared in the 1940s and as a result the wood was invaded by sycamore, which has crowded out native plants and which the Woodland Trust is now bringing under control, as a preliminary to reintroducing coppicing.

A stream runs through the wood and floods in winter, creating several marshy patches, which makes for some interesting flora.

Since 1981, 41 bird species have been recorded as breeding: marsh tit and spotted flycatcher are still there but willow tit and hawfinch have been lost. Siskins and sometimes redpolls feed in the alders in winter.

Sparrowhawk: sometimes breeds in The Mores
Alan Williams

Visiting

Take the A128 Ongar road north from Brentwood and turn left on to a minor road to Bentley. Turn right after the church in Bentley and the entrance is on the left 300m or so on. Parking by St Paul's church, off Snakes Hill. Alternatively, follow the public footpath that runs north from Weald Park, turning left at Coxtie Green Road and then right again a short way along.

Buses from Brentwood to Stondon Massey and Ongar run along the A128.

Accessible at all times.

Spring for early flowers and songbirds; autumn for fungi.

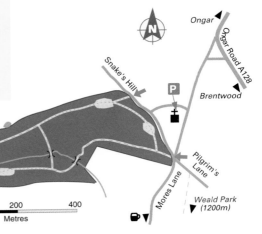

Weeleyhall Wood

78ac/31ha   OS Ex184/La169   GR 156 212   SSSI

ESSEX
Wildlife Trust

Weeleyhall Wood is one of the finest surviving woods in Tendring, although it suffered severely in the 1987 storm. Standard oaks provide most of the timber but there are about eight acres of sweet chestnut coppice, a similar area of Scots and Corsican pine plantation, an area of hazel coppice, and alder glades with an important ground flora that includes moschatel. It is owned by Essex Wildlife Trust.

In spring the bluebells, which carpet almost half the wood, yellow archangel and climbing corydalis make a fine display. Several fern species are also to be found.

The wood has good numbers of woodland birds – including nightingales which have increased with the re-introduction of coppicing – and the commoner butterflies.

A major clearance was undertaken after the 1987 storm. A large non-intervention area has been left; others have been allowed to regenerate naturally. Coppicing has been reintroduced and the pine plantation is being thinned.

Visiting

The reserve is just off the B1441 Colchester to Clacton road. Park where indicated near Weeley Church, then follow signs to the reserve across (privately owned) fields.

Several bus services to/from Clacton run along the B1441.

Accessible at all times

May for early flowers and breeding birds.

Call the warden on 01255 861625 or Essex Wildlife Trust HQ on 01206 735456.

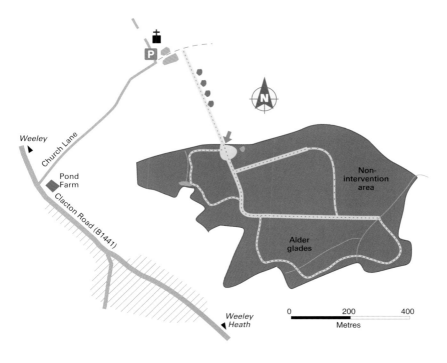

Westhouse Wood

7ac/3ha   OS Ex184/La168   GR 974 272

ESSEX
Wildlife Trust

This small wood on the outskirts of Colchester is managed by Essex Wildlife Trust. Despite its small size it contains a wide range of trees and shrubs. Hazel is the dominant coppice species, and small-leaved lime, crab apple and rowan are scattered among fine oak and ash standards, along with sweet chestnut, holly and field maple.

As a result of coppicing, blue-bells and wood anemones carpet the wood in spring, and there are fine displays of foxgloves in areas that have recently been cleared. Work has also been carried out to keep water in two small ponds throughout the summer months.

Visiting

The entrance is down a slip road on the left off the B1508 Colchester–Sudbury road, just before it passes over the A12 at Braiswick, north-west of Colchester.

Bus services from Colchester to Bures and Sudbury run past the entrance.

Accessible at all times.

Call the warden on 01206 573118 or Essex Wildlife Trust HQ on 01206 735456.

Wheatley Wood

84ac/34ha   OS Ex175/La178   GR 788 914

WOODLAND
TRUST

Wheatley Wood is former farmland given to the Woodland Trust by Rochford Council and planted up as part of the Trust's 'Woods on your Doorstep' millennium project. The trees include oak, ash, hornbeam and willow, and shrubs such as hawthorn and guelder rose. The meadow areas are cut for hay.

Visiting

Reached via Little Wheatley Chase, on the right 600m past the roundabout where the A129 Wickford–Rayleigh road meets the A130.

Rayleigh station (Liverpool Street–Southend is about 10 minutes' walk).

Accessible at all times.

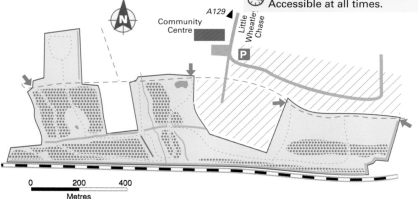

Whet Mead

25ac/10ha   OS Ex183/La168   GR 829 137   LNR

This is a former rubbish tip that has been restored and is now a Local Nature Reserve managed by Braintree Council. Much of it is rough meadow with a wide range of flowering plants, bordered by some scrub and young woodland and containing three linked lagoons. This attracts a good range of the commoner butterflies and dragonflies, and seed-eating birds like skylark and goldfinch.

It is bordered on two sides by the Rivers Blackwater and Brain, which have plants like water figwort and flowering rush growing on their banks and support water voles, grey herons and kingfishers.

Visiting

 Access is via Blackwater Lane which leaves Maldon Road (B1018) eastwards just north of Saul's Bridge over the River Brain and follows the river through a tunnel under the Witham bypass.

Regular Witham–Maldon buses run along Maldon Road.

Accessible at all times.

Take care when walking as tipped material may project out of the ground. Young children should be accompanied as the site is remote and river and lagoon banks are very steep.

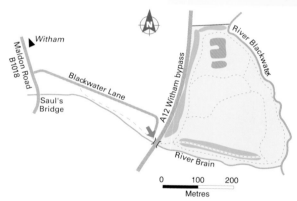

Witton Wood Spinney

0.5ac/0.2ha OS Ex184/La169   GR 235 204

ESSEX Wildlife Trust

This small spinney opposite the entrance to Frinton-on-Sea railway station provides a quiet, urban retreat for birds and insects. It contains a number of tree species, both native and introduced, and is at its most colourful in late spring when the hawthorn blossom contrasts with the white umbels of cow parsley and the yellow of alexanders.

It is managed by Essex Wildlife Trust.

Visiting

No visiting is possible: the reserve serves principally as a defence against advancing concrete.

Wivenhoe Wood

56ac/22ha   OS Ex184/La168   GR 035 223

Wivenhoe Wood is a fine old coppice woodland on the east bank of the River Colne near Wivenhoe, alongside grassland and scrub that once belonged to Lower Lodge Farm and a section of tidal foreshore with saltmarsh, all managed by Colchester Council.

It is likely that the sweet chestnut trees in the wood were planted by the Romans, who introduced the tree to this country from southern Europe as a source of food and rot-resistant timber ideal for fence posts and the like. Coppicing creates a diverse woodland rich in wildlife, and the grassland and scrub nearby adds further variety.

An area of saltmarsh to the west of the railway line can be reached via a level crossing. This is used by wading birds such as redshank and greenshank.

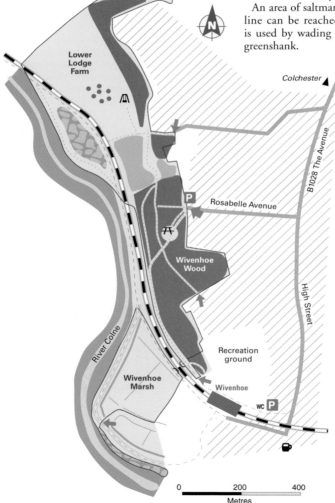

Wivenhoe Marsh

13ac/5ha   OS Ex184/La168   GR 034 217   pLNR, SSSI

This public open space is an area of former grazing marsh alongside the River Colne at Wivenhoe, which Colchester Council proposes (at publication time) to make a Local Nature Reserve.

From the sea wall path there are good views of the inner estuary of the Colne and over the ditches, dykes and ponds of the marsh. Unusual plants like strawberry clover and slender hare's-ear grow here, and it has a rich insect life, with many dragon- and damselflies on the wing in summer and stag beetles wandering in from Wivenhoe Wood to the north. Whitethroats, reed warblers and sedge warblers nest in the dense vegetation.

Visiting

Access via Rosabelle Avenue, a turning off The Avenue (B1028) north of Wivenhoe centre, or from the south via the sea wall path or public footpaths alongside the railway.

Wivenhoe station is a few minutes' walk from Wivenhoe Marsh and from the southern tip of Wivenhoe Wood. Regular buses run from Colchester to Wivenhoe.

Accessible at all times.

May/June for birdsong in the woods and scrub; July/August for insects along the woodland edge and in clearings, and around the marsh and foreshore.

A surfaced path runs from the car park at the end of Rosabelle Avenue to the picnic site. The footpath west of the railway is surfaced also.

available from Council offices or call 01206 853588.

Writtle Forest scene
Tony Gunton

Writtle Forest

500ac/200ha OS Ex183/La167   *GR 638 012*

Sizeable parts of what was once Writtle Forest survive in private ownership and are still being coppiced commercially. These woods have all the diversity and also much of the wildness that you might have found in mediæval woods – areas dense with bracken and bramble and others where the woodland floor is dark and bare; little streams and bogs; occasional glades. The trees are mainly sweet chestnut coppice, with oak and hornbeam in the damper parts, and maple, spindle, and dogwood on the fringes.

Unlike Hatfield Forest, Writtle Forest had the woods in the middle and the 'plains' – open areas used for grazing – around the outside. Mill Green Common is a surviving part of the plains. It has been heavily invaded by birch and other trees, but still has some heather in the open parts, which are alive with insects in summer.

Maple Tree Lane is a broad ancient green lane, bounded for much of its length by massive ditches and banks topped with huge coppice stools of hornbeam and massive oaks. Short sections have been surfaced, but for most of the way the tracks followed by horses and (with more difficulty) people meander round patches of bramble and scrub and occasional pools and boggy areas.

Visiting

A few miles west of Chelmsford, between the roads from Chelmsford to London (A12/A1016) and Ongar (A414). Leave the A12 at Ingatestone and take the minor road from the centre of Ingatestone to Fryerning. Turn right and follow Mill Green Road to Mill Green, or turn left and follow Blackmore Road to reach Fryerning Wood and Maple Tree Lane.

Accessible at all times.

May–June for early flowers and birdsong; July–August for flowers and butterflies.

Many of the paths are heavily used by horses and can be boggy and wet even in the summer.

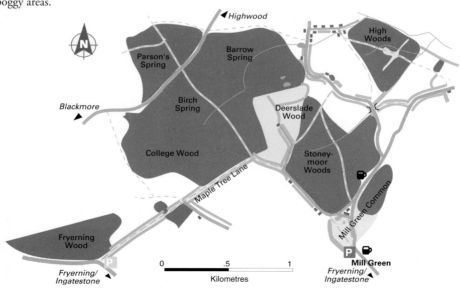

Highwood

High Woods

Barrow Spring

Parson's Spring

Blackmore

Birch Spring

Deerslade Wood

College Wood

Stoney-moor Woods

Maple Tree Lane

Mill Green Common

Fryerning Wood

Fryerning/ Ingatestone

Mill Green

Fryerning/ Ingatestone

0   .5   1

Kilometres

Indexes

Duncan Bridges

Kestrel
Alan Williams

Island
ncer

Index of sites
and summary of facilities

Additional sites mainly of local interest

	Location	Ha	GR	Contact	Summary
Beckton Park	Newham	30	419 814	020 8430 3598	Public park with wildflower meadow, lake and young scrub and woodland
Brickfield & Long Meadow	Earl's Colne	3	860 285	01206 282478	Grassland, pond & brook in Colne Valley
Brockwell Meadows	Kelvedon	5	867 187	01376 570508	Fen grassland on River Blackwater flood plain
Bull Meadow	Colchester	1	997 258	01206 853588	Waterside meadow
Bully Point NR	Lee Valley (Newham)	5	377 852	01992 702200	Educational reserve with grassland and pond
Causeway Meadow	Maldon	6	849 078	01621 875823	Grassland, formerly grazed
Chelmer Valley Park	Gt Dunmow	8	633 219	01371 872406	Rough grassland bordering the River Chelmer
Claypits Plantation	Saffron Walden	1	541 368	01799 510461	Mixed woodland with glades
Cranham Brickfields	Upminster	8	582 874	01708 433809	Ancient hornbeam wood, rough grassland and scrub
Elms Farm Park	Maldon	10	847 080	01621 875823	Amenity and rough grassland next to the Blackwater & Chelmer canal
Gosbecks	Colchester	50	968 228	01206 282932	Archaeological park with grassland used by skylarks
Grove House Wood	Stanford-le-Hope	2	686 818	01375 390000	Woodland with small reedbed
Grove Woods	Rayleigh	1	825 901	01702 318100	Woodland with open areas (former plotland)
Heybridge Creek	Maldon	1	859 076	01621 875823	Large reed bed close to the Blackwater Estuary
Hullbridge foreshore	Hullbridge (Rochford)	4	801 954	01702 546366	Woodland and grassland overlooking Crouch Estuary
Hylands Park	Chelmsford	200	683 043	01245 606812	Formal park with a recreational woodland
Kennington's Park	Aveley (Thurrock)	40	560 813	01708 641880	Restored gravel pit/landfill site with lakes, willow carr and new woodland
Kingley Wood	Rayleigh	2	794 900	01702 546366	Ancient woodland and wildflower meadow
Linford Wood	Linford (Thurrock)	4	676 797	01375 844281	Woodland with mature thorn scrub and a small fen
Magnolia Nature Park	Hawkwell (Rochford)	9	860 923	01702 546366	Mixture of grassland, scrub and woodland with a pond
Pickers Ditch	Tendring	3	178 171	01255 425501	Grassland with hedges, scrub and mature trees
Pimp Hall	Waltham Forest	1	389 940	020 8527 5544 ex 6019	'Natural park' on site of mediæval Pimp Hall manor
Southend-on-Sea foreshore	Southend	848	880 845	01702 215692	Intertidal mudflats and saltmarsh, with eelgrass beds
Thundersley Glen	South Benfleet	11	787 878	01268 792711	Woodland with glades and scrub (former plotland)
Warley Hall Woods	nr Upminster	1	601 888	01708 433809	Ancient coppice woodland

Index of species photos and terms